PAN CHANCHO BAKERY
44

the PAN CHANCHO cookbook

BOOKMAKERS PRESS INC.

For Zal and Rose,

who gave us the spark we would never have known

Published by Bookmakers Press Inc.

Second printing 2007

Library and Archives Canada Cataloguing in Publication

Yanovsky, Zoe, 1967- The Pan Chancho cookbook / Zoe Yanovsky.

Includes index. ISBN-13: 978-1-896451-02-2 ISBN-10: 1-896451-02-0

1. Cookery. 2. Pan Chancho Bakery. I. Pan Chancho Bakery II. Title.
TX714.Y345 2006 641.5 C2006-906332-X

Pan Chancho Bakery
44 Princess Street
Kingston, ON K7L 1A4
(613) 544-7790
pigpan@kingston.net

Produced and published by
Bookmakers Press Inc.
12 Pine Street
Kingston, ON K7K 1W1
(613) 549-4347
tcread@sympatico.ca

Design by Janice McLean
Front cover photograph: Bernard Clark
Back cover photograph: Janice McLean

Printed by Dollco Printing
Ottawa, ON

acknowledgements

Putting together a cookbook is a huge endeavour, especially when a place wears as many hats as does the Pan Chancho Bakery. So while it's impossible to salute all the people, both past and present, who have played a part in making *The Pan Chancho Cookbook* a reality, we'd like to pay special tribute to the following:

Chefs Laura Charrette, Tibrata Gillies and Anne Linton, for their creativity, care and collegiality in the kitchen and their attention to detail in putting so many of Pan Chancho's recipes down on paper; pastry chef Stefanie Killen and assistant pastry chef Joy McBride, who keep all things light and sweet in the desserts department; bakers Paul Muller and Carel Vanderlinden, who've kept the home fires burning; and Victoria Newbury, who once again proved a galvanizing editorial presence.

Pandora De Greene, Cuong Ly, Susan Newbury, Viên Hoang, Reyna Belsham, Hilbert Buist, Stev George and Christyne Flynn, for sharing their love of food and their recipes.

Our hardworking production staff June and William Wu, Manuel Ventura, Ping Lee and Mariela Santamaria; all the prep cooks who've juiced, peeled, scaled and shelled; the line cooks who've stood at their stations day after day putting up the food with the same devotion and precision; the pastry staff who've whisked, whipped, rolled, folded and answered the phone; the bakers who've worked the midnight hour; and the friends and colleagues who helped test these recipes.

Pan Chancho's manager Veronica Desjardins, who graciously makes it all work; the welcoming staff who've worked the front of the house — Stephanie Mitchell, Korinne Peachey and Alyson Charrette; Chris Lawrence, who keeps the building going, day after day; and Paul Varty and Rick Coombes, who deliver our daily bread.

Nick Waterfield and Susan Silver, for their behind-the-scenes dedication.

The people at Bookmakers Press: editor Tracy Read, who promised Rose a cookbook and can now rest easy; art director Janice McLean, for her beautiful design and food photography; and Laurel Aziz, Susan Dickinson and Mary Patton, who pulled out all the stops to bring this book to print.

Photographer Bernard Clark and his assistant David Kennedy, for capturing the spirit of Pan Chancho's staff and regulars.

George Montague, Sonny Sadinsky and Julia Allen Manheim — a heartfelt thank you.

And, most of all, our loyal customers, who make it all worthwhile.

—Zoe Yanovsky

contents

contents

introduction

In the early-morning hours of March 8, 2002, there was an unusual flurry of activity not far from the Lake Ontario waterfront in downtown Kingston. Against an overcast sky, a warm, golden light filtered through the floor-to-ceiling windows of the elegant two-and-a-half-storey limestone that towers over lower Princess Street. For weeks, the day had been marked on calendars all over town, and a throng of visitors was only too happy to brave the cold, determined to be among the first in line to explore the venue and sample the wares.

The bright spot on that late-winter cityscape was the grand opening of the new Pan Chancho Bakery at 44 Princess Street. At seven in the morning, it was one of the few downtown establishments open for business, and anticipation of the day had kept Kingston buzzing for more than a year. Now the building was steadily filling up with eager customers. Regulars from the bakery's

Zal and Rose had a gift for bringing together members of the community in the name of good food and fellowship. With Pan Chancho, they were working their magic once again.

old location and newcomers alike casually mingled, sipping cappuccinos and lattes, taking in the store's lofty ceilings and breathing in the tantalizing aromas from the wall-to-wall racks filled with loaves of fresh-baked breads and breakfast pastries. They toured the cold cases of artfully created savoury prepared foods and a mouth-watering selection of desserts and cheeses.

At the centre of it all were Pan Chancho's owners, Zal Yanovsky and Rose Richardson, looking happy, if just a little shell-shocked. In their unique styles, they warmly greeted friends, accepted best wishes on their new venture and encouraged visitors to sample the food. By 2002, of course, with the success of Chez Piggy, Zal and Rose had well-established reputations as restaurateurs extraordinaire. They had a special gift for bringing together members of the community in the name of good food and fellowship. Now, with the new Pan Chancho, they were working their magic once again.

Since that day, Pan Chancho has become much more than a "bright spot" in downtown Kingston. Today, it is a veritable beacon, a destination for Kingston residents and the thousands of visitors who come through our doors each year, captivated by the thriving food culture. Housed in one of the most spectacular buildings in town, the new 10,000-square-foot Pan Chancho is not simply a bakery but a retail food shop, café, dining room, catering service and wholesale supplier of artisanal bread.

The first chapter in the story of Pan Chancho, however, begins almost a decade earlier at a little shop a few blocks away. In the early 1990s, Zal and Rose hit upon the idea of setting up a satellite operation that would satisfy Chez Piggy's hearty appetite for good bread. To justify the bakery storefront, they would also sell sandwiches and soup to a bustling lunch crowd. Zal and Rose had always shown a genius for nurturing young talent, and as they brought together a creative, enthusiastic staff, they prepared to launch the new enterprise. Pan Chancho would produce bread according to exacting Old World methods, creating a flavourful selection of handmade loaves each day using organic hard flours, spring water, sea salt and fresh baker's yeast — all baked in humid gas ovens to give each loaf its signature crust.

But even before the doors opened in 1994, the original concept of a bread-and-lunch shop had exploded into a European-style food store and catering service with a substantial menu of à la carte dishes along with baked goods prepared, as always, from the best local ingredients. The retail area soon boasted a selection of specialty gourmet foods, such as Mennonite salami, raw milk French cheeses, exotic olives and an ever-present round of Parmigiano-Reggiano.

Pan Chancho was imprinted with Zal and Rose's trademark standards and style, but the bakery was never meant to be a mirror image of Chez Piggy. It offered the early-morning service that had eluded the restaurant's already jammed lunch and dinner business as well as an eclectic cuisine unavailable anywhere else in town. People wanted good food, but there was a growing desire to enjoy that food in the comfort of their own homes. Zal and Rose knew instinctively that Pan Chancho could satisfy that trend.

Anybody dropping by the crowded Johnson Street location on a Saturday morning, however, could see that the bakery was rapidly becoming a victim of its own success. By 1999, Pan Chancho had outgrown its first home. The line cooks prepped food at a slim chopping bench in the cramped kitchen, and to meet the retail demand within the limited kitchen space, there were shifts for each department: bakery, pastry and savouries. "The old

From first home to new home: Pan Chancho's founding staff, 1994 (courtesy Jack Chiang), and new staff, 2002.

location was bursting at the seams," says Chez Piggy/ Pan Chancho general manager Nick Waterfield. "People were tripping over one another." At the same time, Zal's vision was evolving — he'd been daydreaming about a café where people could stop by for early-morning coffee, chat with friends and "enjoy fresh bread, drink grappa and eat stinky cheese."

The owners and staff soldiered on even as the plan was afoot to find roomier digs. After a two-year search, Zal and Rose found a property whose potential fit their growing business. Zal had an entrepreneur's nose for a good thing, and he had also always been a firm believer in the leap of faith. Neither Zal nor Rose was a bottom-line bean counter willing to sacrifice an idea in order to conform to the established norms of the restaurant industry. On the contrary, they were all about vision first, setting a goal and then piecing together the logistics and staff to make it a booming reality. The little bakery was on the verge of becoming a larger-than-life food emporium, and Zal and Rose rolled up their sleeves for the challenge ahead.

Forty-four Princess Street has a storied past. Built in 1833 for the Commercial Bank, the building was designed in the classical style once favoured by bankers and, over the years, had served as the offices for the Royal College of Physicians and Surgeons, a privately owned apartment complex, an LCBO retail outlet, a department store and a brokerage house. Most recently, it had been home to a fast-food hamburger chain. It was a handsome example of colonial architecture and had always been one of Rose's favourite buildings.

In 2001, Zal and Rose bought the property with a straightforward plan to renovate and update it. But almost 170 years and a checkered chain of custody had left the structure in a state of disrepair. The historic façade had been altered, and the structural integrity of the building was compromised. And, as with most renovations, everything that could go wrong did. The modest retrofit turned into a classic teardown, with every interior wall, stud, beam and all but one staircase slated for replacement. Likewise, all the electrical,

During the renovation, architect Rob Crothers remembers Zal dropping by his office, standing at the bottom of the staircase and calling out, "Squeak! Squeak!"

mechanical and plumbing had to be renewed, upgraded and redesigned for the bakery's specific needs. As the scope of the renovation kept growing, the project went over budget and over time. Architect Rob Crothers remembers Zal regularly dropping by his office, standing at the bottom of the staircase and calling out, "Squeak! Squeak!" For Zal, who never had any trouble attracting attention, it was just another way to lightheartedly move the process forward. For Kingstonians, the familiar sight of a dusty Zal decked out in a hard hat only fed the excitement about what was to come.

More than a year later, with the hard slogging of reconstruction behind them, Zal and Rose were ready to make the place their own. Huge new gleaming hand-painted wood-trimmed windows opened the view onto Princess Street. Exposed limestone walls and wood floors were warmed with elaborate lighting, and traditional design partnered with postmodern, as boldly coloured industrial girders spanned the room. Behind the public space, the building concealed a series of high-tech kitchens, prep rooms and offices. At the rear, an enclosed stone patio with three original poplar trees was devised as a peaceful oasis in the downtown core. What visitors on that March morning in 2002 appreciated first was the sheer scale of 44 Princess Street — an appropriate canvas for Zal and Rose's artistry. The finished building reflected their sophistication as gourmets and restaurateurs, but it also embodied their belief that good food, good company and beautiful surroundings are important parts of what make life worth living.

Which brings us to this book. With the success of 1998's *Chez Piggy Cookbook*, Zal and Rose almost immediately began to think about producing a concise volume of recipes that would represent the young Pan Chancho.

What no one could ever have predicted was that we would lose both Zal and Rose before the book was completed and the story of Pan Chancho written. Zal died suddenly of heart failure in December 2002, and in March 2005, Rose died from cancer. That profound loss makes the completion of this cookbook and the growing success of Pan Chancho all the more poignant.

The two founders continue to occupy the hearts and minds of the Pan Chancho staff, and their spirits inhabit the very walls of the stunning new bakery, a living tribute to their dream. "Zal and Rosie are the reference point for everything we make and do. We talk about them all the time," says their daughter Zoe Yanovsky. "They had an incredibly high standard for both themselves and the people who worked with them, and even though staff members come and go, there will always be a core of us who know how they'd like things to be done. Everything we do is influenced by them. At the same time, they created something organic at Pan Chancho, and their legacy is part of the sense of purpose and inspiration that informs each day at the bakery."

Today, Pan Chancho hums 24/7. The building is a hive of activity by day, but even at night, the joint is jumping — as the bakers arrive for the night shift, the sounds of jazz, blues, rock and roll and hip hop start to resonate through the building. With more than 70 people on staff and Zal and Rose's hand-picked chefs in the kitchen, Pan Chancho is rolling ahead. Themed dinners celebrate the food traditions of countries all over the world, just as Zal and Rose did, and have allowed the chefs to expand their repertoires. On weekends, as regulars rise early to pick up their favourite pastry, bread, cheese or an order of dragon noodles, there are lineups out the front door. And although there may be fewer grappa orders in the café than Zal might have considered

Clockwise from bottom left: One of the first steps in restoring 44 Princess Street was to remove the remnant exterior of its former occupants. To restore the building's classical splendour, demolition crews also took the interior back to the sticks to create a clean slate for the massive task of reconstruction (photographs courtesy Rob Crothers).

ideal, he'd be pretty happy to know that in Kingston, Pan Chancho is where you can count on meeting an old friend and catching up with the news. It's become a part of the fabric of life here.

As with all Zal and Rose's projects, *The Pan Chancho Cookbook* has become, well, bigger. So here it is, a full-sized companion to the award-winning *Chez Piggy Cookbook*, a portable tribute to the place and the chefs who make it great and to the unforgettable couple who inspired an entire community for nearly three decades. The book you see before you represents the collective creativity of all who have worked at Pan Chancho — both locations — over the past 12 years. We've included the standards that bring customers in the door each day along with a wide selection of recipes suited for special occasions and holiday seasons. We've covered the complete range of foods, from soups, appetizers and salads to main courses, desserts and baked goods. Our culinary secrets are now revealed.

As Zal might have said: It's a mo' better book.

breads

pain ordinaire, page 20

breads

sourdough starter

You need patience and a large mixing container to make a sourdough starter. And to keep it active and ready to use, you must "feed" it every day. At Pan Chancho, it's the start of many great breads.

days 1 + 2

1 cup	unbleached hard white flour	250 mL
$1\frac{1}{2}$ cups	spring water, room temperature	375 mL

day 3

1 cup	unbleached hard white flour	250 mL
1 cup	spring water, room temperature	250 mL

day 4

$\frac{1}{2}$ cup	unbleached hard white flour	125 mL
$\frac{1}{2}$ cup	spring water, room temperature	125 mL

caveat baker

Bread making is part art, part science, and home bakers should remember that they're contending with fluctuating levels of humidity and temperature. Today's rainy-day failure may well be tomorrow's sunny triumph. Don't be discouraged.

Days 1 + 2. To make starter: In a large bowl, mix flour and water together. Cover with a tea towel or cheesecloth, and allow to stand for 2 days at room temperature.

Day 3. Feed starter: In a small bowl, mix flour and water together (this is called a slurry). Stir starter, then mix in slurry, and blend thoroughly. At end of Day 3, mixture should be bubbly and smell a little boozy. If it doesn't, allow to stand for another day or two before feeding again with a slurry.

Day 4. Before you feed starter, discard all but 1 cup (250 mL). From now until Day 7, feed starter its volume in flour and water.

Day 5. Feed starter a slurry of 1 cup (250 mL) flour and 1 cup (250 mL) water.

Day 6. Feed starter 2 cups (500 mL) flour and 2 cups (500 mL) water.

Day 7. Starter is ready to use at room temperature. If you are baking frequently, continue to feed starter once a day. If you bake only once a week, store starter in refrigerator until needed. (To limit the size of the ever-growing starter, remove and discard 1 cup/250 mL starter before each weekly feeding.) To reactivate starter, bring it (or a portion of it) to room temperature and feed for a few days.

Once starter has become active, it can also be stored in portions in the freezer; it can then be reactivated as needed.

dried ancho chili + cocoa bread

The combination of ingredients might sound a little strange, but this bread makes a great sandwich and delicious French toast, especially when served with crème fraîche flavoured with orange zest.

2 tsp.	fresh (cake) yeast or 1 tsp. (5 mL) active dry yeast	10 mL
$1\frac{1}{2}$ cups	water	375 mL
$1\frac{1}{2}$ cups	Sourdough Starter (see page 16), room temperature	375 mL
3 cups	hard wheat flour	750 mL
$\frac{3}{4}$ cup	Dutch Process Cocoa Powder	175 mL
2 tsp.	sea salt	10 mL
$\frac{1}{2}$ tsp.	freshly ground black pepper (optional)	2 mL
$\frac{1}{4}$ cup	finely chopped dried ancho chili, seeds removed	50 mL

don't rush it

Allow this bread to cool completely before slicing, as it is very dense and will appear gummy and underbaked if sliced while warm.

If using fresh yeast, crumble into room-temperature water and stir until small bubbles appear. To proof active dry yeast, water should be warm. Proof yeast in $\frac{1}{2}$ cup (125 mL) of the water; when creamy, stir in rest of water.

Place starter in a large bowl, and stir in yeast mixture. Mix well. Add remaining ingredients, and mix at medium speed with the dough hook on an electric mixer for 10 minutes or by hand for 20 minutes, until dough is sticky and elastic. Transfer dough to a lightly oiled bowl, turning dough to coat with oil, and cover with plastic wrap. Let rise at room temperature for 4 hours or in the refrigerator overnight, until doubled in size.

Punch down dough, and transfer to a lightly floured surface. Gently shape into a round free-form loaf. Place on a lightly oiled baking sheet, cover with a clean tea towel, and let rise in a warm place for $1\frac{1}{2}$ to 2 hours.

Preheat oven to 425°F (220°C), and place pizza stone in the bottom third of oven. Gently move loaf onto a floured peel or board. Make a cut in top of loaf with a sharp serrated knife to allow dough to rise while baking.

Spritz water inside oven to form steam, and slide loaf onto pizza stone. Bake for 30 to 40 minutes, until crust is dark and loaf sounds hollow when tapped. Cool on wire rack.

Makes 1 large round loaf

variation

Substitute 2 cups (500 mL) chopped dried apricots or dried cherries for the ancho chili.

olive + rosemary sourdough

We can put almost anything on this bread and it sells, but it's especially good with tuna salad or any grilled cheese.

$3\frac{1}{2}$ cups	unbleached hard white flour	875 mL
1 tsp.	chopped fresh rosemary	5 mL
$\frac{2}{3}$ cup	Sourdough Starter (see page 16), room temperature	150 mL
1 cup	spring water, room temperature	250 mL
$\frac{1}{2}$ tsp.	sea salt	2 mL
$\frac{1}{2}$ cup	chopped kalamata olives	125 mL

In a medium bowl, mix flour and rosemary together. In a large bowl, add starter to water. Gradually add flour mixture, mixing by hand and bringing ingredients together to form a loose ball.

Let dough rest for at least 5 minutes to let flour absorb water and to allow gluten to start developing. Dough should be smooth, soft and fairly sticky.

Add salt, turn out onto a floured surface, and knead for 5 to 10 minutes, until dough has a silky texture. Mix in olives. (You may need to add a small amount of flour at this point to offset moisture from olives.)

Form dough into a ball, and place in a large, lightly oiled bowl, turning dough to coat with oil. Cover with plastic wrap, and let stand for 1 hour at room temperature. Transfer to refrigerator, and leave overnight to allow flavours to develop.

Remove dough from refrigerator 2 hours before baking. Turn out onto a lightly floured surface. Shape dough into a free-form loaf. Place on a rimless floured baking sheet, cover with a clean tea towel, and let rise at room temperature until nearly doubled in size, about 1 to $1\frac{1}{2}$ hours.

An hour before baking, preheat oven to 500°F (260°C) and place a pizza stone in bottom third of oven. Pour 1 cup (250 mL) water into a baking pan, and set on oven floor 15 minutes before baking.

When loaf is ready to bake, move onto a floured peel or board and cut a circular cap on dome of dough using a razor blade or an extremely sharp knife. Slide loaf onto pizza stone, and reduce oven temperature to 450°F (230°C). Bake for 10 minutes, then reduce oven temperature to 400°F (200°C), and bake for 10 minutes more.

Remove pan of water, and continue to bake for 20 to 35 minutes. The finished loaf should make a hollow sound when you thump the bottom. Let cool completely on wire rack before slicing.

Makes 1 loaf

pita bread

A Greek-style bread, this pita is part of our signature sandwich, Cumin-Spiced Lamb Pita (see page 122). We brush it with olive oil on each side, heat it in a pan and then sprinkle it with za'atar or oregano.

2 scant Tbsp.	active dry yeast	25 mL
1/4 tsp.	white sugar	1 mL
2 cups	warm water	500 mL
1/3 cup	extra-virgin olive oil	75 mL
4 tsp.	sea salt	20 mL
5 1/2 cups	all-purpose flour	1.4 L
1/2 cup	whole wheat flour	125 mL
	Fine cornmeal	

In a large bowl, dissolve yeast and sugar in 1/2 cup (125 mL) of the water, and allow to proof in a warm place until yeast begins to foam. Stir in remaining 1 1/2 cups (375 mL) water, olive oil and salt, and mix in flours 1 cup (250 mL) at a time. Turn dough out onto a lightly floured surface, and knead until smooth and elastic, about 10 minutes.

Grease a large bowl with butter. Place dough in bowl, and turn to coat all sides. Cover, and let rise in a warm place until doubled in size.

Punch dough down, and let rest on a floured surface for 10 minutes. Divide into 8 pieces, and shape each piece into a ball. Cover with a clean tea towel, and let rest for 30 minutes. Using a rolling pin, flatten each ball into an 8-inch (20 cm) circle.

Preheat oven to 500°F (260°C), and sprinkle a baking sheet or pizza stone with cornmeal. Bake pitas (probably a few at a time, depending on the size of your stone) on the lowest oven rack for 5 minutes, then transfer to a higher rack for 3 to 5 minutes, until pitas have puffed up and are lightly browned.

Makes 8 pitas

pain ordinaire

We think this bread should really be called "pain extraordinaire." Our bakers use the dough in everything from baguette and bâtarde to Italian stretch and pizza crust. Although you can make Pain Ordinaire in as little as two days, the flavour improves when the process is extended over three.

day 1
starter

1 Tbsp.	active dry yeast	15 mL
2 cups	warm water	500 mL
2 cups	unbleached hard white flour	500 mL

day 2
dough

1 Tbsp.	active dry yeast	15 mL
1 cup	warm water	250 mL
	Starter from Day 1	
	Pinch ascorbic acid crystals or 1/4 tsp. (1 mL) lemon juice	
4–5 cups	unbleached hard white flour	1–1.25 L
1 Tbsp.	sea salt	15 mL

Day 1. In a large bowl, stir yeast into water until dissolved. Gradually add flour, stirring until well mixed. Cover with plastic wrap, and refrigerate over night.

Day 2. In a large bowl, stir yeast into water. Add starter and ascorbic acid or lemon juice. Add flour 1 cup (250 mL) at a time, up to 4 cups (1 L). Reserve 1 cup (250 mL) flour for kneading dough. Blend by hand or with a hand mixer on low speed until you have a rough dough.

Scrape out onto a well-floured work surface. Sprinkle salt over top, and knead, gradually incorporating the remaining 1 cup (250 mL) flour. The kneaded dough should be silky and satiny but slightly sticky. Resist adding too much flour. Place in a large oiled bowl, turning dough to coat with oil. Cover with plastic wrap, and refrigerate overnight.

Day 3. Remove dough from refrigerator, and punch down. Divide dough in two. (If shaping by hand into free-form loaves, see "Stoned Heat," facing page, for baking instructions.) Place in two loaf pans coated with cooking spray. Cover with a clean tea towel, and let rise at room temperature for 1 1/2 to 2 hours.

Preheat oven to 450°F (230°C). Ideally, you want to begin baking the loaves before they have doubled in size; otherwise, they will fall when they come into contact with the heat.

When loaves are about three-quarters risen, slash tops of loaves with a razor blade. Just before you put bread into oven, place a pan of boiling water on bottom rack. Bake loaves for 10 minutes, then reduce oven temperature to 375°F (190°C), and remove pan of water. Continue to bake for 30 to 35 minutes.

Check loaves throughout baking process, and if they get too dark on top, cover loosely with aluminum foil. If you are baking the bread in loaf pans, turn loaves out onto oven rack, bottoms up or on their sides, for the last 10 minutes to firm up bottom and sides.

Makes 2 loaves

stoned heat

If you decide to bake bread free-form rather than in a loaf pan, it can be baked on a pizza stone dusted with cornmeal. Preheat oven, and place pizza stone in the bottom third of oven. Gently move loaf onto a floured peel or board, then slide loaf onto pizza stone. Baking on a hot stone ensures that your bread will have a brown bottom.

spelt bread

Made from the flour of an ancient African wheat grain, this bread has a nuttier flavour than North American wheat strains. We get our organic spelt, whole wheat and rye flours from Mountain Path in eastern Ontario.

11 cups	spelt flour	2.75 L
2 Tbsp.	fresh (cake) yeast	25 mL
	or 1 Tbsp. (15 mL) active dry yeast	
5 cups	water	1.25 mL
2 Tbsp.	sea salt	25 mL
2 Tbsp.	honey	25 mL
1/2 cup	hulled sunflower seeds, plus more for top of loaf	125 mL
1/2 cup	spelt kernels, soaked for 20 minutes + drained	125 mL

Spray two loaf pans with cooking spray, and set aside. Place 10 cups (2.5 L) of the flour in a large bowl, and make a well in centre.

If using fresh yeast, crumble into room-temperature water and stir until small bubbles appear. To proof active dry yeast, water should be warm. Proof yeast in 1/2 cup (125 mL) of the water; when creamy, stir in rest of water. Add salt and honey, and quickly stir together. Immediately start pouring yeast mixture into well in flour, stirring by hand to mix as you pour, until all the flour has been incorporated and you have a rough dough. Fold in remaining 1 cup (250 mL) flour, sunflower seeds and spelt kernels.

Turn dough out onto a lightly floured surface, and knead for 5 to 6 minutes, until it is smooth and elastic. Divide dough into two equal portions, and place in loaf pans. Smooth the surface with wet fingertips. Sprinkle top of loaf with remaining sunflower seeds. Cover with a clean tea towel, and let rise in a warm, draft-free place for 50 to 60 minutes, until dough has almost doubled in size.

Meanwhile, preheat oven to 400°F (200°C). Bake loaves for 40 to 50 minutes. Finished loaves should sound hollow when tapped on bottom.

Let cool completely on wire rack before slicing. This bread tastes best 18 to 24 hours after baking.

Makes 2 large loaves

light rye bread

This aromatic rye loaf gets its extra-sweet flavour from buttermilk. The inside texture of the loaf is smooth, while the crust is satisfyingly crunchy. You may need a countertop mixer to blend the dough.

day 1
milk sour

1½ cups	buttermilk, room temperature	375 mL
¾ cup	whole rye flour	175 mL

day 2
rye starter

2½ tsp.	active dry yeast	12 mL
1 cup	warm water	250 mL
	Milk sour from Day 1	
2 cups	unbleached hard white flour	500 mL
½ cup	whole rye flour	125 mL

day 3
dough

	Rye starter from Day 2	
½ cup	water	125 mL
1 tsp.	honey	5 mL
1 Tbsp.	sea salt	15 mL
3 cups	unbleached hard white flour	750 mL
1	large egg, beaten with 1 Tbsp. (15 mL) water to make egg wash	1
3 Tbsp.	caraway seed	40 mL

Day 1. In a large bowl, mix buttermilk and flour by hand until there are no lumps. Cover with plastic wrap, and let stand at room temperature overnight.

Day 2. In a small bowl, stir yeast into water. Let stand for 5 minutes, until bubbles start to form on surface. Add yeast mixture to milk sour. Gradually add flours, and mix well. Cover with plastic wrap, and refrigerate overnight. Dough should nearly triple in size.

Day 3. Bring rye starter to room temperature. Mix by hand or in the bowl of a stand-up mixer with paddle attachment on low speed. Blend in water, honey and salt, and gradually incorporate flour.

Turn dough out onto a floured surface. Dust hands with flour, and knead. Dough should be sticky, so try not to add more flour. Cover with a clean tea towel, and let rise at room temperature for 1 hour.

Punch dough down, and divide in two. Shape into round or oval loaves, cover with a clean tea towel, and let rise at room temperature for 40 minutes.

Preheat oven to 400°F (200°C), and place pizza stone in bottom third of oven. Slash tops of loaves with a razor blade, and brush lightly with egg wash. Sprinkle caraway seed on top. Bake on pizza stone for 15 minutes. Reduce oven temperature to 375°F (190°C), and continue to bake for 25 minutes more.

Makes 2 loaves

dark army rye

Cocoa, molasses and coffee give this bread a lusty full-bodied flavour. Grill it with extra-old Cheddar to wake up your taste buds.

soaker

1 cup	water	250 mL
$1^1/_2$ cups	cracked rye	250 g

pre-ferment

1 scant cup	Sourdough Starter (see page 16)	200 g
$^3/_4$ cup + 2 Tbsp.	water	200 mL
$^3/_4$ cup + 2 Tbsp.	organic rye flour	250 g

dough

$5^1/_4$ cups	organic white flour	850 g
1 Tbsp.	fennel seed, toasted + ground	15 mL
1 Tbsp.	cocoa powder	15 mL
1 Tbsp.	instant coffee powder	15 mL
4 tsp.	sea salt	20 mL
	Soaker	
	Pre-ferment	
$1^1/_3$ cups + 2 Tbsp.	water	350 mL
1 Tbsp.	fresh (cake) yeast	15 mL
1 Tbsp.	fancy molasses	15 mL

To make soaker, pour water over cracked rye in a small bowl, and let soak at room temperature for 6 hours.

To make pre-ferment, stir starter, water and flour together in a large bowl until smooth. Starter must be fully blended with flour. Cover with plastic wrap, and allow to ferment at room temperature for 3 hours or in refrigerator overnight.

To make dough, combine flour with fennel, cocoa, coffee and salt. In a large bowl, combine soaker and pre-ferment with water and yeast. Add molasses, then start adding flour mixture, 1 cup (250 mL) at a time. Stir strongly in a circular motion until dough is too stiff to mix in bowl. Turn out dough onto a lightly floured surface, and knead, dusting surface and dough with flour to keep dough soft and pliable and just slightly tacky. After 10 to 12 minutes, dough should be silky and smooth with a bounce-back resilience.

Place dough in a lightly oiled bowl, turning dough to coat with oil. Cover with plastic wrap, and let rise at room temperature for $2^1/_2$ to 3 hours or in refrigerator overnight, until doubled in size.

Divide dough into three pieces, being careful not to let too much gas out of dough. Place each piece on a lightly floured surface, and flatten slightly. Fold each piece in two overlapping folds toward the centre so that dough has three "layers." Turn seam side down, and press air out of loaf. Dust each loaf with a mixture of rye and white flours, and place seam side down in lightly oiled bread pans. Cover with a clean tea towel, and let bread rise for $1^1/_2$ hours, until doubled in size.

Meanwhile, preheat oven to 400°F (200°C). Spritz water inside oven to form steam, and place loaves on middle rack. Bake for 10 minutes, misting oven with spritzer two more times. Reduce oven temperature to 350°F (180°C), rotate bread and move to lower rack. Bake for 30 to 35 minutes, until bread sounds hollow when tapped. Cool loaves on wire rack for at least 1 hour before slicing.

Makes 3 loaves

croûtes

1/4 cup	extra-virgin olive oil	50 mL
1 1/2 tsp.	minced fresh rosemary	7 mL
1 1/2 tsp.	finely minced garlic	7 mL
1/2 tsp.	sea salt	2 mL
1/4 tsp.	freshly ground black pepper	1 mL
	Baguette	

Preheat oven to 400°F (200°C). In a small bowl, mix together olive oil, rosemary, garlic, salt and pepper.

Cut baguette into 1/2-inch (1 cm) slices. Lightly brush slices on one side with flavoured oil (be careful — too much oil will drench the croûte). Place slices on a cookie sheet, and bake for about 20 minutes, until golden brown and crispy all the way through.

whole wheat bread

Moist and tasty, this is a perfect sandwich bread — and it works with anything you put in it or on it.

day 1
starter

2 Tbsp.	active dry yeast	25 mL
3/4 cup	warm water	175 mL
2/3 cup	buttermilk	150 mL
1 3/4 cups	unbleached hard white flour	425 mL

day 2
starter

2 cups	warm water	500 mL
	Starter from Day 1	
2 1/2 cups	whole wheat flour	625 mL
2 1/4 cups	unbleached hard white flour	550 mL
2/3 cup	wheat germ	150 mL

day 3
dough

1 1/2 cups	starter	375 mL
1 1/2 cups	warm water	375 mL
1 Tbsp.	active dry yeast	15 mL
2 1/2 cups	whole wheat flour	625 mL
2 cups	unbleached hard white flour	500 mL
1 Tbsp.	sea salt	15 mL
2 Tbsp.	honey	25 mL

Day 1. In a large bowl, stir yeast into water until dissolved. Add buttermilk, and gradually add flour, mixing until smooth. Cover with plastic wrap, and let stand in a cool place overnight.

Day 2. Stir water into starter. Gradually add flours, then wheat germ, mixing thoroughly. Cover with plastic wrap, and refrigerate overnight.

Day 3. Place starter in a large bowl (remaining starter will keep in refrigerator for a few days). Add remaining ingredients, and mix well with a stand-up mixer or by hand. Turn out onto a lightly floured surface, and knead until smooth.

Cover with plastic wrap, and let rise at room temperature until nearly doubled in size. Punch dough down, and divide in two. Shape into free-form loaves (see "Stoned Heat," page 21, for baking instructions), or put into loaf pans coated with cooking spray. Cover with a clean tea towel, and let rise again until dough is not quite doubled in size.

Preheat oven to 425°F (220°C). Slash tops of loaves with a razor blade. A few minutes before putting bread in oven, place a pan of boiling water on bottom rack. Bake for 15 minutes, then reduce oven temperature to 375°F (190°C), and remove pan of water. Bake for 25 minutes more or until loaves are evenly browned.

Makes 2 loaves

pumpkin seed bread

Appreciate the nuttiness of the pumpkin seeds in this version, or leave them out and make a lovely Pain de Campagne.

day 1
starter

1 Tbsp.	active dry yeast	15 mL
2½ cups	warm water	625 mL
1½ cups	whole rye flour	375 mL
1 cup	unbleached hard white flour	250 mL

day 2
seed mix

½ cup	hulled sunflower seeds	125 mL
½ cup	sesame seeds mixed with 2 tsp. (10 mL) tamari sauce	125 mL
1 cup	pumpkin seeds	250 mL
1 tsp.	cumin seed, ground	5 mL

dough

2½–3 cups	unbleached hard white flour	625–750 mL
2 tsp.	sea salt	10 mL

Starter from Day 1

Extra sunflower and pumpkin seeds to top loaves

Day 1. In a large bowl, dissolve yeast in water, then gradually stir in flours. Cover with plastic wrap, and refrigerate overnight.

Day 2. In a small bowl, mix seeds together. Set aside.

Gradually add flour and salt to starter, and mix into a soft dough. Add seed mix. Turn out onto a lightly floured surface, and knead for 4 to 5 minutes. Cover with a clean cloth, and let rise until doubled in size, about 1 hour.

Preheat oven to 350°F (180°C), and place pizza stone in bottom third of oven. Punch dough down, and divide in two. Shape into free-form oval loaves, cover with a clean tea towel, and let rise again until not quite doubled. Slash tops of loaves with a razor blade, press seeds into tops, and bake on pizza stone for 45 minutes. (See "Stoned Heat," page 21, for baking instructions.)

Makes 2 loaves

cornmeal, cilantro + jalapeño rings

Despite its name, this is a mild bread with a soft crust and a chewy texture. Enjoy it with chilies, stews and pâtés.

sponge

1 tsp.	fresh (cake) yeast	5 mL
	or $1/2$ tsp. (2 mL) active dry yeast	
$1/2$ cup	water	125 mL
$1/2$ cup	organic white flour	125 mL
$1/4$ cup	whole wheat flour	50 mL

dough

	Sponge	
$2\frac{1}{2}$ cups	water	625 mL
1 tsp.	fresh (cake) yeast	5 mL
	or $1/2$ tsp. (2 mL) active dry yeast	
$1\frac{1}{4}$ cups	fine yellow cornmeal,	300 mL
	plus more for tops of loaves	
1 Tbsp.	sea salt	15 mL
$1/4$ cup	chopped cilantro	50 mL
$1/3$ cup	medium-diced jalapeños	75 mL
1 Tbsp.	coarsely ground black pepper	15 mL
4-$4\frac{1}{2}$ cups	organic white flour	1–1.125 L

To make sponge: If using fresh yeast, crumble yeast into room-temperature water and stir until small bubbles appear. To proof active dry yeast, water should be warm. Proof yeast in $1/4$ cup (50 mL) of the water, and when creamy, stir in rest of water. Add flours, and stir until strands of gluten stretch from spoon, about 100 strokes. Scrape down sides of bowl, and cover with plastic wrap. Allow to rise in a warm (80°F/27°C), draft-free place for $1\frac{1}{2}$ to $2\frac{1}{2}$ hours or in refrigerator overnight. Sponge should be bubbly, have a wheatish aroma and be doubled in size.

To make dough, scrape sponge into a larger bowl, if necessary, and add water and yeast. Stir until sponge breaks up and a slight foam appears on surface. Add cornmeal, and stir until combined. Add salt, cilantro, jalapeños and pepper. Add enough flour to make a thick dough that is hard to stir. Turn dough out onto a lightly floured surface, and knead in remaining flour. Dough should be soft and smooth after 15 to 20 minutes of kneading and spring back quickly when pressed with a finger.

Form dough into a ball. Lightly oil a large, clean bowl, place dough in centre, and turn to coat with oil. Cover with plastic wrap, and allow to rise at room temperature for 2 to 3 hours or in refrigerator overnight, until dough is doubled in size. At this point, your finger leaves an indentation when dough is lightly pressed.

Gently scrape dough onto a lightly floured surface, and divide into three equal pieces. Shape each piece into a loose ball, and lightly flour the surface. Place your elbow in centre of ball, and gently force the knob of your elbow through the dough while rotating in a circular motion until you have a hole 1 to 1½ inches (2.5-4 cm) wide in middle. Pick up ring, and finish shaping by hand until it is an even thickness all around. Spritz with water, and sprinkle with cornmeal.

Place rings on a floured surface, and cover with a clean, damp tea towel and plastic wrap to avoid a dry skin forming. Let rise in a warm place until rings have almost doubled in size, about 1 hour.

Meanwhile, preheat oven to 400°F (200°C), and place a pizza stone in centre of oven for most even heat distribution. Gently move each ring onto a floured peel or board, and lightly press top with a little cornmeal. Spritz water inside oven to form steam, then slide rings onto pizza stone. Bake for 3 minutes, then spritz oven again. Bake for 15 minutes more, until some browning occurs, then reduce oven temperature to 350°F (180°C). Bake for 15 to 20 minutes more, until golden brown with darker top and bottom. You should hear a hollow sound when the bottom is tapped. Cool completely on wire rack.

Makes 3 rings

croissants

We use the sponge method to bake our croissants, and we feel it's what elevates our croissants above the rest. First developed by Viennese bakers and introduced to the French in the 1820s, it has been abandoned by most commercial bakeries in favour of a quicker straight-dough technique with no fermentation. (Please note: This recipe is so sensitive that, with the exception of the yeast, the dry measures must be weighed in grams for complete accuracy.)

sponge

1 Tbsp. (15 mL) fresh (cake) yeast
225 g water
225 g organic hard white flour

dough

225 g spring water, room temperature
Sponge
725 g organic white flour
120 g white sugar
20 g sea salt
2 Tbsp. (25 mL) fresh (cake) yeast
1 large egg
20 g powdered milk
50 g unsalted butter,
plus 450 g, chilled, for folding dough
10 g malt
1 large egg beaten with
1 Tbsp. (15 mL) water to make egg wash

time-out

If you are incredibly motivated, you can make this an all-day enterprise, but there are two obvious junctures where you can rest the dough in the refrigerator overnight and give yourself a well-deserved break. Very laid-back bakers could even stretch this process over three days.

To make sponge, combine yeast with water in a large bowl. Add flour, and stir until strands of gluten stretch from spoon, about 100 strokes. Scrape down sides of bowl, and cover with plastic wrap. Allow to rise in a warm, draft-free place for approximately 2 hours or in refrigerator overnight. When sponge starts to sag in the middle (known as "the drop"), it's ready.

To make dough, pour water around sides of bowl containing sponge to loosen it from bowl. Transfer to a larger bowl, and add remaining ingredients. Stir until dough comes together into a rough ball. Transfer to a lightly floured surface, and knead for about 8 to 10 minutes, until smooth, silky and soft. Lightly dust with flour to prevent dough from sticking to the work surface. Place dough in a large, lightly oiled bowl, turn dough to coat with oil, cover, and let rise at room temperature for 1 hour. Refrigerate for 20 minutes to cool a bit.

Slice 450 g chilled butter into 6 even pieces, and place between two sheets of plastic wrap. Work butter with your hands into one seamless, evenly thick rectangle roughly 9 by 13 inches (23 x 33 cm). Flatten dough into a rectangle about 10 by 20 inches (25 x 50 cm), then proceed with the folding technique on facing page.

Preheat oven to 345°F (175°C), and line a baking pan with parchment paper. Brush croissants again with egg wash, and bake for 7 minutes. Rotate baking pan, reduce temperature to 325°F (160°C), and bake croissants for 5 to 6 minutes, until golden brown and flaky.

Makes 12-15 croissants

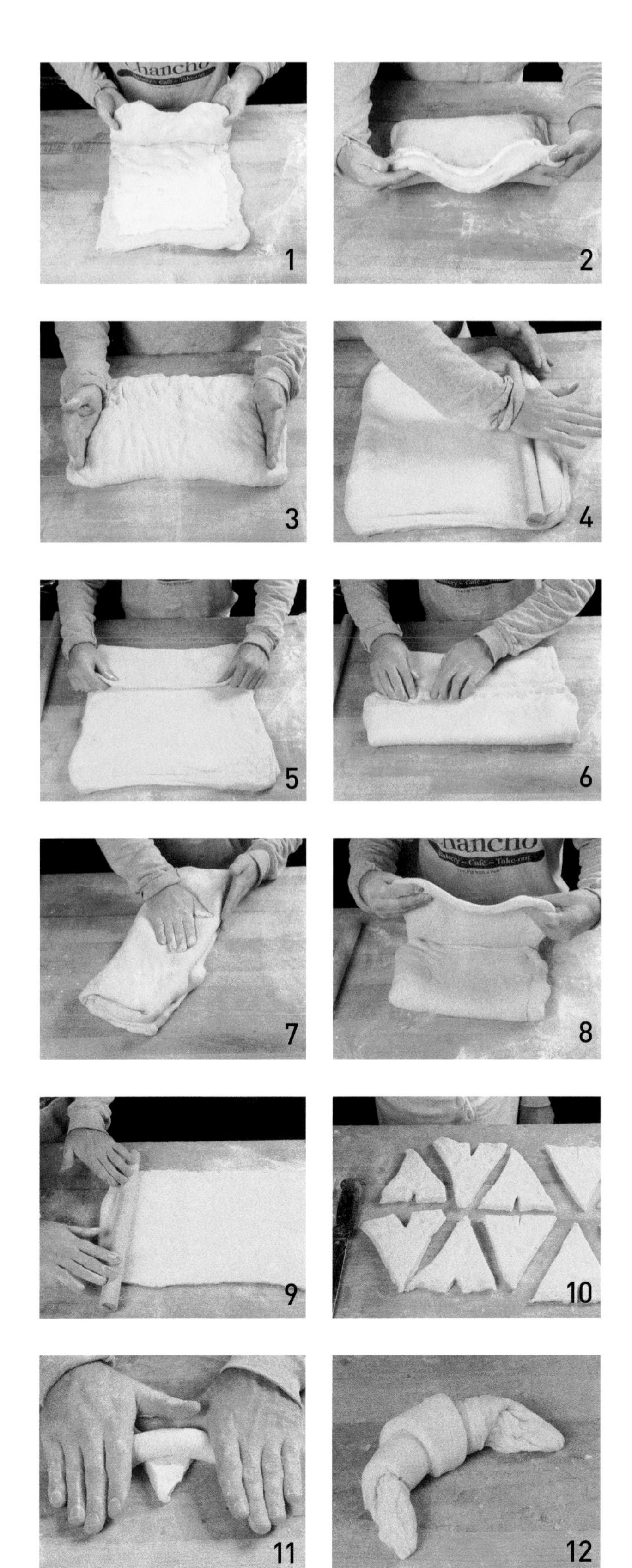

folding technique

Place rectangle of butter on two-thirds of dough, leaving top third clear and $\frac{1}{2}$ inch (1 cm) at sides and bottom. Fold top third over middle third **(1)**, then bottom third over that **(2)**. Pinch sides and top edge to keep butter in **(3)**. Lightly press dough with your hand to flatten, making sure butter stays inside. Turn one of the seams toward your body, and with a rolling pin, roll dough into a 12-by-24-inch (30 x 60 cm) rectangle **(4)**. To make your first fold, fold two outer quarters toward centre so that ends meet **(5 + 6)**. Then fold dough in half, making sure dough is even **(7)**. Place on a lightly oiled tray, cover with a damp cloth and plastic wrap so that it is airtight, and let rise at room temperature for $1\frac{1}{2}$ to 2 hours or in the refrigerator overnight.

If dough was refrigerated, remove and let sit at room temperature for 20 minutes so that butter is warm and malleable. Roll into a 14-by-26-inch (35 x 65 cm) rectangle. Fold into thirds **(8)**, cover with plastic wrap, and let rest in refrigerator for 45 to 60 minutes.

Cut dough exactly in half. Roll each piece into a 12-by-20-inch (30 x 50 cm) rectangle, roughly $\frac{1}{4}$ inch (6 mm) thick **(9)**. Cut into triangles 4 inches (10 cm) wide by 6 inches (15 cm) long. Cut a notch in bottom of each triangle **(10)**. Put any extra bits of dough in the middle of the triangle, above notch. Take the bottom corners of the widest part of the triangle and stretch away from the notch as you roll up croissant toward the point of the triangle. Tip of triangle should be on bottom of croissant when you finish **(11)**. Tweak ends down in a crescent shape **(12)**. Brush croissants with egg wash, cover with a clean tea towel, and let rise at room temperature for $1\frac{1}{2}$ to 2 hours.

Croissants are now ready to bake.

apple + cider bread

Moist and pretty, this is our bread of choice for French toast, served with Apple-Butter Crème Fraîche (see page 110).

sponge

2 Tbsp.	fresh (cake) yeast	25 mL
	or 1 Tbsp. (15 mL) active dry yeast	
$1\frac{1}{4}$ cups	water	300 mL
$1\frac{1}{4}$ cups	apple cider, room temperature	300 mL
$1\frac{1}{2}$ cups	organic hard white flour	375 mL
1 cup	organic rye flour	250 mL

dough

	Sponge	
1 Tbsp.	fresh (cake) yeast	15 mL
	or $1\frac{1}{2}$ tsp. (7 mL) active dry yeast	
$2\frac{1}{2}$–3 cups	organic hard white flour	625–750 mL
$2\frac{1}{4}$ tsp.	sea salt	11 mL
2 tsp. + 1 Tbsp.	flax seed	10 mL + 15 mL
3	unpeeled apples, medium dice	3
	(preferably McIntosh, Ida Red or Granny Smith)	
1 Tbsp.	organic rye flour	15 mL

To make sponge: Crumble yeast into room-temperature water and cider in a large bowl, and stir until small bubbles appear. If using dry yeast, proof yeast in $\frac{1}{2}$ cup (125 mL) warm water. When creamy, mix in remaining $\frac{3}{4}$ cup (175 mL) warm water and the cider.

Mix in flours, a small amount at a time, and stir vigorously until mixture is relatively smooth and strands of gluten stretch from the spoon. Cover with plastic wrap, and let rise at room temperature for $2\frac{1}{2}$ hours or in refrigerator overnight.

To make dough, scrape sponge into a large bowl and crumble in fresh yeast or stir in dry yeast. Sift hard white flour and salt together, and stir in 2 tsp. (10 mL) flax seed. Add flour mixture to sponge, a handful at a time, stirring to incorporate flour after each addition. When all but $\frac{1}{2}$ cup (125 mL) flour has been added, turn dough out onto a lightly floured surface. Flatten dough, and work apples into dough along with remaining $\frac{1}{2}$ cup (125 mL) flour. This should take about 10 minutes of kneading and folding. The dough should be smooth and elastic, with chunks of apple sticking out of it.

Place dough in a large, lightly oiled bowl, and turn dough to coat with oil. Cover with plastic wrap, and let rise in a warm place for 2 to $2\frac{1}{2}$ hours, until doubled in size.

In a small bowl, mix together 1 Tbsp. (15 mL) flax seed and rye flour. Set aside.

Turn dough out onto a lightly floured surface, and flatten, gently pushing air out of dough. Shape dough into an oval loaf by folding it onto itself several times, sealing the seam each time with the heel of your hand. Sprinkle and roll loaf in flax seed and flour mixture, and place in a loaf pan coated with cooking spray. Cover with a damp cloth, and let dough rise in a warm place for 1½ to 2 hours, until doubled in size. At this point, your finger leaves an indentation when dough is lightly pressed.

Meanwhile, preheat oven to 350°F (180°C). Bake loaf for about 45 minutes, until you hear a hollow sound when loaf is tapped. Cool completely on a wire rack.

Makes 1 loaf

pain au chocolate

For chocolate lovers, this is the croissant's better half. For best results, use high-quality, imported European chocolate.

Dough for Croissants (see page 30)

1½ cups	bittersweet chocolate chips	375 mL
1	large egg, beaten with 1 Tbsp. (15 mL) water to make egg wash	1
	Turbinado sugar	

Follow the instructions for making croissants until you complete step **(8)**, folding the dough into thirds. Cover with plastic wrap, and let rest in refrigerator for 45 to 60 minutes.

Cut dough in half. Roll first piece into a strip about 8 by 30 inches (20 x 75 cm) with square ends. Distribute chocolate chips in two lines lengthwise, 2 inches (5 cm) in from each edge. Cut dough crosswise into 6 or 7 rectangular pieces. Roll up each piece, and place seam side down, on a parchment-lined baking sheet. Repeat with remaining dough. Brush with egg wash, cover, and let rise at room temperature for 1½ to 2 hours.

Preheat oven to 345°F (175°C). Brush dough again with egg wash, sprinkle with sugar, and bake for 7 minutes. Rotate baking sheet, reduce temperature to 325°F (160°C), and bake for 5 to 6 minutes, until golden brown and flaky.

Makes 12-14 pain au chocolate

arugula + gruyère crumpets

A great weekend breakfast or brunch bread. And don't stint on the butter!

$1\frac{1}{2}$ cups	2% milk	375 mL
$1\frac{1}{2}$ tsp.	white sugar	7 mL
2 Tbsp.	fresh (cake) yeast	25 mL
$2\frac{1}{2}$ cups	all-purpose flour	625 mL
	Pinch sea salt	
$\frac{1}{2}$ tsp.	baking soda	2 mL
$\frac{3}{4}$ cup + 1 Tbsp.	spring water, room temperature	190 mL
$\frac{3}{4}$ cup	grated Gruyère cheese	175 mL
$\frac{1}{2}$ cup	minced shallots	125 mL
1 tsp.	kosher sea salt	5 mL
$\frac{1}{2}$ cup	chopped arugula	125 mL
$\frac{1}{3}$ cup	unsalted butter, melted	75 mL

Heat milk in a small saucepan over low heat until it is lukewarm. Stir in sugar and yeast, remove from heat, and let stand for 10 minutes. In a large bowl, combine flour and salt, and stir in yeast mixture. Cover with a clean tea towel, and let rise in a warm place until doubled in size, about 1 hour.

Mix baking soda with water, and pour into flour mixture. Beat vigorously with a wooden spoon. Fold in cheese, shallots, salt and arugula.

Brush a large cast-iron frying pan and 4 metal crumpet rings ($3\frac{1}{2}$ inches/9 cm in diameter by 2 inches/5 cm deep) with melted butter. Place rings in pan over medium-high heat, and fill each ring with $\frac{1}{3}$ cup (75 mL) batter. Reduce heat to low, and cook for 5 minutes, until large bubbles form on surface of crumpets. Remove rings, turn crumpets over, and cook for 5 minutes more. Remove crumpets, and repeat process until all the batter is gone.

Makes 12 crumpets

savoury brioche

Light yet rich and sophisticated. What better companion for stews, soups and sandwiches? And the chocolate brioche can only be described as transcendent.

3–4 cups	all-purpose flour	750 mL–1 L
1 tsp.	sea salt	5 mL
3 Tbsp.	white sugar	40 mL
1 cup	butter, room temperature	250 mL
5	large eggs	5
2 Tbsp.	fresh (cake) yeast or 1 Tbsp. (15 mL) active dry yeast	25 mL
3 tsp.	chopped fresh Italian parsley	15 mL
1 tsp.	chopped fresh sage	5 mL
2 tsp.	chopped fresh chives	10 mL
2 tsp.	chopped fresh rosemary	10 mL
1	thinly sliced scallion	1
1/2 cup	grated Cheddar cheese	125 mL
1/2 tsp.	freshly ground black pepper	2 mL
1	large egg, beaten with 1 Tbsp. (15 mL) water to make egg wash	1

Sift flour, salt and sugar together. In a mixer fitted with a paddle attachment, whip butter, add 3 of the eggs, then the flour mixture, 1 cup (250 mL) at a time, while continuing to beat. Add remaining 2 eggs, one at a time, while mixer is blending. (If you add all the eggs at once, the eggs and butter may not bind together.) Add yeast. Beat mixture on high for 1 minute more. Dough will be shiny and elastic. Blend in herbs, cheese and pepper at low speed. Wrap dough in plastic wrap, and refrigerate for 6 hours or overnight to firm the butter.

Preheat oven to 350°F (180°C), and lightly grease two large muffin tins. Place dough on a lightly floured surface. Divide dough into 24 pieces, and pinch a small bit off each piece to top brioche. Hand-roll large and small pieces into balls. Place large balls in muffin tins, press a hole into top of each, and press in smaller ball. Cover with a damp tea towel and plastic wrap to avoid a dry skin forming, and let rise in a warm place until doubled in size, about 1 hour. Brush with egg wash, and bake for 8 minutes. Rotate pans, and bake for 8 minutes more. Pop brioches out of muffin tins, and cool on wire rack.

Makes 24 brioches

note

To make mini brioche, use mini muffin tins and roll dough into marble-sized balls. Bake for 9 minutes or until browned on top.

chocolate brioche

To make chocolate brioche, add 1 1/2 cups (375 mL) bittersweet chocolate chips instead of the herbs, cheese and pepper.

apple ginger muffins

Apples mingle with the warm flavour of ginger, making these muffins an excellent treat on a crisp fall day.

2	large eggs	2
1/3 cup	packed brown sugar	75 mL
1/2 cup	vegetable oil	125 mL
1/2 cup	apple juice	125 mL
2 cups	chopped peeled apples	500 mL
1 tsp.	vanilla extract	5 mL
3/4 cup	whole wheat flour	175 mL
3/4 cup	all-purpose flour	175 mL
1 Tbsp.	baking powder	15 mL
1/2 tsp.	baking soda	2 mL
1/2 tsp.	salt	2 mL
1 1/2 tsp.	ground ginger	7 mL

topping

1 1/2 tsp.	unsalted butter, chilled	7 mL
1	piece crystallized ginger	1
1 Tbsp.	brown sugar	15 mL
2 1/2 tsp.	rolled oats	12 mL
2 tsp.	all-purpose flour	10 mL
1/4 tsp.	ground cinnamon	1 mL

Preheat oven to 375°F (190°C), and spray 8 to 10 muffin cups with vegetable spray or line with paper cups.

In a small bowl, whisk together eggs, brown sugar, oil and apple juice. Make sure there are no lumps in sugar. Stir in apples and vanilla.

In a large bowl, mix together flours, baking powder, baking soda, salt and ground ginger. Add egg mixture, and gently stir until flour is incorporated. Do not overmix.

To make topping, cut butter into very small chunks, and dice ginger into tiny pieces. Place butter and ginger in a small bowl, and add brown sugar, rolled oats, flour and cinnamon. Mix together, rubbing ingredients through your fingers to incorporate butter.

Portion batter into muffin cups, and sprinkle topping over each muffin. Bake for 20 to 25 minutes, until a small knife inserted in centre comes out clean with moist crumbs attached.

Makes 8-10 muffins

raisin bran muffins

Some devoted out-of-towners actually make weekly trips to pick up these muffins from Pan Chancho. They're that good.

3	large eggs	3
1/2 cup	packed brown sugar	125 mL
1/4 cup	fancy molasses	50 mL
3/4 cup	unsalted butter, melted	175 mL
1 tsp.	vanilla extract	5 mL
2 cups	buttermilk	500 mL
2 1/4 cups	bran	550 mL
1/2 cup	dark raisins	125 mL
1 cup	all-purpose flour	250 mL
1 cup	whole wheat flour	250 mL
2 tsp.	baking powder	10 mL
2 tsp.	baking soda	10 mL

Preheat oven to 350°F (180°C), and spray 12 to 15 muffin cups with vegetable spray or line with paper cups.

In a medium bowl, whisk together eggs, brown sugar, molasses, butter, vanilla, buttermilk and bran. In a large bowl, stir together raisins, flours, baking powder and baking soda. Add buttermilk mixture, stirring only until flour is incorporated. Do not overmix.

Fill muffin cups three-quarters full, and bake for 25 to 30 minutes, until tops spring back when lightly tapped.

Makes 12-15 large muffins

lemon raspberry fruit loaves

There's a lovely marriage of sweet and tart in this dense, moist loaf—perfect for a tea or coffee break.

3 1/3 cups	all-purpose flour	825 mL
1 1/3 cups	white sugar	325 mL
4 tsp.	baking powder	20 mL
1/2 tsp.	salt	2 mL
1 Tbsp.	lemon zest	15 mL
2	large eggs	2
2 cups	2% milk	500 mL
1/2 cup	melted butter	125 mL
2 tsp.	vanilla extract	10 mL
2 1/4 cups	fresh raspberries	550 mL

Preheat oven to 325°F (160°C), and grease two 9-by-5-inch (2 L) loaf pans. Sift flour, sugar, baking powder and salt together into a large bowl. Add lemon zest, and set aside.

In a medium bowl, whisk together eggs and milk, then stir in butter and vanilla. Add to flour mixture, and begin to stir. Add raspberries before flour is completely mixed through, and stir just until dry ingredients are incorporated. Fill pans evenly with batter, and bake for 1 to 1 1/4 hours, until a small knife inserted in centre comes out clean, with moist crumbs attached. Cool in pan for 10 minutes, then turn out onto rack to finish cooling.

Makes 2 loaves

appetizers

appetizers

duck confit with orange-onion marmalade on savoury brioche, page 45

artichoke heart, roasted garlic + arugula spread

Serve this tangy spread with a crusty baguette.

5	cloves garlic, peeled	5
1 Tbsp.	extra-virgin olive oil	15 mL
1	14 oz. (398 mL) can artichoke hearts, rinsed + drained	1
3 Tbsp.	chopped arugula	40 mL
1 Tbsp.	chopped fresh Italian parsley	15 mL
1/4 cup	chèvre	50 mL
1 Tbsp.	unsalted butter, room temperature	15 mL
1 heaping Tbsp.	cream cheese, room temperature	15 mL
1 Tbsp.	lemon juice	15 mL
1/2 tsp.	sea salt	2 mL
3/4 tsp.	freshly ground black pepper	4 mL

Preheat oven to 400°F (200°C). Place garlic on a piece of heavy-duty aluminum foil, and drizzle with olive oil. Wrap garlic in foil, and roast for 20 minutes. Allow to cool before using.

Blend all ingredients together in a food processor.

Makes 2 1/2 cups (625 mL)

caramelized onion + sherry spread

No chip can resist this dip. Its rich, creamy texture makes this spread a real crowd-pleaser and one of our best sellers.

8 oz.	cream cheese	225 g
3 tsp.	dry sherry	15 mL
2 tsp.	sherry vinegar	10 mL
	Pinch sea salt	
	Pinch freshly ground black pepper	
3/4 cup	Caramelized Onions (see page 226)	175 mL

Blend cream cheese, sherry, vinegar, salt and pepper in a food processor until smooth. Add caramelized onions, and purée.

Makes 1 1/4 cups (300 mL)

chopped chicken liver

If you were lucky, you had a chance to make and eat this dish with Zal, whose joy and enthusiasm turned the experience into a major event. So this one's for Zal, from Sonny and Vicki, with a whole lotta love.

1 cup	finely diced fresh chicken-fat pieces	250 mL
$2^1/_4$ cups	finely chopped cooking onion	550 mL
1 lb.	fresh chicken livers, trimmed of fat	450 g
	Extra-virgin olive oil (optional)	
3 + 1	hard-boiled eggs, finely chopped	3 + 1
2 Tbsp.	chopped fresh Italian parsley	25 mL
1 tsp.	sea salt	5 mL
$^1/_4$ tsp.	freshly ground black pepper	1 mL
	Lettuce leaves	

In a cast-iron frying pan over low heat, cook chicken fat until pieces have rendered most of their fat, about $^1/_2$ cup (125 mL), and the solid bits are browned. Strain, and reserve both rendered fat and crispy bits.

In the same pan over medium heat, fry $^1/_4$ cup (50 mL) of the onion with 1 Tbsp. (15 mL) of the rendered fat until onion is crisp and brown. Remove from heat, strain off fat, and place onion bits on a paper towel to drain.

Place chicken livers in the same pan in oven about 4 inches (10 cm) from broiler, and broil for 4 minutes on each side to cook through. Remove from oven, remove livers, allow to cool, then chop coarsely, and set aside.

Measure remaining rendered fat and add olive oil, if necessary, to make $^1/_2$ cup (125 mL). Add to pan, place over medium heat, and cook remaining 2 cups (500 mL) onion until translucent, about 10 minutes. Stir in liver and 3 of the chopped eggs, and immediately remove from heat. Transfer to a large bowl containing parsley, salt and pepper, and mix thoroughly. Firmly press mixture into a small bowl, cover and chill.

Unmould chopped liver onto a bed of lettuce, and garnish with remaining chopped egg and reserved crispy fat and onion bits. Serve with baguette or rye bread.

Serves 4

marinated feta with honey

Salty, peppery and sweet — all features that make this a very popular dish on the café's breakfast menu.

2 Tbsp.	mixed peppercorns (red, green + black)	25 mL
4–5	fresh rosemary sprigs	4–5
4–5	fresh thyme sprigs	4–5
1 lb.	goat's milk feta, cut into 1/2-inch (1 cm) slices	450 g
4 cups	extra-virgin olive oil (enough to cover feta slices)	1 L
	Liquid honey for garnish	

Place half of the peppercorns and herbs in a shallow serving dish. Layer feta slices on top, drizzle with olive oil to cover, and sprinkle with remaining peppercorns and herbs. Cover dish, and allow feta to marinate in the refrigerator for 2 days.

To serve, remove from refrigerator and allow to come to room temperature. Remove feta slices from oil, and arrange on a serving plate. Drizzle with some marinade and honey, and garnish with the marinated peppercorns. Serve with slices of baguette on the side.

Serves 8-10

herbed goat-cheese balls

Small in size but big in taste, these cheese balls make an excellent addition to an antipasto plate.

1 lb.	chèvre, crumbled	450 g
1/3	bunch fresh chives, finely chopped	1/3
2	cloves garlic, minced	2
1/4 tsp.	crushed dried chilies	1 mL
1/4	Preserved Lemon, finely chopped (see page 216)	1/4
1 cup	finely chopped fresh Italian parsley	250 mL

In a medium bowl, mix chèvre, chives, garlic, dried chilies and lemon thoroughly, then form into 3/4-inch (2 cm) balls, and roll in parsley.

Makes 36 cheese balls

homestyle bacalao

The star ingredient in this dish is bacalao, or salt cod. Just one delectable bite puts you oceanside.

$1\frac{1}{2}$ lb.	salt cod	680 g
2 Tbsp.	pine nuts	25 mL
1 lb.	Yukon Gold potatoes, peeled + finely diced	450 g
$\frac{1}{2}$ cup	extra-virgin olive oil	125 mL
2	cooking onions, thinly sliced	2
4	cloves garlic, thinly sliced	4
5 cups	canned whole tomatoes, crushed by hand	1.25 L
$\frac{1}{4}$ cup	chopped fresh Italian parsley	50 mL
3 Tbsp.	rinsed capers	40 mL
3 Tbsp.	coarsely chopped golden raisins	40 mL
$\frac{1}{3}$ cup	coarsely chopped pitted green olives	75 mL
3	roasted red peppers, julienned	3
	Freshly ground black pepper	
	Chopped fresh Italian parsley for garnish	

Soak cod in cold water for 6 to 8 hours, changing water once. Pinch a piece of fish from the thickest portion, and taste for saltiness. If it is too salty, change water and allow to sit for 1 to 2 hours more, then test again. Repeat if still too salty.

Place pine nuts in a small, dry frying pan over low heat, and toast, shaking pan, until lightly golden. Remove from heat, and set aside.

Cook potatoes in boiling salted water for 5 to 6 minutes, until tender but not disintegrating. Drain, and set aside.

Drain cod, place in a saucepan, and cover with water. Bring water to a low boil, and cook for 4 to 5 minutes, until fish is flaky. Drain, cool, and shred.

Heat olive oil in a large pan over medium heat, add onions and garlic, and cook until onions are soft, about 10 minutes. Add tomatoes and parsley, and simmer for 10 minutes. Add capers, raisins, pine nuts and potatoes, and continue to simmer until sauce has thickened, 5 to 10 minutes. Add cod, and simmer for 5 minutes. Add olives, roasted peppers and pepper to taste. Place in a serving bowl, garnish with parsley, and serve with crusty bread or Croûtes (see page 25).

Makes $5\frac{1}{2}$ cups (1.4 L)

smoked whitefish mousse

"Jingle bells, Pan Chancho sells / So order right away / Dips and spreads, smoked whitefish heads / All arranged on trays. Hey!" So went the radio jingle cowritten by Zal and staff. Silly? You bet. But there's nothing silly about this most excellent spread. Perfect for everyday snacking and special occasions.

1/2 lb.	deboned smoked whitefish	225 g
1 1/2 tsp.	lemon zest	7 mL
2 Tbsp.	lemon juice	25 mL
1 cup	35% M.F. cream	250 mL
4 tsp.	chopped fresh chives	20 mL
	Sea salt	

In a food processor, process whitefish, lemon zest and juice. Add 1/2 cup (125 mL) of the cream, and blend for a second. Place in a bowl, and fold in 3 tsp. (15 mL) of the chives and remaining 1/2 cup (125 mL) cream until consistency is light and airy. Add salt to taste. Garnish with remaining 1 tsp. (5 mL) chives, and serve on your favourite crackers.

Makes 3 cups (750 mL)

stuffed piquillo peppers

A small, mild red pepper about the size of a large jalapeño, the piquillo pepper is available canned.

1 lb.	chèvre	450 g
1 tsp.	chopped fresh thyme	5 mL
1 Tbsp.	chopped fresh chives	15 mL
1 Tbsp.	chopped fresh Italian parsley	15 mL
2 tsp.	lemon zest	10 mL
1 tsp.	minced garlic	5 mL
12–15	canned piquillo peppers	12–15

In a medium bowl, blend together all ingredients, except peppers, using a wooden spoon. Place mixture in a piping bag, and pipe into each pepper.

Serves 6-8

duck confit with orange-onion marmalade on savoury brioche

Affectionately known as "duck burgers," these mini sandwiches are a popular item on our catering menu. Duck lovers can store unused duck confit in the refrigerator for use later as a main-course dish.

duck confit

3	whole heads garlic	3
2 Tbsp.	coarse sea salt	25 mL
2 tsp.	black peppercorns	10 mL
1	whole nutmeg	1
1	bay leaf	1
1	star anise	1
2	fresh thyme sprigs	2
6	Muscovy duck legs	6
	Canola oil or duck fat	

orange-onion marmalade

4 cups	very thinly sliced cooking onion	1 L
1/4 cup	extra-virgin olive oil	50 mL
1 1/2 cups	orange juice	375 mL
	Pinch sea salt	

24	mini Savoury Brioche (halve recipe on page 35)	24
1	large egg	1
1 Tbsp.	10% M.F. cream	15 mL
2–3	duck legs confit, shredded	2–3
1 cup	orange-onion marmalade	250 mL

just ducky

To enjoy duck confit as a main course, preheat oven to 400°F (200°C). Warm fat to remove legs from pan, scraping off any residual fat. Heat an oven-proof pan over medium-high heat, and fry legs until skin is crispy. Transfer pan to oven for 10 to 15 minutes, until meat is hot. Serve with mashed potatoes and a favourite vegetable.

Preheat oven to 325°F (160°C). To confit duck legs, place garlic, salt, peppercorns, nutmeg, bay leaf, star anise and thyme in an ovenproof saucepan large enough to hold duck legs. Place legs in pan, skin side up, and cover with oil or duck fat. Bring to a simmer over medium-low heat, cover, and transfer pan to oven. Cook for 2 to 2 1/2 hours, until meat is tender.

Remove from oven, remove 3 of the legs, and set aside. (Remaining 3 legs, once cool, can be refrigerated, still completely covered in oil or fat, for future use. See "Just Ducky," below.) When legs are sufficiently cool, remove skin, shred meat and set aside.

To make marmalade, cook onion in olive oil in a heavy-bottomed frying pan over low heat, stirring occasionally, until onion is completely soft and translucent. Add orange juice and salt. Increase heat to medium to reduce liquid, stirring frequently to prevent sticking, and simmer for 15 to 20 minutes, until mixture has reached a jamlike consistency. Makes about 1 1/4 cups (300 mL).

To make mini brioches, preheat oven to 350°F (180°C). In a small bowl, whisk together egg and cream to make egg wash. Follow brioche recipe directions, using marble-sized pieces of dough. Brush dough with egg wash, and bake for 7 to 10 minutes. Brioches should sound hollow when tapped.

To assemble mini sandwiches, slice brioches in half, divide shredded meat among brioches, and top each with a dollop of marmalade.

Serves 6

pâté de campagne with foie gras

This chunky, coarse-textured terrine makes any occasion special and is perfect for holiday entertaining.

3	chicken legs	3
6 cups	water	1.5 L
8–10	bay leaves	8–10
2	fresh Italian parsley sprigs	2
1	small cooking onion, chopped	1
4 oz.	rind from fatback	115 g
1/3 cup	dry white wine	75 mL
2 Tbsp.	extra-virgin olive oil	25 mL
3 tsp.	chopped fresh thyme	15 mL
2 tsp.	chopped fresh rosemary	10 mL
2	slices stale bread, crusts removed	2
1/4 cup	chopped fresh Italian parsley	50 mL
1	clove garlic, minced	1
12 oz.	veal, finely chopped	340 g
12 oz.	pork, finely chopped	340 g
12 oz.	ground pork	340 g
7 oz.	prosciutto, finely diced	200 g
6 oz.	cold fresh fatback, rind removed, diced	170 g
1/3 cup	cognac	75 mL
	Pinch ground allspice	
	Pinch ground mace	
	Sea salt	
	Freshly ground black pepper	
10–12	bacon slices	10–12
4–5 oz.	foie gras, thinly sliced	115–140 g

Separate chicken legs into drumsticks and thighs. Skin and debone thighs, reserving skin and bones. Set thigh meat and drumsticks aside.

In a large stockpot, place water, drumsticks, reserved skin and bones, 1 of the bay leaves, parsley sprigs, onion and rind from fatback. Bring to a simmer over medium-high heat, then reduce heat to low, and simmer for 2 1/2 hours. Remove from heat, strain, and discard solids. Skim off fat, and return stock to pot. Boil to reduce stock to 1/2 cup (125 mL). Allow stock to cool, then refrigerate to chill.

Thinly slice thigh meat, place in a shallow dish, and marinate in wine, olive oil, 1 tsp. (5 mL) of the thyme, 1 tsp. (5 mL) of the rosemary and 1 of the bay leaves for 3 hours.

Preheat oven to 325°F (160°C). In a food processor, pulse bread to make coarse crumbs. In a large bowl, thoroughly mix breadcrumbs, parsley, remaining 2 tsp. (10 mL) thyme, remaining 1 tsp. (5 mL) rosemary, garlic, veal, chopped and ground pork, chilled stock, prosciutto, fatback, cognac, allspice and mace. Season liberally with salt and pepper. Fry about 1 Tbsp. (15 mL) of this mixture, let cool, and taste. Add more salt and pepper, if needed.

Line a 6-cup (1.5 L) terrine with bacon slices, and pat one-third of the meat mixture in the bottom. Then layer as follows: marinated thigh meat, one-third meat mixture, foie gras and remaining one-third meat mixture. Top with remaining bay leaves. Cover pâté with parchment or waxed paper, pressing down to pack terrine tightly. Cover with aluminum foil. Using the tip of a knife, poke holes in the foil and paper to allow steam to escape.

Place terrine in a baking dish half filled with boiling water (a bain-marie). Bake for 2 to 2½ hours, then remove from bain-marie. Remove foil, leaving parchment or waxed paper in place, and drain off liquid. Weight the pâté as it cools. Chill completely before serving.

Serves 10-12

portobello + chèvre pâté

An earthy marriage of chèvre and portobello mushrooms, this pâté can also be used as a sandwich spread.

2 Tbsp.	unsalted butter	25 mL
¼ cup	finely diced cooking onion	50 mL
1 tsp.	minced fresh rosemary	5 mL
1 tsp.	minced garlic	5 mL
¼ cup	dry white wine	50 mL
1	large portobello mushroom cap, gills removed, large dice	1
¼ tsp.	sea salt	1 mL
	Pinch freshly ground black pepper	
6–7 oz.	chèvre, crumbled, room temperature	170–200 g
1 Tbsp.	chopped fresh Italian parsley	15 mL

In a saucepan over medium heat, melt butter. Add onion, rosemary and garlic, and cook until onion is soft, about 10 minutes. Add wine, and reduce by half, 3 to 5 minutes. Add mushroom, salt and pepper, increase heat to medium-high, and cook until most of the liquid released from the mushroom has evaporated, about 5 minutes.

Remove from heat, and stir in chèvre and parsley. Mix thoroughly. Taste, and add more salt and pepper, if needed. Mould in a bowl.

Serve with fresh baguette or Croûtes (see page 25).

Makes about 2 cups (500 mL)

roasted red pepper + feta hummus

A richer, more complex variation on traditional hummus — and a perpetual favourite.

2	medium roasted red peppers, peeled, seeded + coarsely chopped	2
1	19 oz. (540 mL) can chickpeas, drained	1
2	cloves garlic, minced	2
3 Tbsp.	lemon juice	40 mL
1 Tbsp.	tahini (sesame paste)	15 mL
1 Tbsp.	extra-virgin olive oil	15 mL
1/4 cup	cow's milk feta	50 mL
1/4 tsp.	freshly ground black pepper	1 mL
	Pinch sea salt (optional)	

Blend all ingredients together in a food processor. Taste, and add salt, if needed. Serve with toasted pita dusted with za'atar.

Makes 2 1/2 cups (625 mL)

sicilian caponata

Reminiscent of puttanesca, this dish does double duty — as a pasta sauce and as a dip. The anchovy paste introduces a rich saltiness that salt alone just can't provide.

1 Tbsp.	pine nuts	15 mL
1	cooking onion, finely diced	1
2	stalks celery, finely diced	2
2 Tbsp.	extra-virgin olive oil	25 mL
4	cloves garlic, minced	4
1 tsp.	sea salt	5 mL
1 Tbsp.	tomato paste	15 mL
1/2 tsp.	anchovy paste	2 mL
1	medium eggplant, peeled, small dice (about 3 cups/750 mL)	1
1 1/2 cups	canned diced tomatoes, drained	375 mL
1 Tbsp.	red-wine vinegar	15 mL
1 tsp.	white sugar	5 mL
6	green olives, pitted + sliced	6
1/4 cup	drained capers	50 mL
1/2 tsp.	freshly ground black pepper	2 mL
1 Tbsp.	chopped fresh oregano	15 mL

Place pine nuts in a small, dry frying pan over low heat, and toast, shaking pan, until lightly golden. Remove from heat, and set aside.

In a large saucepan over medium heat, cook onion and celery in olive oil for 10 minutes, until softened. Stir in garlic, salt, tomato paste and anchovy paste. Cook for 2 minutes, then add eggplant, and cook for 15 minutes. Add tomatoes, vinegar and sugar, and cook until eggplant is soft, about 10 minutes. Stir in olives, capers and pepper. Remove from heat, allow to cool, then refrigerate to chill.

Just before serving, add oregano and pine nuts. Can be stored in refrigerator for up to 5 days.

Makes 3 cups (750 mL)

tzatziki

By draining low-fat yogurt, you get the rich taste and thicker texture of sour cream without paying the high-fat price.

3 cups	2% M.F. yogurt	750 mL
1	medium English cucumber	1
4	cloves garlic, minced	4
2 Tbsp.	chopped fresh dill	25 mL
2 Tbsp.	chopped fresh mint	25 mL
3 Tbsp.	lemon juice	40 mL
	Sea salt	
	Freshly ground black pepper	

Spoon yogurt into a clean coffee filter, place in a strainer over a bowl, and allow to drain for 1 hour. Discard liquid. Grate cucumber, and similarly drain, again discarding liquid. In a medium bowl, mix together yogurt, cucumber, garlic, dill, mint and lemon juice. Add salt and pepper to taste. Serve as a dip with toasted pita sprinkled with oregano.

Makes 3 cups (750 mL)

sun-dried tomato tapenade

You just can't put enough love in with a food processor. To get the right texture, we chop everything by hand.

2 cups	sun-dried tomatoes, soaked in hot water for 20 minutes	500 mL
3	cloves garlic, minced	3
3 Tbsp.	chopped drained capers	40 mL
2 Tbsp.	chopped lightly toasted pine nuts	25 mL
3/4 cup	extra-virgin olive oil	175 mL
4 tsp.	balsamic vinegar	20 mL

Drain tomatoes, and finely chop. In a medium bowl, thoroughly mix tomatoes with remaining ingredients. Cover, and refrigerate; can be stored for up to 10 days.

Makes about 2 cups (500 mL)

chicken chimichangas with guacamole + pickled red onions

Delicious Mexican street food all dressed up in its city clothes.

2	small cooking onions, thinly sliced	2
3	cloves garlic, minced	3
2 Tbsp.	extra-virgin olive oil	25 mL
2–4 Tbsp.	Mexican Chili Paste (see page 228)	25–50 mL
2 cups	shredded cooked chicken	500 mL
2 Tbsp.	chopped cilantro	25 mL
1 Tbsp.	lime juice	15 mL
1½ cups	grated Monterey Jack cheese	375 mL
8	6-inch (15 cm) flour tortillas	8
	Canola oil for deep-frying	
1 cup	Guacamole (see page 230)	250 mL
1 cup	Pickled Red Onions (see page 227)	250 mL

In a heavy-bottomed saucepan over medium heat, cook onions and garlic in olive oil until soft, about 10 minutes. Stir in chili paste, and remove from heat. Allow to cool, then combine in a medium bowl with chicken, cilantro and lime juice.

Place equal portions of chicken mixture and cheese in centre of each tortilla. Fold edges of tortilla toward the middle (about a 2-inch/5 cm fold), then roll tortilla from bottom to make an enclosed packet. Secure with two toothpicks. Deep-fry in hot oil until golden brown, 3 to 4 minutes. Remove, and drain on paper towels.

To serve, remove toothpicks, cut each chimichanga in half and top with guacamole and onions.

Serves 8

variation

Substitute shredded cooked pork or cooked mushrooms for the chicken.

chorizo empanadas

All chorizo is not created equal, so find a supplier who can provide a sausage that is moist and not too fatty. These tender pastries will be all the better.

1/4 cup	finely diced cooking onion	50 mL
1 tsp.	chopped garlic	5 mL
1 Tbsp.	extra-virgin olive oil	15 mL
1	chorizo sausage, small dice	1
2/3 cup	canned crushed tomatoes	150 mL
	Pinch sea salt	
	Pinch freshly ground black pepper	
2 tsp.	chopped fresh Italian parsley	10 mL
1 tsp.	chopped fresh thyme	5 mL
1	large egg	1
1 Tbsp.	10% M.F. cream	15 mL
	Sour Cream Pastry (see page 203)	

In a heavy-bottomed pan over medium-high heat, cook onion and garlic in olive oil until onion is transparent, about 2 minutes. Add chorizo, increase heat to high, and cook for 5 minutes. Reduce heat to medium, add tomatoes, and cook for 10 to 15 minutes, until mixture is thick. Remove from heat, and stir in salt, pepper, parsley and thyme. Allow to cool, then refrigerate to chill.

Preheat oven to 400°F (200°C), and line a baking sheet with parchment paper. In a small bowl, whisk egg and cream together until frothy. Set aside.

Roll pastry to a thickness of 1/8 inch (3 mm), and cut into 3-inch (7.5 cm) circles. Lay pastry rounds on a flat surface, prick with a fork, and brush edges with egg wash. Place about 1 tsp. (5 mL) chorizo mixture in centre of each round, then fold in half and crimp edges. Place empanadas on baking sheet, and bake for 15 minutes, until golden brown.

Makes about 24 empanadas

pork + shrimp samosas

The combination of pork and shrimp reflects the colonial Dutch influence on the island of Sri Lanka. All the curry-powder spices are toasted before they are ground, imparting a deeper, nuttier flavour. Buy samosa wrappers at an Asian market.

sri lankan curry powder

1 cup	coriander seed	250 mL
1/2 cup	cumin seed	125 mL
1 Tbsp.	fennel seed	15 mL
1 tsp.	fenugreek seed	5 mL
1	2-inch (5 cm) stick cinnamon	1
1 tsp.	whole cloves	5 mL
1 tsp.	cardamom seed	5 mL
2 Tbsp.	dried curry leaves	25 mL
4 Tbsp.	basmati rice	50 mL
2 tsp.	chili powder	10 mL

cilantro dipping sauce

4 cups	loosely packed cilantro	1 L
2 Tbsp.	lime juice	25 mL
5 Tbsp.	canola oil	65 mL
4–5	Thai chilies, finely minced	4–5
2	cloves garlic, minced	2

To make curry powder, toast coriander seed, cumin seed, fennel seed and fenugreek seed in separate batches in a dry frying pan over low heat until seeds are browned. Set aside.

Break up cinnamon stick, and grind together with cloves, cardamom seed, curry leaves and rice in a spice grinder or with a mortar and pestle.

In a small bowl, stir together browned seeds, cinnamon mixture and chili powder. Store in an airtight container for up to 6 months. Makes 1 1/2 cups (375 mL).

To make dipping sauce, place all ingredients in a blender, and blend until smooth. Makes 3/4 cup (175 mL).

To make samosas, parboil potato in boiling salted water, until it is soft, 5 to 7 minutes. Drain and spread on a clean towel to cool and dry.

In a heavy-bottomed pot over low heat, gently cook onion, ginger and garlic in clarified butter or ghee until soft, about 20 minutes. Add pork, increase heat to medium, and cook thoroughly, breaking apart any lumps. Add shrimp, and continue to cook until shrimp turns pink, about 2 minutes. Stir in curry powder, salt and pepper, and set aside to cool.

Stir potato, cilantro and lime juice into cooled meat mixture. Taste, and add more salt and pepper, if needed.

Meanwhile, in a small bowl, whisk egg white and cream together until frothy. Place rectangular samosa wrappers side by side on a large cutting board, and brush lightly

samosas

1 cup	finely diced Yukon Gold potato	250 mL
2 cups	finely diced cooking onion	500 mL
1 Tbsp.	minced fresh ginger	15 mL
2	cloves garlic, minced	2
2 Tbsp.	clarified butter or ghee	25 mL
6 oz.	ground pork	170 g
4 oz.	shrimp, peeled, deveined + coarsely chopped	115 g
1 Tbsp.	Sri Lankan curry powder	15 mL
1 tsp.	sea salt	5 mL
1/2 tsp.	freshly ground black pepper	2 mL
2 Tbsp.	chopped cilantro	25 mL
1 Tbsp.	lime juice	15 mL
1	large egg white	1
1 Tbsp.	10% M.F. cream	15 mL
40	samosa wrappers	40
	Canola oil for deep-frying	

with egg wash. Work in small batches to prevent egg wash from drying out once applied to wrappers. Place about 1 Tbsp. (15 mL) meat mixture on bottom right-hand corner of wrapper, then fold diagonally from the bottom corner to the opposite side, making a triangular shape. Continue triangular folding pattern to the top of the wrapper until filling is enclosed. (You're folding wrappers as you would a flag.) Deep-fry samosas in hot oil until lightly browned, 2 to 3 minutes. Drain on paper towels. Serve with dipping sauce.

Makes 40 samosas

vegetable samosas

Use 3 cups (750 mL) finely diced cooking onion, 3 Tbsp. (40 mL) clarified butter or ghee and only 1 Tbsp. (15 mL) chopped cilantro. Follow instructions for Pork + Shrimp Samosas, leaving out the pork and shrimp and adding 1 cup (250 mL) frozen peas with the parboiled potato.

caramelized onion + cheddar cheese tarts

We can barely keep up with the demand for these savoury tarts.

48	2-inch (5 cm) prebaked tart shells (double recipe for Sour Cream Pastry; see page 203)	48
2 cups	Caramelized Onions (see page 226)	500 mL
1 1/3 cups	grated extra-old Cheddar cheese	325 mL
1 Tbsp.	minced fresh chives	15 mL

Preheat oven to 350°F (180°C). Fill tart shells with onions, and top with cheese. Bake for 5 to 7 minutes to melt cheese and lightly brown. Garnish with chives, and serve hot or at room temperature.

Makes 48 tarts

tofu fritters with shrimp + smoked bacon

Unbeknownst to the mainstream population, tofu has been keeping culinary company with meat for centuries. Buy fresh tofu cakes at Asian markets and health-food stores.

dipping sauce

1/2 cup	rice-wine vinegar	125 mL
1/2 cup	white sugar	125 mL
2	cloves garlic, minced	2
1/4 tsp.	sea salt	1 mL
1 1/2 tsp.	crushed dried chilies	7 mL

fritters

4	fresh tofu cakes (about 1 1/2 lb./680 g)	4
3 Tbsp.	finely diced carrot	40 mL
2 Tbsp.	finely diced red bell pepper	25 mL
1 1/2 Tbsp.	minced fresh ginger	20 mL
2	large cloves garlic, minced	2
2	Thai chilies, minced	2
3	slices bacon or 2 slices triple-smoked bacon, finely diced + cooked	3
4	cooked shrimp, finely diced	4
1	large egg, beaten	1
2	scallions, thinly sliced	2
1/4 cup	cornstarch	50 mL
1 Tbsp.	chopped cilantro	15 mL
1/2 tsp.	sea salt	2 mL
1/8 tsp.	freshly ground black pepper	0.5 mL
	Canola oil for deep-frying	

To make dipping sauce, bring vinegar and sugar to a boil in a small saucepan, reduce heat to medium, and simmer for 3 to 5 minutes. Stir in garlic, salt and dried chilies. Set aside to cool.

To make fritters, press tofu cakes between paper towels. Weight, and place in a strainer over a bowl to drain. Refrigerate overnight. Discard liquid.

In a large bowl, mash tofu thoroughly with a fork. Add remaining ingredients, and mix well. Drop about 2 Tbsp. (25 mL) fritter batter at a time into a deep fryer, and cook until golden brown. Serve hot with dipping sauce.

Serves 4–6

variation

For a vegetarian variation, simply omit the bacon and shrimp.

siu mai

The best way to make siu mai is with family and friends — the work goes faster and the siu mai seems tastier. Pork is an essential ingredient here, but we leave it to you to decide upon a preferred ratio of pork to seafood.

1 lb.	ground pork + ground fresh raw shrimp	450 g
1 tsp.	sea salt	5 mL
8	water chestnuts, finely chopped	8
4 tsp.	chopped fresh ginger	20 mL
1/4 cup	cornstarch	50 mL
1/4 cup	Chicken Stock (see page 60)	50 mL
2 1/2 tsp.	Kung Fu soy sauce	12 mL
2 tsp.	finely chopped salted turnip (sold in Asian markets)	10 mL
2 Tbsp.	white sugar	25 mL
1/2 tsp.	dry sherry	2 mL
1/2 tsp.	toasted sesame oil	2 mL
1/4 cup	chopped cilantro	50 mL
1/4 cup	chopped scallions	50 mL
1	large egg	1
1 Tbsp.	cold water	15 mL
60	round won ton skins or Chinese dumpling wrappers	60

In a food processor, mix pork and shrimp, salt, water chestnuts, ginger, cornstarch, stock, soy sauce, turnip, sugar, sherry, sesame oil, cilantro and scallions until thoroughly combined.

In a small bowl, whisk together egg and water until frothy. Lay won ton skins or dumpling wrappers on a flat surface, and brush edges with egg wash. Work in small batches to prevent egg wash from drying out once applied to wrappers. Place about 1 tsp. (5 mL) pork mixture in centre of each wrapper, and gather up sides to form a pouch. Lightly squeeze top together while tapping bottom to flatten slightly. Repeat until all wrappers are filled.

Steam dumplings in batches in a covered bamboo steamer for 15 to 20 minutes. Serve hot with Ginger Dipping Sauce (see page 56).

Makes 60 dumplings

note

You can make these dumplings ahead of time and freeze them. After steaming the dumplings, allow to cool, then arrange on a baking sheet lined with parchment paper so that dumplings are not touching. Freeze, then store in freezer bags for up to 6 months. To reheat, steam for 15 to 20 minutes.

variation

Substitute frozen crab or lobster meat for the shrimp, but be sure the meat is squeezed dry. Use only 1 tsp. (5 mL) soy sauce in filling, and omit sugar.

shiitake potstickers with ginger dipping sauce

A heavenly little taste of a dim sum classic that offers the best of both worlds: a soft, chewy top and a crispy bottom.

ginger dipping sauce

1/2 cup	Kung Fu soy sauce	125 mL
3 Tbsp.	rice-wine vinegar	40 mL
4 tsp.	minced fresh ginger	20 mL
1 tsp.	minced garlic	5 mL
1	scallion, finely chopped	1
1 Tbsp.	toasted sesame oil	15 mL

potstickers

2 cups	sliced shiitake mushrooms	500 mL
1 Tbsp.	minced garlic	15 mL
1 Tbsp.	minced fresh ginger	15 mL
5 Tbsp.	canola oil	65 mL
	Pinch five-spice powder	
1 Tbsp.	dry sherry	15 mL
1	leek, quartered, thinly sliced + rinsed	1
1/2 cup	finely diced carrot	125 mL
	Sea salt	
1	scallion, thinly sliced	1
2 Tbsp.	dried porcini mushrooms	25 mL
1 tsp.	Kung Fu soy sauce	5 mL
1	large egg	1
1 Tbsp.	cold water	15 mL
30	round won ton skins or Chinese dumpling wrappers	30
	Canola oil for frying	

To make ginger dipping sauce, whisk all ingredients together in a small bowl. Set aside. Makes 3/4 cup (175 mL).

In a large, heavy-bottomed frying pan over medium-high heat, cook mushrooms, garlic and ginger in 2 Tbsp. (25 mL) of the oil, stirring frequently, until lightly browned, 4 to 5 minutes. Season with five-spice powder, and deglaze pan with sherry. Remove mushrooms, place in a medium bowl, and set aside.

In same pan over medium-high heat, cook leek and carrot in 2 Tbsp. (25 mL) of the oil until carrot is slightly softened. Season with salt, and add scallion. Cook for 2 minutes, then stir into mushroom mixture.

Meanwhile, soak dried mushrooms in 1/4 cup (50 mL) hot water for 10 to 15 minutes. Remove mushrooms from soaking liquid with a slotted spoon. Strain liquid,

and reserve. Finely chop porcini mushrooms, and sauté in frying pan with remaining 1 Tbsp. (15 mL) oil for 1 minute. Deglaze pan with reserved soaking liquid. Cook until most of the liquid is boiled off, about 1 minute more. Add to mushroom-leek mixture. Stir in soy sauce, and allow to cool.

In a small bowl, whisk together egg and water until frothy. Lay won ton skins or dumpling wrappers on a flat surface, and brush edges with egg wash. Work in small batches to prevent egg wash from drying out once applied to wrappers. Place about 1 tsp. (5 mL) mushroom mixture in centre of each wrapper, and gather up sides to form a pouch. Lightly squeeze top together while tapping bottom to flatten slightly. Repeat until all wrappers are filled.

Bring a large stockpot of salted water to a boil, and drop a small batch of potstickers gently into water. When potstickers float to top, transfer to a greased baking sheet, leaving space between each one so that they won't stick together. Repeat until all potstickers are cooked.

Meanwhile, heat about 1 inch (2.5 cm) oil in a deep cast-iron pot. Fry potstickers, bottoms down, until bottoms are crispy but tops remain soft. Serve hot with dipping sauce.

Makes 30 potstickers

more, please

Once you've tasted these potstickers, you'll realize there are never, ever enough. To satisfy a sudden craving, double the recipe and keep a stash on hand in the freezer. Simply place uncooked potstickers on a baking sheet lined with parchment paper, leaving generous space between them to prevent sticking, and freeze. Once frozen, store in freezer bags for up to 6 months. To cook, drop frozen potstickers into boiling salted water, adjusting heat to bring water back to a gentle boil. Then proceed as with fresh potstickers.

soups

saffron fennel soup with parmesan crisps, page 66

soups

vegetable stock

For a well-balanced flavour, use this light-coloured stock in vegetable soups, vegetarian sauces and starch dishes, such as risotto or polenta, that call for a stock.

2	leeks (white part only), finely chopped + rinsed	2
2	medium cooking onions, finely chopped	2
4	medium carrots, finely chopped	4
4	stalks celery, finely chopped	4
4	cloves garlic, lightly bruised	4
1	medium fennel bulb, finely chopped	1
1/4 cup	canola oil	50 mL
2	large potatoes, peeled + thinly sliced (optional)	2
2	bay leaves	2
3	fresh thyme sprigs	3
3	fresh Italian parsley sprigs	3
2	whole cloves	2
1/2 tsp.	black peppercorns	2 mL
4 qt.	cold water	4 L

In a large stockpot over low heat, cook leeks, onions, carrots, celery, garlic and fennel in oil until softened, about 10 minutes. Add remaining ingredients (the potatoes add body to this stock, but if you want a clear stock, do not add). Increase heat to medium-low, and bring to a simmer. Cook, uncovered, for 45 minutes, skimming off any impurities as they rise to the top.

Strain stock through a fine-mesh sieve or a colander lined with cheesecloth, and discard solids. If stock is not being used immediately, cool quickly by setting pot in a sink filled with ice water. Refrigerate stock for 2 to 3 days, or freeze in airtight containers for up to 6 months.

Makes 3 1/2 quarts (3.5 L)

chicken stock

4 lb.	chicken bones, rinsed to remove any blood	1.8 kg
4 qt.	cold water	4 L
2	medium cooking onions, coarsely chopped	2
1	clove garlic	1
1	medium carrot, coarsely chopped	1
1	stalk celery, coarsely chopped	1
1	fresh Italian parsley sprig	1
1	fresh thyme sprig	1
1	bay leaf	1
1/2 tsp.	black peppercorns	2 mL
2	whole cloves	2

Place bones in a large stockpot, and add water. Slowly bring to a simmer over medium heat, skimming off any impurities as they rise to the top. Add remaining ingredients, reduce heat to medium-low, and simmer, uncovered, for 3 to 4 hours.

Remove and discard bones. Strain stock through a fine-mesh sieve or a colander lined with cheesecloth, and discard solids. If stock is not being used immediately, cool quickly by setting pot in a sink filled with ice water. Refrigerate stock for 2 to 3 days, or freeze in airtight containers for up to 6 months.

Makes 3 1/2 quarts (3.5 L)

brown stock

Use this stock as a starting point when making any soup, stew or sauce that needs a rich, caramelized colour and flavour. Roasting the bones and vegetables first develops a more pronounced taste, while the tomato paste adds extra depth to the colour.

4 lb.	beef or veal bones	1.8 kg
2	medium cooking onions, coarsely chopped	2
1	clove garlic	1
1	medium carrot, coarsely chopped	1
1	stalk celery, coarsely chopped	1
4 qt.	cold water	4 L
1	fresh Italian parsley sprig	1
1	fresh thyme sprig	1
1	bay leaf	1
1/2 tsp.	black peppercorns	2 mL
2	whole cloves	2
1 cup	tomato paste (optional)	250 mL

stock tip

When making stock, the goal is to get as much gelatin from the bones as possible without allowing the fat to become emulsified into the liquid. The key is to keep your stock as still as possible. Never allow it to come to a boil. Simmering it and constantly skimming off impurities will ensure that your stock does not become cloudy.

Preheat oven to 375°F (190°C). In a large roasting pan, arrange bones in a single layer. Roast, turning occasionally, for about 30 minutes. Add onions, garlic, carrot and celery, and roast, uncovered, for 30 minutes, or until bones and vegetables are well browned but not burned.

Transfer bones and vegetables to a large stockpot. Deglaze roasting pan by adding 2 cups (500 mL) of the water and placing pan over medium heat on stovetop, stirring and scraping to remove any brown bits. Add this liquid to stockpot along with remaining water and rest of ingredients. Reduce heat to medium-low, and slowly bring to a simmer, skimming off any impurities as they rise to the top. Simmer, uncovered, for 6 to 8 hours, adding more water as necessary to keep bones completely covered.

Remove and discard bones. Strain stock through a fine-mesh sieve or a colander lined with cheesecloth, and discard solids. If stock is not being used immediately, cool quickly by setting pot in a sink filled with ice water. Refrigerate stock for 2 to 3 days, or freeze in airtight containers for up to 6 months.

Makes 3 1/2 quarts (3.5 L)

chilled beet + apple soup

This gorgeous soup celebrates the perfectly paired flavours of beet and apple. Our biggest challenge at Pan Chancho is getting it made before the cooks gobble up the roasted beets.

6	medium beets (about 2 lb./900 g)	6
1 Tbsp.	canola oil	15 mL
	Sea salt	
	Freshly ground black pepper	
2	green apples	2
1/2	small red onion	1/2
1 Tbsp.	pickled ginger	15 mL
2 1/2 cups	apple juice	625 mL
3 cups	water	750 mL
2 Tbsp.	prepared horseradish	25 mL
1 tsp.	white-wine vinegar	5 mL
1 cup	sour cream	250 mL

Preheat oven to 400°F (200°C). Coat unpeeled beets with oil, and place in a baking pan. Sprinkle with salt and pepper, and roast for 1 to 1 1/4 hours, until a knife can be inserted into the centre of the beets with no resistance.

Allow beets to cool, then peel, and cut into 1-inch (2.5 cm) dice. Peel apples, and cut into 1-inch (2.5 cm) dice. Cut onion into 1-inch (2.5 cm) dice.

In a blender or food processor, chop beets, apples, onion and ginger, and slowly add just enough apple juice to purée ingredients. When mixture is smooth, transfer to a large bowl, and stir in water and any remaining apple juice. Taste, and add more salt and pepper, if needed. Refrigerate soup until well chilled.

In a small bowl, whisk together horseradish, vinegar and sour cream. Refrigerate until needed.

To serve, ladle chilled soup into individual bowls and top with a dollop of sour-cream mixture.

Serves 4–6

chilled smoked tomato + chipotle soup

In this spicy soup, paprika, roasted tomatoes and chipotle chilies bring home the smoky heat.

20	small plum tomatoes	20
1	medium cooking onion	1
3 Tbsp.	extra-virgin olive oil	40 mL
3	cloves garlic, minced	3
1/2 tsp.	smoked paprika	2 mL
2	chipotle chilies in adobo sauce, rough-chopped	2
1 tsp.	adobo sauce	5 mL
1 Tbsp.	brown sugar	15 mL
2 cups	Vegetable Stock (see page 60)	500 mL
1/8 tsp.	sea salt	0.5 mL
	Sour cream for garnish	

Over direct medium heat on a charcoal barbecue, roast tomatoes, turning to cook on all sides, until skin blisters, about 10 minutes. Allow to cool slightly, then peel, seed and rough-dice (you should have about 3 1/2 cups/875 mL), reserving any juice. Set aside.

Meanwhile, char whole onion with its skin on, turning to cook on all sides, until onion is soft, about 20 minutes. Allow to cool slightly, then peel and rough-chop. Set aside.

In a large pot over low heat, cook onion in olive oil with garlic, paprika, chipotles and adobo sauce for about 5 minutes. Add tomatoes and reserved juice, and stir in sugar. Simmer for 10 minutes. Add stock, increase heat to medium-high, and bring to a boil. Reduce heat to low, and simmer for 10 to 15 minutes, until slightly thickened. Add salt.

Purée mixture using blender, immersion blender or food processor. Refrigerate until well chilled, or cool quickly by setting pot in a sink filled with ice water.

To serve, ladle soup into individual bowls and garnish with a dollop of sour cream.

Serves 4–6

creamy cheddar with three onions

Sharp, tangy two-year-old Cheddar teams up with sweet caramelized onions for a mellow meeting.

2	shallots, minced	2
1	stalk celery, minced	1
1/4 cup	unsalted butter	50 mL
1/3 cup	all-purpose flour	75 mL
5 cups	2% milk	1.25 L
1 cup	dry white wine	250 mL
3/4 cup	minced Caramelized Onions (see page 226)	175 mL
1 lb.	old Cheddar cheese, grated	450 g
1 Tbsp.	Dijon mustard	15 mL
	Sea salt	
	Freshly ground black pepper	
1/2	bunch fresh chives, finely chopped	1/2

In a large pot over medium heat, cook shallots and celery in butter until vegetables are softened, about 10 minutes. Reduce heat slightly, and stir in flour. Cook for 2 minutes, stirring constantly.

To prevent lumps from forming, gradually whisk in milk. Increase heat to medium, and cook, stirring, until mixture begins to thicken, 12 to 15 minutes.

When mixture has the consistency of light cream, add wine, onions, cheese, mustard and salt and pepper to taste. Cook, stirring, until cheese is melted and incorporated into soup.

To serve, ladle soup into individual bowls and sprinkle liberally with chives.

Serves 4-6

east indian dahl with fresh curry leaves

In this hearty rendition of a dish found on menus throughout India, the high-protein lentil is brought to life by aromatic curry leaves and spices. It's at its most flavourful when refrigerated and reheated and served the next day.

1/2 cup	ghee or clarified butter	125 mL
1 1/2 tsp.	black mustard seed	7 mL
1/2 cup	finely diced cooking onion	125 mL
1/4 cup	minced garlic	50 mL
6	cloves garlic, whole	6
1/4 cup	minced fresh ginger	50 mL
13	fresh curry leaves	13
4	green cardamom pods, cracked	4
4	whole cloves	4
1	1-inch (2.5 cm) stick cinnamon	1
1/4 cup	Madras Curry Paste (see page 229)	50 mL
1 cup	canned diced tomatoes, with juice	250 mL
5 cups	Chicken Stock or Vegetable Stock (see page 60)	1.25 L
1 cup	red lentils, picked + rinsed	250 mL
1/2	bay leaf	1/2
1/2	lemon, seeds removed	1/2
1 tsp.	sea salt	5 mL
1/4 tsp.	freshly ground black pepper	1 mL

In a medium pot over medium heat, melt ghee or clarified butter, add mustard seed, and cook, shaking pan, until seeds pop. Reduce heat to low, and add onion, minced and whole garlic, ginger and curry leaves, and cook, stirring occasionally, until aromatics are soft, 15 to 20 minutes. Add cardamom, cloves and cinnamon, and cook for 2 minutes. Stir in curry paste and tomatoes, and simmer for 5 minutes. Remove from heat, and set aside.

Meanwhile, in a large pot over medium-high heat, bring stock to a boil. Add lentils, bay leaf and lemon, and allow to cook at a rolling boil to prevent lentils from settling to bottom of pot, where they would stick and burn. Cook uncovered, stirring occasionally, until lentils disintegrate, 30 to 45 minutes.

Stir in reserved curry mixture, reduce heat to medium-low, and simmer, uncovered, for 15 minutes. Add salt and pepper. Before serving, remove cinnamon stick, bay leaf and lemon.

Serves 4-6

saffron fennel soup with parmesan crisps

A little Pernod helps deepen the delicate licorice flavour that the fennel bulb and seeds bring to this soup.

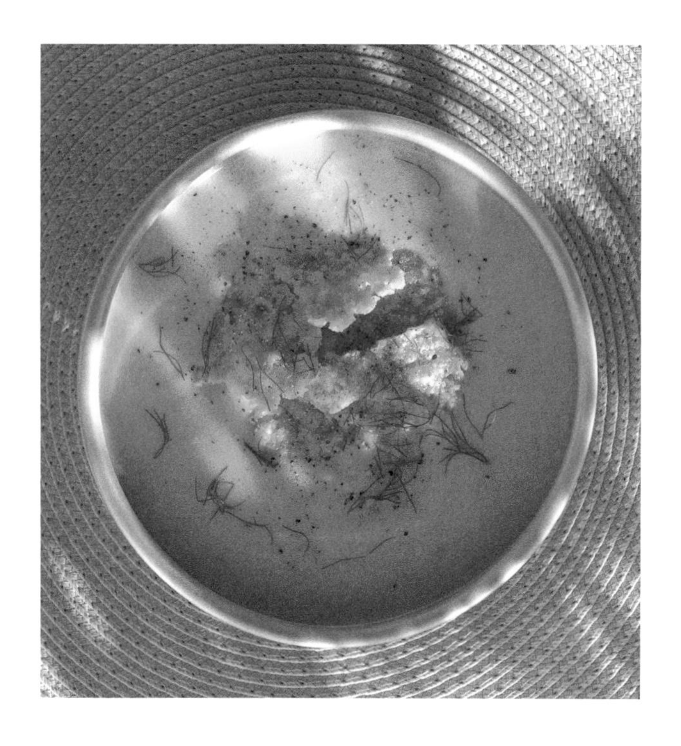

parmesan crisps

$1\frac{1}{2}$ cups	freshly grated Parmigiano-Reggiano	375 mL

soup

$\frac{1}{4}$ tsp.	fennel seed	1 mL
1	medium cooking onion, thinly sliced	1
2	cloves garlic, minced	2
2 Tbsp.	unsalted butter	25 mL
1	medium potato, peeled + thinly sliced	1
1	fennel bulb, thinly sliced	1
	Small pinch saffron threads	
$\frac{1}{2}$ cup	dry white wine	125 mL
5 cups	Vegetable Stock (see page 60)	1.25 L
$\frac{1}{2}$ cup	35% M.F. cream	125 mL
	Sea salt	
	Freshly ground black pepper	
2 Tbsp.	Pernod	25 mL

To make Parmesan crisps, preheat oven to 375°F (190°C) and line a baking sheet with parchment paper. Parmesan must be hand-grated, rather than finely ground. Sprinkle cheese over baking sheet, and lightly shake to ensure that it is evenly spread. Bake for 10 to 12 minutes, until cheese is golden. Allow to cool, then break into pieces. Set aside.

To make soup, toast fennel seed in a small, dry frying pan over medium heat for 2 to 3 minutes. Keep pan moving, but do not toss seeds. Remove from heat, and allow to cool. Grind seeds to a powder using a spice grinder or a mortar and pestle. Set aside.

In a large pot over medium-low heat, cook onion and garlic in butter until softened but not browned, about 10 minutes. Add potato, fennel bulb, saffron, wine and stock. Increase heat to medium-high, and bring to a boil. Reduce heat, and simmer uncovered, stirring occasionally, for 45 minutes. Stir in cream, fennel seed and salt and pepper to taste.

Purée soup using blender, immersion blender or food processor. Return soup to pan, and place over low heat to keep warm.

Just before serving, heat Pernod in a shallow pan over high heat, and ignite. Immediately remove from heat, and allow flame to burn off. Stir into soup. Ladle into individual bowls, and garnish with Parmesan crisps.

Serves 4–6

carrot + red pepper soup with parmesan

Roasted red peppers and a Parmesan cheese garnish give this everyday soup a sophisticated disposition.

1/4 cup	unsalted butter	50 mL
1	medium cooking onion, small dice	1
3	cloves garlic, minced	3
2 1/2 tsp.	sea salt	12 mL
1/4 tsp.	freshly ground black pepper	1 mL
1/2 Tbsp.	finely chopped fresh thyme	7 mL
1 lb.	carrots, peeled, medium dice	450 g
2	roasted red peppers, coarsely chopped	2
7 1/2 cups	Vegetable Stock (see page 60)	2 L
1 1/2 tsp.	red-wine vinegar	7 mL
1/2 cup	freshly grated Parmigiano-Reggiano	125 mL

Melt butter in a large pot over medium-low heat. Add onion, garlic, salt and pepper. Reduce heat to low, and cook, stirring occasionally, until mixture is softened, about 10 minutes. Add thyme, carrots and roasted red peppers, and cook, stirring occasionally, for 10 minutes.

Add stock, increase heat to medium-high, and bring to a low, rolling boil. Cook until carrots are soft enough to purée, about 15 minutes.

Purée soup using immersion blender, food processor or blender. Return soup to pan, and place over low heat to keep warm. Stir in vinegar. Add more salt and pepper to taste.

To serve, ladle soup into individual bowls and garnish with cheese.

Serves 4-6

parsnip + pear soup with toasted almonds

The pears sweeten and lighten the earthiness of the parsnips, while the almond garnish adds crunch and texture.

	Sliced almonds for garnish	
1	medium cooking onion, sliced	1
2 Tbsp.	unsalted butter	25 mL
1 lb.	parsnips, peeled, trimmed + thinly sliced	450 g
2	pears, peeled, cored + sliced	2
1/4 cup	dry white wine	50 mL
4 cups	Vegetable Stock (see page 60)	1 L
1 cup	35% M.F. cream	250 mL
	Sea salt	
	Freshly ground black pepper	

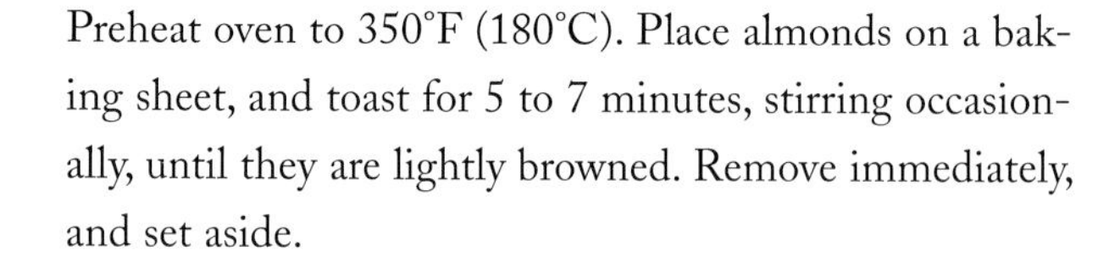

Preheat oven to 350°F (180°C). Place almonds on a baking sheet, and toast for 5 to 7 minutes, stirring occasionally, until they are lightly browned. Remove immediately, and set aside.

In a large pot over medium-low heat, cook onion in butter until soft but not browned, about 10 minutes. Add parsnips, pears, wine and stock, increase heat to medium-high, and bring to a boil. Reduce heat to low, and simmer, uncovered, for 45 minutes.

Stir in cream, and heat through. Add salt and pepper to taste. Purée soup using blender, immersion blender or food processor, return soup to pan, and place over low heat to keep warm.

To serve, ladle soup into individual bowls and garnish with almonds.

Serves 4-6

butternut squash + vanilla soup with cardamom crème fraîche

Cardamom and vanilla step up to bring this soup its warm, spicy and sweet flavour.

cardamom crème fraîche

1/2 cup	Crème Fraîche (see page 230)	125 mL
1/4 tsp.	ground cardamom	1 mL
	Pinch sea salt	

soup

1/4 cup	unsalted butter	50 mL
4 cups	diced butternut squash	1 L
1 cup	finely diced cooking onion	250 mL
1 cup	finely diced carrot	250 mL
1/2	red bell pepper, small dice	1/2
1/2	vanilla bean	1/2
2 cups	Vegetable Stock (see page 60)	500 mL
1 cup	apple juice	250 mL
1/2 cup	35% M.F. cream	125 mL
1 tsp.	sea salt	5 mL
1/8 tsp.	white pepper	0.5 mL
	Cardamom crème fraîche for garnish	

To make cardamom crème fraîche, blend together crème fraîche, cardamom and salt in a small bowl. Refrigerate until ready to use.

To make soup, melt butter in a large pot over medium heat, and cook squash, onion, carrot and red pepper for about 5 minutes. Split vanilla bean and scrape out seeds. Add seeds and pod to pot along with stock and apple juice. Reduce heat to low, and simmer, uncovered, for 25 to 35 minutes, until squash is tender.

Remove vanilla pod, and purée soup using blender, immersion blender or food processor. Stir in cream and salt and pepper. Return soup to pot over low heat to keep warm.

To serve, ladle soup into individual bowls and garnish with a dollop of crème fraîche.

Serves 4-6

pricey spicy

A member of the ginger family, cardamom is native to India but is also cultivated in tropical regions such as Thailand and Central America. By weight, it's one of the most expensive spices in the world, but since a little of its intensely aromatic flavour goes a long way, it's easy to be frugal. Cardamom seeds begin to lose their essential oils when they are ground, so cardamom is best stored in seed or pod form.

bitter greens + potato soup

Soul-soothing and good for you too: After a bowl of this restorative soup, you'll just feel like a better person.

2 Tbsp.	unsalted butter	25 mL
1	medium cooking onion, small dice	1
4	cloves garlic, minced	4
2	stalks celery, small dice	2
$^1/_8$ tsp.	ground nutmeg	0.5 mL
2	Yukon Gold potatoes, peeled, medium dice	2
2 Tbsp.	dry white wine	25 mL
$7^1/_2$ cups	Vegetable Stock (see page 60)	2 L
3 cups	packed bitter greens (frisée, escarole or dandelion greens)	750 mL
$1^1/_2$ cups	packed baby spinach	375 mL
1 Tbsp.	sea salt	15 mL
$^1/_4$ tsp.	freshly ground black pepper	1 mL

In a large pot, melt butter over medium-low heat. Add onion, garlic, celery and nutmeg. Reduce heat to low, and cook, stirring occasionally, until vegetables are softened, about 10 minutes.

Add potatoes, wine and stock. Increase heat to medium-high to bring to a low, rolling boil. Cook until potatoes are soft enough to purée. Add bitter greens and spinach, and purée using blender, immersion blender or food processor. Return to pot, and place over low heat for about 3 minutes to heat through. Add salt and pepper, and serve.

Serves 4-6

smoked trout chowder

The brothlike base of this true Canadian chowder gives it a delicacy that distinguishes it from heartier versions.

1/2 cup	unsalted butter	125 mL
1/2 cup	finely diced cooking onion	125 mL
1/2 cup	finely diced carrot	125 mL
1/2 cup	finely diced celery	125 mL
1/2 cup	finely diced fennel bulb	125 mL
1 tsp.	dried thyme	5 mL
2 Tbsp.	all-purpose flour	25 mL
1/2 cup	dry white wine	125 mL
6 cups	Fish Stock (see below)	1.5 L
1 cup	finely diced potato	250 mL
1/2 cup	35% M.F. cream	125 mL
	Sea salt	
	Freshly ground black pepper	
2–3 cups	flaked smoked trout	500–750 mL
2 Tbsp.	chopped fresh thyme for garnish	25 mL

In a large pot over medium heat, melt butter. Add onion, carrot, celery, fennel and dried thyme, and cook, stirring occasionally, until vegetables are softened, about 10 minutes. Stir in flour, and cook, stirring constantly, for 2 to 3 minutes.

In a small saucepan over medium heat, reduce wine by about half. Add wine and stock to vegetable mixture, increase heat to medium-high, and bring to a boil. Reduce heat to low so that soup comes to a simmer. Add potato, and cook, uncovered, until potato is tender, about 10 minutes. Stir in cream and salt and pepper to taste.

To serve, place 1/2 cup (125 mL) trout in each bowl, ladle chowder over top, and garnish with fresh thyme.

Serves 4-6

fish stock

2	medium cooking onions, finely chopped	2
1	medium carrot, finely chopped	1
1	stalk celery, finely chopped	1
1	medium fennel bulb, finely chopped	1
1/4 cup	canola oil	50 mL
4 lb.	bones + trimmings of white-fleshed, nonoily fish, such as halibut, snapper or haddock	1.8 kg
2	bay leaves	2
2	fresh thyme sprigs	2
2	fresh Italian parsley sprigs	2
1/2 tsp.	whole cloves	2 mL
1 tsp.	black peppercorns	5 mL
3 1/2 qt.	cold water	3.5 L

In a large stockpot over low heat, cook onions, carrot, celery and fennel in oil until softened, about 10 minutes. Add remaining ingredients, increase heat to medium-low, and bring to a simmer. Cook, uncovered, for 35 to 45 minutes, skimming off any impurities as they rise to the top.

Remove bones and discard. Strain stock through a fine-mesh sieve or a colander lined with cheesecloth, and discard solids. If stock is not being used immediately, cool quickly by setting pot in a sink filled with ice water. Refrigerate stock for 2 to 3 days, or freeze in airtight containers for up to 6 months.

Makes 3 1/2 quarts (3.5 L)

greek lamb soup with feta + honey

Honey rounds out the gamy lamb flavour, and feta gives this soup a salty kick. We use lamb left over from our Cumin-Spiced Lamb Pita (see page 122), which features the same seasonings, but any slow-braised lamb will do.

1/2 tsp.	cumin seed	2 mL
2 Tbsp.	extra-virgin olive oil	25 mL
1	medium cooking onion, small dice	1
2	cloves garlic, minced	2
1	2-inch (5 cm) stick cinnamon	1
1/2 tsp.	dried tarragon	2 mL
1	28 oz. (796 mL) can diced tomatoes, with juice	1
1/2 cup	dry red wine	125 mL
2 cups	Chicken Stock (see page 60)	500 mL
1 Tbsp.	honey	15 mL
1/4 lb.	shredded cooked lamb	115 g
1/4 tsp.	crushed dried chilies	1 mL
1/8 tsp.	sea salt	0.5 mL
1/2 cup	crumbled cow's milk feta for garnish	125 mL

Place cumin seed in a small, dry frying pan over medium heat, and toast, shaking pan, until seeds become fragrant, about 2 minutes. Allow to cool, then grind using a spice grinder or a mortar and pestle. Set aside.

In a large pot, heat olive oil over medium-low heat. Add onion, garlic, cumin, cinnamon and tarragon. Reduce heat to low, and cook, stirring occasionally, until onion and garlic are softened, about 10 minutes. Stir in remaining ingredients, except feta.

Increase heat to medium-high to bring soup to a simmer. Reduce heat to low, and continue to simmer, uncovered, for 15 to 20 minutes. Taste, and add more salt, if needed. Remove cinnamon stick.

To serve, ladle soup into individual bowls and garnish with feta.

Serves 4-6

corn chowder with double-smoked bacon

To deepen the colour of this chowder, Zal's trick was a hit of saffron. The flavour is unaffected, but the yellow pops.

	Small pinch saffron threads	
1/2 cup	dry white wine	125 mL
3	1/4-inch-thick (6 mm) strips double-smoked bacon, small dice	3
2 Tbsp.	unsalted butter	25 mL
1	small cooking onion, finely diced	1
1	stalk celery, finely diced	1
1/2	medium red bell pepper, finely diced	1/2
1/2	medium green bell pepper, finely diced	1/2
2 Tbsp.	all-purpose flour	25 mL
3 cups	Chicken Stock (see page 60)	750 mL
1/2 tsp.	sea salt	2 mL
1/2 tsp.	freshly ground black pepper	2 mL
1 1/2 cups	fresh or frozen corn kernels	375 mL
1 1/2 cups	puréed fresh or frozen corn kernels	375 mL
1	medium potato, small dice	1
1 cup	35% M.F. cream	250 mL

Pulverize saffron threads with a mortar and pestle. Soak saffron in a splash of the wine to cover.

Meanwhile, in a large pot over medium heat, cook bacon until crispy, then remove with a slotted spoon and reserve, leaving bacon fat in pot. Add butter, onion, celery and peppers, and cook until vegetables are softened, about 10 minutes.

Stir flour into vegetables, and cook, stirring, for 2 minutes. Add stock, saffron tea and remaining wine, increase heat to medium-high, and bring soup to a boil. Add salt, pepper, whole and puréed corn and potato. Reduce heat to low, and simmer, uncovered, for 10 to 15 minutes, until potato is tender.

Stir in cream and reserved bacon, and simmer for 5 to 10 minutes to heat through.

Serves 4-6

soupe aux pois canadien-français

To everyone lucky enough to have spent their childhoods watching French-Canadian grandparents work their magic in the kitchen — and to those grandparents — we lovingly dedicate this soup.

1 cup	dried whole yellow peas or 2 cups (500 mL) split yellow peas	250 mL
1 Tbsp.	lard or canola oil	15 mL
1/3 cup	small-diced salt pork or bacon	75 mL
1/2 cup	small-diced cooking onion	125 mL
1/2 cup	small-diced celery	125 mL
1/3 cup	small-diced carrot	75 mL
8 cups	Ham Broth (see facing page)	2 L
2 Tbsp.	pot barley	25 mL
1 cup	shredded cooked pork or diced ham (optional)	250 mL
	Sea salt	
	Freshly ground black pepper	

If using whole peas, soak overnight in 4 cups (1 L) cold water, then rinse five times, drain and set aside. If using split peas, rinse under cold running water until water runs clear, and set aside.

In a large pot, heat lard or oil over low heat, add salt pork or bacon, and cook, stirring, until fat has been rendered. Do not allow to brown.

Add onion, celery and carrot. Increase heat to medium-low, and cook until vegetables are softened, stirring occasionally, about 10 minutes. Add broth, and increase heat to high. When broth comes to a boil, add peas. Allow to come back to a boil, then reduce heat to medium-low, and simmer, uncovered, for 30 minutes, stirring occasionally.

Add barley, and cook for about 15 minutes, stirring occasionally, until peas are soft and barley is tender. Stir in pork or ham, if using, and add salt and pepper to taste.

Serves 4-6

ham broth

Knowing the secret of a great ham broth just may be part of the Québécois genetic makeup. Here's how we break the code.

1	whole smoked ham hock	1
1/2 lb.	salt pork	225 g
	Ham bone + trimmings (optional)	
7 qt.	Chicken Stock (double recipe on page 60) or water	7 L
5	medium carrots, cut into 1/2-inch (1 cm) slices	5
5	stalks celery, cut into 1/2-inch (1 cm) slices	5
3	medium cooking onions, large dice	3
1	small fennel bulb, large dice	1
7	fresh thyme sprigs	7
7	fresh Italian parsley sprigs	7
13	black peppercorns	13
1	bay leaf	1
5	whole cloves	5

In a large stockpot, place ham hock, salt pork and ham bone and trimmings, if using. Add stock or water, and bring to a boil over high heat. Immediately reduce heat to medium-low so that liquid comes to a low simmer. Skim off any scum or fat that rises to the surface. Add remaining ingredients, and simmer, uncovered, for about 3 hours, until ham hock is tender and meat falls off the bone.

Strain broth through a fine-mesh sieve or a colander lined with cheesecloth, and discard solids. If broth is not being used immediately, cool quickly by setting pot in a sink filled with ice water. Refrigerate broth for 2 to 3 days, or freeze in airtight containers for up to 6 months. Reserve ham-hock meat to use in another dish, such as Soupe aux Pois Canadien-Français (see facing page).

Makes 5 quarts (5 L)

double-strength chicken noodle soup

Made from a stock that is made from a stock, this soup has a seductively intense chicken flavour.

reinforced chicken stock

10 cups	Chicken Stock (see page 60)	2.5 L
5	medium carrots, small dice	5
5	medium cooking onions, small dice	5
5	stalks celery, small dice	5
1 cup	dry white wine	250 mL
7	fresh thyme sprigs	7
7	fresh Italian parsley sprigs	7

soup

1/2 cup	small-diced cooking onion	125 mL
1/2 cup	small-diced celery	125 mL
1/2 cup	small-diced carrot	125 mL
1 Tbsp.	canola oil	15 mL
1 tsp.	dried thyme	5 mL
1/4 cup	dry white wine	50 mL
5 cups	reinforced chicken stock	1.25 L
1/2 cup	fresh or frozen green peas	125 mL
2 cups	diced cooked chicken	500 mL
1 Tbsp.	sea salt	15 mL
1/2 tsp.	freshly ground black pepper	2 mL
1/3 lb.	linguine, broken into 1-inch (2.5 cm) pieces	150 g
	Extra-virgin olive oil	

To make reinforced chicken stock, combine all ingredients in a large stockpot, place over medium-high heat, and bring to a simmer. Reduce heat to medium, and continue to simmer, uncovered, until stock is reduced by half, 45 to 60 minutes.

Strain stock through a fine-mesh sieve or a colander lined with cheesecloth, and discard solids. If stock is not being used immediately, cool quickly by setting pot in a sink filled with ice water. Refrigerate stock for 2 to 3 days, or freeze in airtight containers for up to 6 months. Makes approximately 6 cups (1.5 L).

To make soup, cook onion, celery and carrot in oil in a large pot over medium-low heat until vegetables are softened, about 10 minutes. Rub thyme between your palms over the pot to release its essential oils. Add wine, increase heat to high, and reduce wine by half.

Add stock, and bring to a boil. Add peas, chicken, salt and pepper. Reduce heat to low, taste, and add more salt and pepper, if needed.

Meanwhile, in a large pot, bring water and a pinch of salt to a boil (if you have additional stock left over, add to water). Add linguine, and cook until al dente. Drain, and drizzle linguine with a little olive oil to prevent it from sticking together.

To serve, spoon linguine into individual soup bowls and ladle soup over top.

Serves 4–6

chicken tortilla soup

There are probably a hundred different versions of this popular Mexican soup, but this is our very own favourite. Don't hesitate to turn up the heat factor to suit your own taste.

1 Tbsp.	extra-virgin olive oil	15 mL
1	medium onion, small dice	1
4	cloves garlic, minced	4
1/2 tsp.	crushed dried chilies	2 mL
1/2 tsp.	ground cumin	2 mL
1/2 tsp.	dried oregano	2 mL
1/2 tsp.	chili powder	2 mL
1/4 cup	diced canned mild green chilies	50 mL
1 1/4 cups	canned diced tomatoes, with juice	300 mL
3/4 cup	frozen corn kernels	175 mL
2 Tbsp.	chopped cilantro	25 mL
2 Tbsp.	lime juice	25 mL
6 cups	Chicken Stock (see page 60)	1.5 L
2 cups	shredded cooked chicken	500 mL
1 1/2 tsp.	sea salt, plus more to sprinkle tortillas	7 mL
4	corn tortillas for garnish	4
	Canola oil to fry tortillas	

Heat olive oil in a large pot over medium-low heat, and add onion, garlic, dried chilies, cumin, oregano and chili powder. Reduce heat to low, and cook, stirring occasionally, until onion and garlic are softened, about 10 minutes.

Stir in green chilies, tomatoes, corn, cilantro, lime juice and stock. Increase heat to medium-high to bring soup to a simmer, then reduce heat to low, and simmer for 5 minutes. Add chicken and salt, and simmer for 3 minutes to warm through. Taste, and add more salt, if needed.

Meanwhile, cut tortillas in half, then into 1/2-inch (1 cm) strips. Add 1/2 inch (1 cm) oil to a large frying pan, and place over medium-high heat. Add tortilla strips, and fry until golden and crisp. Remove with a slotted spoon, place on paper towels to drain, and sprinkle with salt.

To serve, ladle into individual soup bowls and garnish with tortilla crisps.

Serves 4–6

coconut-lime chicken soup

Warm and calming, this is the Asian equivalent of chicken noodle soup — a complete comfort food.

1 Tbsp.	canola oil	15 mL
1	medium cooking onion, cut in half lengthwise + thinly sliced	1
2	cloves garlic, minced	2
1 Tbsp.	minced fresh ginger	15 mL
2½ tsp.	minced fresh lemongrass	12 mL
2	Thai chilies, stems removed, minced	2
2	fresh or frozen kaffir lime leaves, stems removed, minced	2
2 cups	shredded cooked chicken	500 mL
¼ cup	lime juice	50 mL
6 cups	Chicken Stock (see page 60)	1.5 L
1 cup	unsweetened coconut milk	250 mL
1 Tbsp.	sea salt	15 mL
½ cup	chopped cilantro for garnish	125 mL

Heat oil in a large pot over medium-low heat. Add onion, garlic, ginger, lemongrass, chilies and lime leaves. Reduce heat to low, and cook, stirring occasionally, until mixture is very soft, about 10 minutes. Do not brown.

Add chicken, and simmer for 3 minutes to heat through. Stir in lime juice, stock and coconut milk, increase heat to medium-high, and bring soup to a simmer. Reduce heat to low, and continue to simmer for 5 minutes. Add salt.

To serve, ladle soup into individual bowls and garnish with cilantro.

Serves 4–6

vietnamese hot + sour pineapple chicken with rice vermicelli

This recipe was developed by Viên Hoang, a much-loved, longtime cook at Chez Piggy and Pan Chancho with a great sense of humour. When Viên made this soup, everybody was very, very happy. Both Tom Yum Hot and Sour Paste and Sour Shrimp Paste can be purchased at your local Asian market.

1/4 cup	canola oil	50 mL
1	small cooking onion, finely diced	1
1	small carrot, finely diced	1
1	stalk celery, finely diced	1
1 cup	canned unsweetened pineapple chunks, with juice	250 mL
1 cup	canned diced tomatoes, with juice	250 mL
4 cups	Chicken Stock (see page 60)	1 L
3–4 Tbsp.	fish sauce	40–50 mL
2 Tbsp.	Tom Yum Hot and Sour Paste	25 mL
2 Tbsp.	Sour Shrimp Paste	25 mL
2 Tbsp.	lime juice	25 mL
1 cup	diced cooked chicken	250 mL
4 oz.	rice vermicelli	115 g
2 Tbsp.	chopped scallions for garnish	25 mL
2 Tbsp.	chopped cilantro for garnish	25 mL

Place oil in a large pot over low heat, add onion, carrot and celery, and cook until vegetables are softened, about 10 minutes. Add pineapple, tomatoes, stock and fish sauce, increase heat to medium-high, and bring to a boil.

In a small bowl, thin the two pastes by stirring in a bit of hot liquid from pot, then add to soup. Reduce heat to low, and cook, uncovered, for 5 to 10 minutes to incorporate flavours. Stir in lime juice and chicken.

Meanwhile, bring a medium pot of water to a boil, add a little salt and the vermicelli. Cook for 2 to 3 minutes. Drain and rinse in cold water to prevent vermicelli from sticking together.

To serve, divide vermicelli among individual bowls and ladle soup on top. Garnish with scallions and cilantro.

Serves 4-6

variation

Substitute cooked rice for the rice vermicelli and/or cooked shrimp for the chicken.

soy beef soup with lime leaf + thai basil

The lime leaf is a critical ingredient in this soup, so please don't leave it out. Available fresh or frozen from Asian markets, it contributes an intense concentrated lime flavour that nothing else can duplicate.

1 Tbsp.	toasted sesame oil	15 mL
2 Tbsp.	canola oil	15 + 15 mL
1	small cooking onion, sliced	1
2	Thai chilies, minced	2
5 cups	Chicken Stock or Brown Stock (see pages 60 and 61)	1.25 L
1/3 cup	Kikkoman soy sauce	75 mL
2	stalks fresh lemongrass, bruised + cut into 2-inch (5 cm) pieces	2
3	fresh or frozen kaffir lime leaves	3
2 cups	sliced shiitake mushroom caps	500 mL
1 1/4 cups	diced cooked roast beef	300 mL
2 Tbsp.	lemon juice	25 mL
	Sea salt	
	Fresh Thai basil leaves for garnish	

Heat sesame oil and 1 Tbsp. (15 mL) canola oil in a large pot over medium-low heat. Add onion and chilies, and cook, stirring, until softened, about 10 minutes. Add stock, soy sauce, lemongrass and lime leaves. Increase heat to medium-high, and bring to a boil. Reduce heat to low, and simmer, uncovered, for 45 minutes.

Meanwhile, in a frying pan over high heat, sauté mushrooms in remaining 1 Tbsp. (15 mL) canola oil, stirring occasionally. Add mushrooms, beef and lemon juice to soup. Add salt to taste. Increase heat to medium-high, and heat through, about 3 minutes.

To serve, ladle soup into individual bowls and garnish with basil.

Serves 4–6

beer, beef + onion soup

With its abundance of onions and croûte garnish, this hearty soup is a tasty play on classic French onion soup.

7	medium cooking onions, cut into 1/4-inch (6 mm) slices	7
2 Tbsp.	finely chopped fresh rosemary	25 mL
1/4 cup	unsalted butter	50 mL
1 3/4 cups	honey brown ale	425 mL
6 cups	Brown Stock (see page 61)	1.5 L
2 cups	cubed cooked roast beef or steak (about 1 lb./450 g)	500 mL
1 Tbsp.	sea salt	15 mL
1/2 tsp.	freshly ground black pepper	2 mL
1 cup	grated Gruyère cheese	250 mL
4–6	Croûtes (see page 25)	4–6

In a large pot over medium-low heat, cook onions and rosemary in butter until onions are soft and transparent, 15 to 20 minutes. Do not brown. Add ale, increase heat to medium-high, and bring to a boil, then reduce heat to low, and allow soup to come to a simmer. Add stock, and simmer, uncovered, for 30 minutes, stirring occasionally.

Add meat, and simmer for about 5 minutes, until heated through. Add salt and pepper, then taste, and add more, if needed.

To serve, ladle soup into individual bowls, sprinkle with cheese and place a croûte on top.

Serves 4–6

salads

green beans gremolata, page 89

salads

marinated artichoke-heart salad

Light and easy — the ideal summer salad.

3	sun-dried tomatoes	3
2	14 oz. (398 mL) cans artichoke hearts packed in water, rinsed, drained + quartered	2
2 tsp.	lemon juice	10 mL
2 Tbsp.	chopped fresh Italian parsley	25 mL
1 tsp.	minced garlic	5 mL
1/4 cup	whole Taggiasche olives (or other small black Italian olive)	50 mL
3	pitted green olives, cut into eighths	3
1 tsp.	coarsely chopped drained capers	5 mL
1/4 cup	extra-virgin olive oil	50 mL
	Sea salt	
	Freshly ground black pepper	

Place sun-dried tomatoes in a small bowl, and cover with boiling water. Let soak until tender, up to 20 minutes. Remove from water, cut into slivers, and set aside.

In a medium bowl, toss artichokes with lemon juice. Add parsley, garlic, olives, tomatoes and capers, and toss gently. While tossing, drizzle in olive oil and add salt and pepper to taste.

Serves 4–6

beet salad with fresh horseradish + dill

For beet lovers everywhere — heat, sweetness and good looks, all in one place.

2 lb.	beets, cooked, cooled + peeled	900 g
1/4 cup	finely grated fresh horseradish root	50 mL
1/4 cup	red-wine vinegar	50 mL
1/4 cup	grapeseed oil	50 mL
2 Tbsp.	chopped fresh dill	25 mL
	Pinch sea salt	
	Pinch freshly ground black pepper	

Cut beets into 1/2-inch (1 cm) dice, and place in a large bowl. Add remaining ingredients, and toss to combine. Taste, and add more salt and pepper, if needed.

Serves 4–6

balsamic mushrooms

Good things come to those who wait. These savoury mushrooms take time, but they're more than worth it.

2½ lb.	whole white mushrooms	1.1 kg
½ cup	extra-virgin olive oil	125 mL
¾ cup	balsamic vinegar	175 mL
2 tsp.	sea salt	10 mL
½ tsp.	freshly ground black pepper	2 mL
1	fresh rosemary sprig	1
¼ cup	diced roasted red pepper	50 mL
2 tsp.	chopped fresh Italian parsley	10 mL

Preheat oven to 400°F (200°C). In a large bowl, toss mushrooms with olive oil, vinegar, salt and pepper until well coated. Arrange in a shallow roasting pan in a single layer. Place rosemary sprig in centre of mixture. Roast for about 1 hour, stirring every 10 minutes to recoat mushrooms.

Mushrooms are done when they are a rich dark mahogany colour and most of the liquid has been absorbed. You may have to top up the olive oil and balsamic vinegar in the last stages, as the water content of mushrooms evaporates.

Let cool, and garnish with roasted red pepper and parsley.

Serves 4–6

asian noodles

Mild but delicious and loaded with vegetables, Asian Noodles are wildly popular at Pan Chancho. Use both Asian oil and dragon oil (see facing page) to flavour stir-fries, cooked vegetables and meat dishes.

asian oil

4 cups	canola oil	1 L
1	stalk fresh lemongrass, finely minced	1
1/3 cup	minced garlic	75 mL
2 Tbsp.	minced Thai chili	25 mL
1/3 cup	chopped fresh ginger	75 mL
1/2 tsp.	whole cloves	2 mL
1	star anise	1
1/4 cup	Kung Fu soy sauce	50 mL

salad

1	1 lb. (450 g) pkg. fresh egg noodles (chow mein)	1
1/3 cup	well-mixed Asian oil	75 mL
2 Tbsp.	Kung Fu soy sauce	25 mL
1/2 tsp.	sea salt	2 mL
1/4 tsp.	freshly ground black pepper	1 mL
1 cup	bite-size broccoli florets	250 mL
1 cup	bite-size cauliflower florets	250 mL
1 cup	julienned carrots	250 mL
2 Tbsp.	Asian oil, oil only	25 mL
1 cup	thinly sliced celery (cut on the diagonal)	250 mL
2 cups	julienned green cabbage	500 mL
1/4 cup	chopped fresh mint	50 mL
1/3 cup	coarsely chopped cilantro	75 mL

To make Asian oil, mix all ingredients together in a medium saucepan. Place over medium-high heat, and bring to a boil. Reduce heat to medium-low, and simmer, stirring, for 15 minutes. Remove from heat, allow to cool, then refrigerate until needed. (Asian oil can be stored in refrigerator in a covered container for up to 6 months.) Makes 5 cups (1.25 L).

To make salad, bring a large pot of salted water to a rolling boil. Add noodles, stirring to separate. Boil for 3 minutes only. Drain, and spread on a baking sheet. While noodles are still warm, add the well-mixed Asian oil and soy sauce, and toss to mix thoroughly. Add salt and pepper. Let noodle mixture cool to room temperature.

Meanwhile, blanch broccoli, cauliflower and carrots separately by cooking briefly in boiling salted water, then drain and plunge into cold water. Drain again, and set aside.

Heat the 2 Tbsp. (25 mL) Asian oil (oil only) in a large sauté pan, and add celery and cabbage. Sauté until vegetables are slightly softened but still have a bit of crunch. Remove from heat. Add blanched vegetables, and let cool to room temperature.

In a large bowl, mix together noodles, vegetables, mint and cilantro. Taste, and add more salt and pepper, if needed.

Serves 4–6

dragon noodles

Yes, Dragon Noodles are spicy. Dragon…fire…heat…get it?

dragon oil

3/4 cup	minced garlic	175 mL
3/4 cup	chopped fresh ginger	175 mL
1/4 cup	coarsely chopped fermented black beans	50 mL
1/3 cup	crushed dried chilies	75 mL
4 cups	canola oil	1 L
1 Tbsp.	toasted sesame oil	15 mL

salad

1	1 lb. (450 g) pkg. fresh egg noodles (chow mein)	1
3 Tbsp.	well-mixed dragon oil	40 mL
1 Tbsp.	toasted sesame oil	15 mL
1/4 cup	Kung Fu soy sauce	50 mL
1/2 tsp.	sea salt	2 mL
1/4 tsp.	freshly ground black pepper	1 mL
1/2 cup	chopped cilantro	125 mL
3	scallions, cut in half lengthwise + sliced diagonally	3

To make dragon oil, mix all ingredients together in a medium saucepan. Place over medium-high heat, and bring to a boil. Reduce heat to medium-low, and simmer, stirring, for 15 minutes. Remove from heat, allow to cool, then refrigerate until needed. (Dragon oil can be stored in refrigerator in a covered container for up to 6 months.) Makes 5-6 cups (1.25-1.5 L).

To make salad, bring a large pot of salted water to a rolling boil. Add noodles, stirring to separate. Boil for 3 minutes only. Drain, and spread on a baking sheet. While noodles are still warm, add dragon oil, sesame oil and soy sauce, and toss to mix well. Add salt and pepper. Let noodle mixture cool to room temperature.

Place noodles in a large bowl, and toss in cilantro and scallions. Taste, and add more salt and pepper, if needed.

Serves 4-6

chayote coleslaw

This lightly cooked slaw has a satisfying crunchy texture and a mild Southwestern flavour.

1	small poblano chili	1
1	small red bell pepper	1
1	small yellow bell pepper	1
2	small chayote squash	2
1 Tbsp. + 3 Tbsp.	extra-virgin olive oil	15 mL + 40 mL
2 Tbsp.	sherry vinegar	25 mL
1/2 tsp.	ground cumin	2 mL
1/2 tsp.	freshly ground black pepper	2 mL
1/4 tsp.	ground coriander seed	1 mL
3/4 tsp.	white sugar	4 mL
	Pinch sea salt	
2 Tbsp.	coarsely chopped cilantro	25 mL

Grill peppers on all sides on the barbecue or in the oven under the broiler until skin blisters and blackens. Place peppers in a large bowl, cover with plastic wrap, and allow to stand for a few minutes to loosen skin. When peppers are cool enough to handle, peel, seed and cut into strips. Place in a large bowl, and set aside.

Peel squash, and julienne into matchstick-sized strips. In a large frying pan over high heat, heat 1 Tbsp. (15 mL) olive oil, and fry squash until lightly cooked, about 1 minute. Do not overcook; squash should be crisp but still quite firm. Remove from heat, allow to cool, then add to bowl with peppers.

In a small bowl, whisk together 3 Tbsp. (40 mL) olive oil, vinegar, cumin, pepper, coriander, sugar, salt and cilantro. Toss with vegetables, and chill before serving.

Makes 4 cups (1 L)

marinated bocconcini salad

Without the tomatoes that traditionally keep it company, bocconcini finally gets a real chance to shine.

1 3/4 lb.	bocconcini cheese, sliced into 1/2-inch (1 cm) rounds	800 g
1/4 cup	extra-virgin olive oil	50 mL
2 Tbsp.	lemon juice	25 mL
2	medium roasted red peppers, large dice	2
1/2 cup	roughly chopped fresh basil	125 mL
	Sea salt (optional)	
	Freshly ground black pepper (optional)	

In a medium bowl, toss cheese with olive oil and lemon juice. Add roasted red peppers and basil, and toss gently. Taste, and add salt and pepper, if needed. Serve at room temperature.

Serves 4–6

green beans gremolata

Garlic, parsley and lemon zest put the gremolata (a classic Italian condiment) in this dish.

1½ lb.	green beans, cleaned	680 g
¼ cup	extra-virgin olive oil	50 mL
¾ tsp.	sea salt	4 mL
½ tsp.	cracked black peppercorns	2 mL
½ cup	finely chopped fresh Italian parsley	125 mL
	Zest of 2 lemons, finely chopped	
2	cloves garlic, minced	2

Immerse beans in boiling water. Blanch for 3 minutes, drain, and plunge into cold water to arrest cooking process. Drain again, and pat dry.

Place beans in a large bowl, and toss with remaining ingredients.

Serves 4-6

chickpea, feta + cumin salad

The start of a beautiful relationship: Chickpeas and cumin are a perfect combination, and the salty taste of feta with the smoky taste of roasted red pepper provides an extra flavour dimension.

2	19 oz. (540 mL) cans chickpeas, drained + rinsed	2
1 cup	medium-diced goat's milk feta (about 4 oz./115 g)	250 mL
¾ cup	medium-diced roasted red pepper	175 mL
2 tsp.	toasted cumin seed	10 mL
1 tsp.	sea salt	5 mL
	Pinch freshly ground black pepper	
¼ cup	extra-virgin olive oil	50 mL
1 Tbsp.	lemon juice	15 mL
1 Tbsp.	chopped fresh Italian parsley	15 mL

In a large bowl, combine all ingredients. Taste, and add more salt and pepper, if needed.

Serves 4-6

fattoush

For a real burst of summer flavour, make this Lebanese bread salad when tomatoes are at their peak. It's also a great way to use up leftover pita.

dressing

2 Tbsp.	extra-virgin olive oil	25 mL
1/3 cup	lemon juice	75 mL
3/4 tsp.	sea salt	4 mL
1/8 tsp.	freshly ground black pepper	0.5 mL
2 tsp.	za'atar	10 mL

salad

3	medium tomatoes, cored + seeded, cut into 1-inch (2.5 cm) pieces	3
1	small green bell pepper, cut into 1-inch (2.5 cm) pieces	1
1/2 cup	quartered + sliced English cucumber	125 mL
4	scallions, chopped	4
2 tsp.	chopped fresh Italian parsley	10 mL
2 tsp.	chopped fresh mint	10 mL
2 tsp.	chopped cilantro	10 mL
1	Pita Bread (see page 19)	1
	Extra-virgin olive oil	
	Lemon juice	
	Sea salt	
	Za'atar	

To make dressing, whisk ingredients together in a small bowl, and set aside. Whisk again before adding to salad.

In a medium bowl, toss together tomatoes, green pepper, cucumber, scallions, parsley, mint and cilantro. Set aside.

Preheat oven to 350°F (180°C). Place pita on a baking sheet. Brush both sides of pita with olive oil and lemon juice, and sprinkle with salt and za'atar. Toast in oven until crisp, turning once, about 10 minutes. Remove from oven, and allow to cool. Break into 1-inch (2.5 cm) pieces, add to salad, and toss gently. Pour dressing over salad, and toss until well coated. Serve immediately.

Serves 4–6

ah, za'atar

A Middle Eastern spice blend, za'atar combines sesame seeds, ground sumac, dried thyme and sometimes a little salt. It is sprinkled over meats, vegetables and breads to enhance their flavour. It can also be mixed with olive oil and drizzled over hot bread, used as a dip or made into a paste. You will find it in Middle Eastern shops.

lime-cilantro coleslaw

Thai chilies bring a touch of heat to this creamy Southwestern slaw, which is also served in our Fish Tacos with Salsa Fresca (see page 161).

dressing

1	large egg	1
1 tsp.	sea salt	5 mL
1/4 cup	lime juice	50 mL
3/4 cup	canola oil	175 mL
1–2	Thai chilies, minced	1–2

salad

6 cups	thinly sliced green cabbage	1.5 L
1/4 cup	chopped cilantro	50 mL
2	scallions, chopped	2
	Zest of 2 limes	

To make dressing, use a food processor to combine egg, salt and 1 tsp. (5 mL) of the lime juice. Slowly add oil until mixture is consistency of stiff mayonnaise. Whisk in chilies and remaining lime juice, and set aside.

In a large bowl, combine cabbage, cilantro, scallions and lime zest. Whisk dressing again, then pour over salad and toss until well coated. Refrigerate until ready to serve.

Serves 4-6

greek salad

With its bright colours and fresh tastes, our take on Greek salad is a real celebration of summer.

dressing

1/2 cup	extra-virgin olive oil	125 mL
3/4 cup	canola oil	175 mL
1/3 cup	red-wine vinegar	75 mL
2 Tbsp.	lemon juice	25 mL
1/2 tsp.	dried oregano	2 mL
1/2 tsp.	sea salt	2 mL
1/4 tsp.	freshly ground black pepper	1 mL

salad

1	large red bell pepper, cut into 1-inch (2.5 cm) pieces	1
1	large yellow bell pepper, cut into 1-inch (2.5 cm) pieces	1
1	large green bell pepper, cut into 1-inch (2.5 cm) pieces	1
1/2	medium red onion, cut into 3/4-inch (2 cm) dice	1/2
1/2	quartered English cucumber, cut into 3/8-inch (9 mm) slices	1/2
1 1/2 cups	halved (lengthwise) cherry tomatoes	375 mL
16	whole kalamata olives with pit	16
1/2 tsp.	sea salt	2 mL
1/4 tsp.	freshly ground black pepper	1 mL
1/2 lb.	cow's milk feta, cut into 3/4 -inch (2 cm) cubes	225 g

To make dressing, whisk ingredients together in a small bowl. Set aside.

In a large bowl, gently toss together all salad ingredients except feta. Just before serving, stir dressing well, then add 1/2 cup (125 mL) to salad, and toss. Gently fold in feta. (Remaining dressing will keep in a covered container in refrigerator for several days.)

Serves 4-6

fourme d'ambert + glazed yams on arugula with pecan vinaigrette

A creamy raw cow's milk blue cheese from France, Fourme d'Ambert beautifully complements the sweet yams and spicy arugula. If you can't find it, St. Agur is an excellent substitute.

yams

2–3	medium yams	2–3
1/4 cup	extra-virgin olive oil	50 mL
1/4 cup	lemon juice	50 mL
1/4 cup	packed brown sugar	50 mL
	Sea salt	
	Freshly ground black pepper	

dressing

3/4 cup	canola oil	175 mL
2 Tbsp.	pecan oil	25 mL
1/4 cup	lemon juice	50 mL
3/4 tsp.	Dijon mustard	4 mL
1/4 tsp.	sea salt	1 mL
1/8 tsp.	freshly ground black pepper	0.5 mL

salad

1/2 cup	pecans	125 mL
8 cups	baby arugula	2 L
	Pickled Red Onions (see page 227)	
5 oz.	Fourme d'Ambert cheese	155 g

To prepare yams, preheat oven to 350°F (180°C) and line a baking sheet with parchment paper. Peel yams, and cut off the ends. Cut yams in half lengthwise, then slice each half lengthwise into three or four wedges.

In a large bowl, whisk together olive oil, lemon juice and brown sugar until sugar is dissolved. Add yam wedges, and toss to coat. Place wedges on baking sheet, and drizzle with oil mixture. Season with salt and pepper. Bake for 40 minutes, until yams are just softened. Remove from oven, and allow to cool.

To make dressing, whisk together all ingredients in a small bowl, and set aside. Whisk again just before using.

To toast pecans, preheat oven to 300°F (150°C). Spread pecans evenly on a baking sheet. Bake for 8 to 12 minutes, stirring frequently, until pecans are lightly browned and fragrant. Set aside to cool.

In a large bowl, toss arugula with just enough dressing to moisten. Divide yam wedges among salad plates. Mound arugula in centre, and spoon onions on top. Garnish with pecans and 5 teaspoon-sized chunks of cheese. Drizzle dressing around edge of each salad, and serve.

Serves 4–6

mixed-grain pilaf

Three grains and pumpkin seed oil impart a deep nutty flavour to a pilaf that will make any occasion special.

$^3/_4$ cup	wild rice	175 mL
$^3/_4$ cup	quinoa	175 mL
	Sea salt	
$^3/_4$ cup	bulgur	175 mL
1 cup	medium-diced cooking onion	250 mL
$^1/_2$ cup	dried cranberries	125 mL
1 Tbsp.	extra-virgin olive oil	15 mL
$1^1/_2$ Tbsp.	chopped fresh thyme	20 mL
$^1/_2$ cup	chopped fresh Italian parsley	125 mL
$^1/_4$ tsp.	freshly ground black pepper	1 mL
2 Tbsp.	pumpkin seed oil	25 mL

To clean wild rice, place in a medium bowl and run under cold running water, stirring with your hand, until water is clear. Drain in a colander.

Cook quinoa, uncovered, in $1^1/_2$ quarts (1.5 L) salted (1 tsp./5 mL) water at a rolling boil for 12 minutes. Drain, spread on a baking sheet, and allow to cool to room temperature.

Place bulgur in a small bowl, and add $^3/_4$ cup (175 mL) lightly salted boiling water. Mix well. Cover tightly with plastic wrap, and let sit for 20 minutes or until all liquid is absorbed. Fluff with a fork, and allow to cool to room temperature.

In a medium saucepan, add wild rice to $1^1/_2$ quarts (1.5 L) cold water. Bring to a slow, rolling boil, and cook, uncovered, until rice looks split open and is tender, 50 to 60 minutes. (You may need to add water to keep rice from cooking dry.) Drain well, and spread on a baking sheet to cool to room temperature.

Meanwhile, in a sauté pan over low heat, cook onion and cranberries in olive oil, stirring occasionally, until onion is very soft and transparent, 15 to 20 minutes. Do not brown. Add thyme, and cook for 2 minutes. Remove from heat, and allow to cool to room temperature.

In a large bowl, toss together quinoa, bulgur, wild rice, onion mixture, parsley, 1 tsp. (5 mL) salt, pepper and pumpkin seed oil. Taste, and add more salt and pepper, if needed. Serve at room temperature.

Serves 4–6

warm potato salad with sherry vinegar + crispy leeks

In this Spanish-influenced salad, crispy leeks serve as a contrast in texture and taste to the sweet roasted pepper.

7–8	new red potatoes, quartered	7–8
2	leeks, julienned + washed	2
	Canola oil	
2 Tbsp.	sherry vinegar	25 mL
2 tsp.	minced garlic	10 mL
1 Tbsp.	extra-virgin olive oil	15 mL
1	roasted red pepper, julienned	1
4–5	fresh basil leaves	4–5
	Sea salt	
	Freshly ground black pepper	

Cook potatoes in boiling salted water until tender. Drain and allow steam to evaporate.

In a heavy-bottomed frying pan over medium-high heat, shallow-fry leeks in 1/2 inch (1 cm) canola oil until they are crispy and golden brown. Remove from pan, and drain on paper towels.

In a large bowl, add vinegar and garlic to warm potatoes, stirring gently to coat potatoes completely. Stir in leeks, olive oil, roasted red pepper and basil. Add salt and pepper to taste. Serve warm.

Serves 4

spanish orange + red onion salad

When you're craving a light accent for a more substantial main course, serve this simple and refreshing salad.

6	navel oranges	6
1/2	medium red onion, thinly sliced lengthwise	1/2
2 tsp.	chopped fresh Italian parsley	10 mL
1/4 cup	freshly squeezed orange juice	50 mL
1 Tbsp.	extra-virgin olive oil	15 mL
1 1/2 tsp.	sherry vinegar	7 mL
1/2 tsp.	sea salt	2 mL
1/8 tsp.	freshly ground black pepper	0.5 mL

Cut top and bottom from each orange. With the flat bottom of the orange resting on a cutting board, use a sharp knife to slice away the peel and pith, following the curve of the orange. Slice oranges crosswise into 1/4-inch (6 mm) rounds, and place in a medium bowl. Add onion and parsley, and toss gently.

In a small bowl, whisk together orange juice, olive oil, vinegar, salt and pepper. Pour over orange mixture, and toss gently until well coated. Chill until ready to serve.

Serves 4–6

moroccan chickpeas with mint

Easy to make, this North African-inspired salad is spicy and fresh-tasting. We serve it with Cumin-Spiced Lamb Pita (see page 122), another longtime Pan Chancho favourite.

1¾ cups	medium-diced cooking onion	425 mL
⅓ cup	extra-virgin olive oil	75 mL
	Sea salt	
2 tsp.	sweet paprika	10 mL
2 tsp.	crushed dried chilies	10 mL
1 tsp.	ground cumin	5 mL
¾ tsp.	ground cinnamon	4 mL
1½ Tbsp.	chopped garlic	20 mL
½ cup	tomato paste	125 mL
1½ Tbsp.	chopped fresh Italian parsley	20 mL
1½ Tbsp.	chopped fresh mint	20 mL
2	19 oz. (540 mL) cans chickpeas, drained + rinsed	2

In a large frying pan over medium-low heat, cook onion in olive oil with 1½ tsp. (7 mL) salt, paprika, dried chilies, cumin and cinnamon until onion is soft, about 10 minutes. Add garlic, and cook for 2 minutes. Add tomato paste, mix well, and cook for 5 minutes.

In a large bowl, stir together onion mixture, parsley, mint and chickpeas. Taste, and add more salt, if needed. Serve at room temperature.

Serves 4-6

ptitim with toasted pistachios + apricots

Zal insisted to anyone who would listen that Israeli couscous was not the same thing as ptitim — at least, not the ptitim of his childhood. But you'll probably find it sold under the name Israeli couscous.

dressing

2 Tbsp.	extra-virgin olive oil	25 mL
1 Tbsp.	lemon juice	15 mL
1/4 tsp.	ground cinnamon	1 mL
1/8 tsp.	cayenne	0.5 mL
1 tsp.	sea salt	5 mL
1/8 tsp.	freshly ground black pepper	0.5 mL

salad

1/3 cup	pistachios	75 mL
1 cup	ptitim (or Israeli couscous)	250 mL
1/2	medium red onion, large dice	1/2
1/2	medium red bell pepper, cut into 1-inch (2.5 cm) pieces	1/2
1/2	medium yellow bell pepper, cut into 1-inch (2.5 cm) pieces	1/2
1/2	medium green bell pepper, cut into 1-inch (2.5 cm) pieces	1/2
1 Tbsp.	minced garlic	15 mL
1 Tbsp.	minced fresh ginger	15 mL
1 Tbsp.	extra-virgin olive oil, plus more for tossing vegetables	15 mL
1 cup	large-diced zucchini	250 mL
1 cup	large-diced eggplant	250 mL
	Sea salt	
2 1/2 tsp.	minced Preserved Lemon (see page 216)	12 mL
2 Tbsp.	chopped cilantro	25 mL
6	dried apricots, small dice	6

To make dressing, whisk all ingredients together in a small bowl, and set aside. Whisk again before adding to salad.

In a small, dry frying pan over medium-low heat, toast pistachios, shaking pan, until they are lightly browned. Set aside.

Cook ptitim as you would pasta, in boiling salted water until al dente, 8 to 10 minutes. Drain, place in a large bowl, and set aside.

In a medium sauté pan over low heat, gently cook onion, peppers, garlic and ginger in olive oil until softened, 15 to 20 minutes. Do not brown. Let cool, and toss with ptitim.

Preheat oven to 350°F (180°C). In separate bowls, toss zucchini and eggplant in olive oil. Roast in separate pans in oven until golden and soft, 12 to 20 minutes. Lightly salt, and allow to cool. Add to ptitim mixture with pistachios, preserved lemon, cilantro and apricots, and toss to mix.

Pour dressing over salad, and toss until well combined.

Serves 6

red cabbage + apple salad with fresh horseradish

With freshly grated horseradish and apple cider vinegar, this salad, developed by Jeff Phillips, has zip to spare.

dressing

2½ Tbsp.	extra-virgin olive oil	35 mL
2½ Tbsp.	canola oil	35 mL
⅓ cup	apple cider vinegar	75 mL
2½ Tbsp.	white-wine vinegar	35 mL
½ tsp.	sea salt	2 mL
2 Tbsp.	brown sugar	25 mL
	Pinch freshly ground black pepper	

salad

5½ cups	thinly sliced red cabbage	1.4 L
1	medium apple (any crisp red variety), julienned with peel on	1
¼ cup	small-diced red bell pepper	50 mL
¼ cup	small-diced yellow bell pepper	50 mL
1 Tbsp.	finely grated fresh horseradish root	15 mL

To make dressing, whisk all ingredients together in a small bowl until sugar is completely dissolved. Set aside.

In a medium bowl, toss cabbage, apple, peppers and horseradish together. Whisk dressing again, pour over salad, and toss until cabbage is well coated.

Serves 4-6

fennel + apple salad

Much neglected as a fresh ingredient, fennel, when partnered with apple, is a delightful salad accompaniment to smoked salmon.

4 cups	thinly sliced fennel bulb	1 L
1	Granny Smith apple, thinly sliced	1
6 Tbsp.	lemon juice	75 mL
1 cup	thinly sliced red onion	250 mL
¼ cup	extra-virgin olive oil	50 mL
¼ cup	chopped fresh Italian parsley	50 mL
	Sea salt	
	Freshly ground black pepper	

In a large bowl, toss fennel and apple slices with lemon juice. Add onion, olive oil and parsley, and toss. Add salt and pepper to taste.

Serves 4-6

wehani + wild rice salad with feta, sweet potato + rosemary

A reddish brown relative of basmati, Wehani rice splits slightly when cooked and has a mild popcorn aroma.

1 cup	Wehani rice	250 mL
1 cup	wild rice	250 mL
2 1/2 cups	medium-diced peeled sweet potato	625 mL
1 cup	small-diced red onion	250 mL
2 tsp.	minced garlic	10 mL
2 Tbsp.	minced fresh rosemary	25 mL
1 tsp.	sea salt	5 mL
1/4 tsp.	freshly ground black pepper	1 mL
1 Tbsp.	extra-virgin olive oil	15 mL
1/4 cup	balsamic vinegar	50 mL
1 lb.	goat's milk feta, cut into 1/2-inch (1 cm) cubes	450 g

To clean Wehani rice, place in a medium bowl under cold running water, stirring with your hand, until water is clear. Drain in a colander. Repeat process with wild rice.

Place each rice in a separate saucepan with 4 cups (1 L) cold salted water. Bring water to a rolling boil, reduce heat to medium-low, and simmer, uncovered, until rice grains split open and rice is tender — 30 to 40 minutes for Wehani rice, 35 to 45 minutes for wild rice. Drain well, and spread on a baking sheet to cool.

In a medium saucepan, cook sweet potato, uncovered, in boiling salted water until just tender, about 10 minutes. Drain, and allow to cool to room temperature.

Meanwhile, in a large frying pan over medium-high heat, sauté onion, garlic, rosemary, salt and pepper in olive oil until onion is slightly softened, about 5 minutes. Add vinegar, and cook for 2 minutes to reduce.

In a large bowl, combine sweet potato, onion mixture and Wehani and wild rice, mixing well. Gently toss in feta. Taste, and add more salt and pepper, if needed.

Serves 4-6

roasted corn, smoked paprika + lime salad

On the morning menu at the café, this salad always accompanies our breakfast wrap, along with refried beans, sour cream and Chili Machismo (see page 223).

4 cups	fresh or frozen corn kernels	1 L
1/4 cup	extra-virgin olive oil	50 mL
1 Tbsp.	fresh lime juice	15 mL
2	cloves garlic, minced	2
1/2	small red onion, finely diced	1/2
1/2	small red bell pepper, finely diced	1/2
1 tsp.	smoked paprika	5 mL
	Sea salt	
	Freshly ground black pepper	
1 Tbsp.	chopped cilantro	15 mL

Preheat oven to 400°F (200°C). On a baking sheet, combine all ingredients, except cilantro, and spread out in a thin layer. Roast for 10 to 12 minutes. Remove from oven, let cool, then mix with cilantro.

Serves 4–6

semi di melone with feta + dill

"Semi di melone" is Italian for "melon pips," and this small seed-shaped pasta produces a far lighter salad than one made with traditional pasta. If you can't find it, substitute orzo.

9	sun-dried tomatoes	9
2 qt.	water	2 L
1 Tbsp. + 1/2 tsp.	sea salt	15 mL + 2 mL
2 cups	semi di melone	500 g
1/2 cup	extra-virgin olive oil	125 mL
3 Tbsp.	white-wine vinegar	40 mL
1/2 cup	thinly sliced red onion	125 mL
1 1/2 tsp.	minced garlic	7 mL
1 Tbsp.	chopped fresh dill	15 mL
1/2 cup	crumbled cow's milk feta	125 mL

Place sun-dried tomatoes in a small bowl, and cover with boiling water. Let soak until tender, up to 20 minutes. Drain tomatoes, cut into slivers, and set aside.

Meanwhile, in a large pot, bring water and 1 Tbsp. (15 mL) salt to a boil. Add pasta, and cook until al dente, about 8 minutes. Drain, toss well with olive oil and vinegar, and spread on a baking sheet to cool.

Place pasta in a large bowl, and add onion, garlic, tomatoes, dill, 1/2 tsp. (2 mL) salt and feta. Toss to mix well. Taste, and add more salt, if needed.

Serves 4–6

thai cucumber salad

This started its life as a green mango salad, so don't hesitate to substitute mangoes for cucumbers if they're in season. For extra crunch in either version, add bean sprouts, and serve right away.

dressing

2 Tbsp.	rice-wine vinegar	25 mL
3 Tbsp.	lime juice	40 mL
2 Tbsp.	fish sauce	25 mL
2 Tbsp.	water	25 mL
1 Tbsp.	white sugar	15 mL
1	clove garlic, minced	1
1	Thai chili, sliced	1

salad

1/4 cup	unsalted peanuts, toasted + crushed	50 mL
1	English cucumber, julienned	1
1/4 cup	small-diced red onion	50 mL
1/4 cup	small-diced red bell pepper	50 mL
1/4 cup	small-diced yellow bell pepper	50 mL
1	Thai chili, minced	1
1 tsp.	chopped fresh mint	5 mL
1 tsp.	chopped fresh basil	5 mL
1 tsp.	chopped cilantro	5 mL

To make dressing, combine vinegar, lime juice, fish sauce, water and sugar in a small saucepan, and heat over low heat until sugar dissolves, about 1 minute. Cool, and stir in garlic and chili. Set aside.

To toast peanuts, place in a small, dry frying pan over medium-low heat. Toast, shaking pan, until peanuts are lightly browned. Allow to cool, then lightly crush.

In a medium bowl, toss together all ingredients, except peanuts. Pour on dressing, and toss until well coated. Garnish with peanuts.

Serves 4-6

sandwiches

lamb burger with feta-dill mayonnaise, page 124

sandwiches

tofu teaser

A former cook playfully dubbed this sandwich the Tofu Teaser, and it stuck. With an organic-tofu spread made with good-tasting yeast, it is an excellent source of B_{12} for vegans and vegetarians.

tofu spread

1/2 lb.	firm, white organic tofu, crumbled	225 g
1/2 tsp.	de-bittered brewer's yeast (or good-tasting yeast)	2 mL
1 tsp.	minced garlic	5 mL
	Pinch cayenne	
2 Tbsp.	extra-virgin olive oil	25 mL
2 Tbsp.	tamari or Japanese soy sauce	25 mL
1	scallion, thinly sliced	1
1 Tbsp.	finely diced carrot	15 mL
1 Tbsp.	finely diced celery	15 mL
1 Tbsp.	roughly chopped cilantro	15 mL
	Sea salt	
	Freshly ground black pepper	

sandwich

8–12 slices Whole Wheat Bread (see page 26)
Tofu spread
Cucumber slices
Tomato slices
Red onion slices
Leaf lettuce

To make tofu spread, place tofu, yeast, garlic and cayenne in a food processor, and combine thoroughly. Add olive oil and tamari or soy sauce, and mix. Transfer mixture to a medium bowl, and stir in scallion, carrot, celery and cilantro by hand. Add salt and pepper to taste. Makes 1 1/2 cups (375 mL).

Sandwich assembly: bread slice, tofu spread, cucumber, tomato, onion, lettuce, tofu spread, bread slice.

Makes 4-6 sandwiches

egg + anchovy salad with leaf lettuce on pain ordinaire

This is an anchovy lover's sandwich and another Zal favourite. Move over caviar — eggs have a new best friend!

egg + anchovy salad

6	hard-boiled eggs	6
1	2 oz. (60 g) can anchovies	1
$^1/_3$ cup	Plain Mayonnaise (see page 231)	75 mL
	Freshly ground black pepper	

sandwich

8 slices Pain Ordinaire (see page 20)
or crusty white bread
Leaf lettuce
Egg + anchovy salad

To make egg salad, peel and chop eggs. Drain anchovies, and coarsely chop. In a small bowl, mix together eggs, anchovies and mayonnaise. Add pepper to taste. Refrigerate until ready to use.

Sandwich assembly: bread slice, lettuce, egg salad, bread slice.

Makes 4 sandwiches

lanark county's dalhousie cheese with garlic purée, roasted tomatoes + fresh basil on pain ordinaire

Here's a tribute to our favourite local artisan cheese producer, Lanark County's Back Forty. If you don't live in eastern Ontario, however, there are a number of other cheeses you can substitute. Try Le Gré des Champs, a raw cow's milk cheese from Québec; a mountain cheese such as Beaufort; Brie de Meaux; or St. Albray, a cow's milk cheese from France.

roasted garlic purée

1	head garlic	1
2 Tbsp.	extra-virgin olive oil	25 mL
	Pinch sea salt	
	Pinch freshly ground black pepper	

roasted tomatoes

4	field or vine-ripened tomatoes, halved	4
2 Tbsp.	extra-virgin olive oil	25 mL
1 Tbsp.	balsamic vinegar	15 mL
	Pinch sea salt	
	Pinch freshly ground black pepper	

sandwich

8 slices Pain Ordinaire (see page 20)
or hearty white bread
Roasted garlic purée
8 generous slices Dalhousie cheese
Roasted tomatoes
Fresh basil leaves

To make garlic purée, preheat oven to 325°F (160°C). Rub garlic head with olive oil, and sprinkle with salt and pepper. Wrap in aluminum foil, and roast for 1 to 1½ hours, until garlic feels soft when gently pressed. Cool, and squeeze garlic buds out of skin into a small bowl. Using a fork, mash garlic into a purée, and set aside.

To make roasted tomatoes, line a baking sheet with parchment paper. Place tomato halves on baking sheet. Drizzle with olive oil and vinegar, sprinkle with salt and pepper, and roast in preheated oven for 15 to 20 minutes, until firm but still moist.

Sandwich assembly: bread slice, garlic purée, 2 cheese slices, 2 roasted tomato halves, basil, bread slice.

Makes 4 sandwiches

say cheese

An unpasteurized sheep's milk cheese produced by Back Forty Artisan Cheese in Lanark County, Ontario, Dalhousie has "a complex range of flavours, with hints of butter, nuts and fruit." According to Back Forty, it's best eaten at three months plus.

grilled cheese bleu with grilled apple on fruit-nut bread

When this sandwich made its debut, we used cherry-almond bread, but as the seasons changed, we switched to cranberry-pecan. Feel free to use whatever fruit-nut bread is currently featured at your local bakery.

grilled apples

2 firm, tart apples
Lemon juice
Extra-virgin olive oil
Sea salt
Freshly ground black pepper

sandwich

8 slices fruit-nut bread
4 generous slices Benedictine Blue cheese
Grilled apples
Butter

To make grilled apples, core apples, leaving peel on, then cut into 1/4-inch (6 mm) slices. In a medium bowl, toss apples with a little lemon juice, olive oil, salt and pepper.

In a heavy-bottomed pan over medium-high heat, cook apples for about 1 minute on each side, until slightly softened. Remove from pan, and allow to cool.

Sandwich assembly: bread slice, cheese slice, apples, bread slice. Butter top and bottom of sandwich, and grill in a heavy-bottomed frying pan over medium heat until bread is golden brown and cheese is melted, 5 to 7 minutes. Serve with Tomato Butter on the side (see page 226).

Makes 4 sandwiches

marinated mediterranean tuna salad on olive + rosemary sourdough

A mayonnaise-free twist on traditional tuna salad, this version uses a vinaigrette-like dressing instead. At Pan Chancho, we prefer the taste of canned Italian tuna in oil or fresh tuna (see Tuna Confit on page 158).

tuna salad

2	7 oz. (200 g) cans light tuna in oil	2
1/4 cup	finely diced red onion	50 mL
2 Tbsp.	finely diced red bell pepper	25 mL
1/4 cup	extra-virgin olive oil	50 mL
1 Tbsp.	minced garlic	15 mL
1 Tbsp.	chopped fresh Italian parsley	15 mL
1 tsp.	lemon zest	5 mL
1 tsp.	lemon juice	5 mL
	Pinch white sugar	
2 Tbsp.	red-wine vinegar	25 mL
1/3 cup	drained canned cannellini beans, rinsed	75 mL
1/4 cup	freshly grated Parmigiano-Reggiano	50 mL
	Sea salt	
	Freshly ground black pepper	

sandwich

8–12 slices Olive + Rosemary Sourdough (see page 18)
Tuna salad
Olive + Caper Relish (see page 223)

To make tuna salad, drain tuna. In a medium bowl, mix together tuna, onion and red pepper. Set aside.

In a small bowl, whisk together olive oil, garlic, parsley, lemon zest and juice, sugar and vinegar. Add dressing to tuna mixture, and toss. Stir in beans and cheese. Add salt and pepper to taste. If not using immediately, refrigerate in a covered container.

Sandwich assembly: bread slice, tuna salad, 1 Tbsp. (15 mL) relish, bread slice.

Makes 4-6 sandwiches

salmon salad with fresh horseradish-apple mayonnaise on pain de campagne

Grate it and weep — you won't regret the tears once you've tasted it. The vinegar in prepared horseradish tends to overwhelm the flavour of this root vegetable, but fresh horseradish is light and hot and has an unexpected sweetness.

horseradish-apple mayonnaise

1 tsp.	Dijon mustard	5 mL
2 tsp.	lemon juice	10 mL
1 tsp.	red-wine vinegar	5 mL
1	apple, peeled + grated	1
3 Tbsp.	grated fresh horseradish root	40 mL
3/4 tsp.	sea salt	4 mL
1/4 tsp.	freshly ground black pepper	1 mL
1	large egg	1
1 cup	canola oil	250 mL

salmon salad

2 cups	flaked cooked fresh salmon	500 mL
1/4 cup	horseradish-apple mayonnaise	50 mL
3 Tbsp.	diced red onion	40 mL
	Sea salt	
	Freshly ground black pepper	

sandwich

8 slices Pain de Campagne
(see page 27)
Leaf lettuce
Salmon salad

To make mayonnaise, place mustard, lemon juice, vinegar, apple, horseradish, salt and pepper in a blender, and purée. Add egg, and purée. While blender is running, slowly drizzle in oil until a thick mayonnaise forms. Taste, and add more salt and pepper, if needed. Refrigerate until ready to use. (Extra mayonnaise can be stored in refrigerator in a covered container for up to 4 days.) Makes about 1 cup (250 mL).

To make salmon salad, mix together salmon, mayonnaise and onion in a medium bowl. Add salt and pepper to taste. If not using immediately, refrigerate in a covered container.

Sandwich assembly: bread slice, lettuce, salmon salad, bread slice.

Makes 4 sandwiches

smoked wild salmon with apple-butter crème fraîche + baby greens on light rye

Simple, elegant and beautiful. A great brunch sandwich. And here's another brunch idea: Double the recipe for this scrumptious apple-butter crème fraîche and serve with French toast.

apple-butter crème fraîche

5 tsp.	apple butter	25 mL
1/4 cup	Crème Fraîche (see page 230)	50 mL

sandwich

6–8 slices Light Rye Bread (see page 23)
Apple-butter crème fraîche
Mixed baby greens
About 30 slices smoked salmon, preferably wild
1/2 red onion, thinly sliced
Fresh fennel sprigs or dill sprigs

To make apple-butter crème fraîche, stir apple butter into crème fraîche in a small bowl. Refrigerate until ready to use.

Open-face sandwich assembly: bread slice, crème fraîche, greens, about 4 salmon slices, onion, fennel or dill.

Makes 6-8 open-face sandwiches

sweet tarts

Apple butter is available at health-food stores, but for an extra dimension of flavour, make your own. Simply peel, core and quarter 12 or more tart apples (the more apples, the more paste). In a heavy-bottomed pan over medium heat, bring apples to a simmer, then reduce heat to low. Cook uncovered, stirring frequently, for several hours, until apples are reduced to a thick, brown paste. Purée. Can be stored in refrigerator in a covered container for up to 2 months.

mediterranean chicken with chive aïoli + balsamic roasted-tomato jam on olive + rosemary sourdough

Pair this sandwich with our Saffron Fennel Soup (see page 66), and call it supper.

roasted-tomato jam

1	28 oz. (796 mL) can diced tomatoes, drained	1
3 Tbsp.	extra-virgin olive oil	40 mL
5 tsp.	balsamic vinegar	25 mL
	Pinch sea salt	
	Pinch freshly ground black pepper	

chive aïoli

1 tsp.	Dijon mustard	5 mL
1 tsp.	lemon juice	5 mL
1 tsp.	red-wine vinegar	5 mL
1	clove garlic, minced	1
3/4 tsp.	sea salt	4 mL
1/4 tsp.	freshly ground black pepper	1 mL
1	large egg	1
1 cup	canola oil	250 mL
3 Tbsp.	chopped fresh chives	40 mL

chicken salad

2 cups	shredded cooked chicken	500 mL
1/2 cup	chive aïoli	125 mL
	Sea salt	
	Freshly ground black pepper	

sandwich

8–12 slices Olive + Rosemary Sourdough (see page 18)
Leaf lettuce
Chicken salad
Roasted-tomato jam

To make tomato jam, preheat oven to 350°F (180°C) and line a baking sheet with parchment paper. In a medium bowl, toss tomatoes with olive oil and vinegar, and add salt and pepper. Spread tomatoes on baking sheet, and roast for 15 minutes. Stir, and roast for 15 minutes more, until tomatoes are a thick, jammy consistency. Set aside. If not using immediately, refrigerate in a covered container for up to 1 week. Makes 1 cup (250 mL).

To make chive aïoli, place mustard, lemon juice, vinegar, garlic, salt and pepper in a blender, and purée. Add egg, and purée. While blender is running, slowly drizzle in oil until a thick mayonnaise forms. Stir in chives. Taste, and add more salt and pepper, if needed. Refrigerate until ready to use. (Extra aïoli can be stored in refrigerator in a covered container for up to 4 days.) Makes about 1 cup (250 mL).

To make chicken salad, mix together chicken and aïoli in a large bowl. Add salt and pepper to taste. If not using immediately, refrigerate in a covered container.

Sandwich assembly: bread slice, lettuce, chicken salad, tomato jam, bread slice.

Makes 4-6 sandwiches

hoisin dynasty chicken breast with orange-anise mayonnaise + scallions on ciabatta

This mayonnaise combines the lively taste of citrus with the tang of white-wine vinegar and anise's licorice hint, making a great counterpoint to the chicken's sweet hoisin glaze.

hoisin glaze

2 Tbsp.	minced garlic	25 mL
2 Tbsp.	minced fresh ginger	25 mL
2 Tbsp.	Kung Fu soy sauce	25 mL
2 tsp.	rice-wine vinegar	10 mL
2 tsp.	toasted sesame oil	10 mL
3/4 cup	hoisin sauce	175 mL
1/4 cup	packed brown sugar	50 mL
2 Tbsp.	oyster sauce	25 mL
1 Tbsp.	dry sherry	15 mL
	Pinch sea salt	

hoisin chicken

4	boneless, skinless chicken breasts	4
1/2 cup	hoisin glaze	125 mL

To make glaze, combine all ingredients in a heavy-bottomed pan over medium heat, and bring to a simmer. Allow sauce to thicken, uncovered, for 5 to 10 minutes, stirring frequently. If not using immediately, refrigerate in a covered container. Makes about 1 1/4 cups (300 mL).

To prepare chicken, preheat oven to 350°F (180°C). Place chicken in a baking pan lined with parchment paper, and bake for 20 minutes. Brush with glaze, and bake for 5 to 10 minutes, until chicken is completely cooked. Allow to cool, and refrigerate until ready to use.

orange-anise mayonnaise

1 tsp.	anise seed	5 mL
2 tsp.	white-wine vinegar	10 mL
1 Tbsp.	orange juice	15 mL
	Zest of 1 orange	
2 tsp.	white sugar	10 mL
3/4 tsp.	sea salt	4 mL
1/4 tsp.	freshly ground black pepper	1 mL
1	large egg	1
1 cup	canola oil	250 mL
2 Tbsp.	finely chopped fresh chives	25 mL

sesame pepper

1	red bell pepper, julienned	1
1 Tbsp.	canola oil	15 mL
1 Tbsp.	toasted sesame oil	15 mL

sandwich

Ciabatta, cut into 4–6 buns + sliced
Orange-anise mayonnaise
Baby spinach
Hoisin chicken, sliced
Sesame peppers
Toasted sesame seeds
2 sliced scallions

To make mayonnaise, toast anise seed in a dry frying pan over medium heat, shaking pan, until fragrant, about 2 minutes. Allow to cool, then grind seed using a spice grinder or a mortar and pestle.

Place anise, vinegar, orange juice and zest, sugar, salt and pepper in a blender, and purée. Add egg, and purée. While blender is running, slowly drizzle in oil until a thick mayonnaise forms. Stir in chives. Taste, and add more salt and pepper, if needed. Refrigerate until ready to use. (Extra mayonnaise can be stored in refrigerator in a covered container for up to 4 days.) Makes about 1 cup (250 mL).

To make sesame pepper, cook red pepper in oils in a cast-iron frying pan over low heat until softened. Remove, and chill.

Sandwich assembly: Spread inside of bun with mayonnaise to taste; then bun bottom, spinach, chicken, sesame pepper, sesame seeds, scallions, bun top.

Makes 4-6 sandwiches

curried chicken with dried apricots + cilantro on ciabatta

Curried comfort: a mild, sweet curried-chicken sandwich with the fresh flavours of lime and cilantro.

curry mayonnaise

1/4 tsp.	Dijon mustard	1 mL
1 tsp.	lemon juice	5 mL
1 tsp.	red-wine vinegar	5 mL
1/2	tart apple, peeled, cored + roughly chopped	1/2
1 Tbsp.	curry powder	15 mL
3/4 tsp.	sea salt	4 mL
1/4 tsp.	freshly ground black pepper	1 mL
1	large egg	1
1 cup	canola oil	250 mL

curried chicken salad

2 1/2 cups	shredded cooked chicken	625 mL
1/2– 3/4 cup	curry mayonnaise	125–175 mL
6	dried apricots, small dice (see box below)	6
1 Tbsp.	chopped cilantro	15 mL
1	scallion, chopped	1
2 Tbsp.	lime juice	25 mL
1 tsp.	lime zest	5 mL
	Sea salt	
	Freshly ground black pepper	

sandwich

Ciabatta, cut into 4 buns + sliced
Curried chicken salad
Mixed baby greens

To make mayonnaise, place mustard, lemon juice, vinegar, apple, curry powder, salt and pepper in a blender, and purée. Add egg, and purée. While blender is running, slowly drizzle in oil until a thick mayonnaise forms. Taste, and add more salt and pepper, if needed. Refrigerate until ready to use. (Extra mayonnaise can be stored in refrigerator in a covered container for up to 4 days.) Makes about 1 cup (250 mL).

To make chicken salad, mix together chicken, mayonnaise, apricots, cilantro, scallion and lime juice and zest in a large bowl. Add salt and pepper to taste. If not using immediately, refrigerate in a covered container.

Sandwich assembly: bun bottom, chicken salad, greens, bun top.

Makes 4 sandwiches

so long, sulphur

The drying process deprives dried apricots of much of their moisture, and they're also treated with sulphur dioxide to preserve their orange colour. To restore some tender plumpness to these tasty fruits and to wash away the preservative, soak dried apricots in hot water before dicing.

chicken salad with avocado crème fraîche on pumpkin seed bread

If you can't find pumpkin seed bread at your local bakery, garnish this sandwich with roasted pumpkin seeds, or pepitas, for a nice, light nutty taste.

avocado crème fraîche

1	small ripe avocado	1
1 Tbsp.	lime juice	15 mL
1/3 cup	Crème Fraîche (see page 230)	75 mL
1/4 tsp.	sea salt	1 mL
	Pinch freshly ground black pepper	

chicken salad

2 cups	shredded cooked chicken	500 mL
1/4 cup	finely diced red onion	50 mL
	Juice of 1 lime	
2 tsp.	lime zest	10 mL
2 Tbsp.	coarsely chopped cilantro	25 mL
	Pinch chili powder	
1/4 tsp.	ground cumin	1 mL
	Avocado crème fraîche	
	Sea salt (optional)	
	Freshly ground black pepper (optional)	

sandwich

8–12 slices Pumpkin Seed Bread (see page 27)
Leaf lettuce
Chicken salad
Sliced tomatoes

To make avocado crème fraîche, cut avocado in half, remove stone, and scoop flesh into a food processor. Add lime juice, and purée. Add crème fraîche, salt and pepper, and purée. Refrigerate until ready to use. Makes about 1 cup (250 mL).

To make chicken salad, mix chicken, onion, lime juice and zest, cilantro, chili powder, cumin and crème fraîche together in a large bowl. Taste, and add salt and pepper, if needed. If not using immediately, refrigerate in a covered container.

Sandwich assembly: bread slice, lettuce, chicken salad, tomatoes, bread slice.

Makes 4–6 sandwiches

mesquite-smoked turkey with chipotle mayonnaise, aged cheddar + lettuce on multigrain

Smoking turkey breasts is a daily ritual at Pan Chancho, and we've been making this sandwich since the bakery first opened in 1994. It continues to be a huge favourite.

spice mixture

1 tsp.	sweet paprika	5 mL
1 tsp.	garlic powder	5 mL
1 tsp.	dried thyme	5 mL
1 tsp.	dried savory	5 mL
1 tsp.	dried oregano	5 mL
1 tsp.	ground coriander seed	5 mL
1 tsp.	ground cumin	5 mL
1 tsp.	freshly ground black pepper	5 mL
1 tsp.	dry mustard	5 mL

smoked turkey

2 cups	mesquite chips	500 mL
1 1/2 lb.	turkey breast	680 g
3 Tbsp.	spice mixture	40 mL
	Sea salt	
	Canola oil for grill	

chipotle mayonnaise

1/4 tsp.	Dijon mustard	1 mL
1 tsp.	lemon juice	5 mL
1 tsp.	red-wine vinegar	5 mL
2	cloves garlic, minced	2
1	small chipotle chili in adobo sauce, finely chopped	1
1 1/2 tsp.	adobo sauce	7 mL
3/4 tsp.	sea salt	4 mL
1/4 tsp.	freshly ground black pepper	1 mL
1	large egg	1
1 cup	canola oil	250 mL

To make spice mixture, mix all ingredients together in a small bowl. Set aside. Makes 3 Tbsp. (40 mL).

To smoke turkey, soak mesquite chips in water for 10 minutes, drain, and wrap in heavy-duty aluminum foil. Punch a few holes in foil, and place package directly on hot coals piled to one side in a charcoal barbecue.

Rub turkey breast with spice mixture, and sprinkle with salt. When package of mesquite chips begins to smoke, oil the grill. Place turkey on grill over indirect heat, and cook for 15 minutes. Turn breast, and cook for 15 minutes more or until breast is cooked through. Remove, and chill in refrigerator.

To make mayonnaise, place mustard, lemon juice, vinegar, garlic, chipotle, adobo sauce, salt and pepper in a blender, and purée. Add egg, and purée. While blender is running, slowly drizzle in oil until a thick mayonnaise forms. Taste, and add more salt and pepper, if needed. Refrigerate until ready to use. (Extra mayonnaise can be stored in refrigerator in a covered container for up to 4 days.) Makes about 1 cup (250 mL).

turkey salad

3 cups	diced smoked turkey	750 mL
	Chipotle mayonnaise	
1/2 cup	finely diced celery	125 mL
1/2 cup	finely diced red onion	125 mL
	Sea salt	
	Freshly ground black pepper	

sandwich

12 slices multigrain bread
Sliced Old Cheddar
Leaf lettuce
Turkey salad

To make turkey salad, mix turkey with enough mayonnaise to achieve desired consistency. Stir in celery and onion, and add salt and pepper to taste. If not using immediately, refrigerate in a covered container.

Sandwich assembly: bread slice, cheese, lettuce, turkey salad, bread slice.

Makes 6 sandwiches

barbecued pulled pork + apple cider slaw on calabrese

Our intensely fragrant spice mixture, partnered with Cuong Ly's wildly popular barbecue sauce, makes this sandwich a taste sensation, especially when served with our crunchy slaw. Keep Ly's sauce on hand for all things barbecue.

apple cider slaw

1/2 cup	apple cider vinegar	125 mL
1/2 cup	packed brown sugar	125 mL
1 tsp.	sea salt	5 mL
1/2 tsp.	freshly ground black pepper	2 mL
3 Tbsp.	canola oil	40 mL
2 cups	shredded green cabbage	500 mL
4	scallions, chopped	4

spice mixture

1 1/2 Tbsp.	ground cumin	20 mL
1 Tbsp.	garlic powder	15 mL
1 tsp.	ground cinnamon	5 mL
2 tsp.	sea salt	10 mL
1 tsp.	freshly ground black pepper	5 mL

ly's barbecue sauce

1 cup	ketchup	250 mL
1/4 cup	beer	50 mL
1/4 cup	fancy molasses	50 mL
2 Tbsp.	oyster sauce	25 mL
1 Tbsp.	Worcestershire sauce	15 mL
1/4 cup	packed brown sugar	50 mL
2 Tbsp.	chopped fresh ginger	25 mL
2 Tbsp.	chopped garlic	25 mL
2 Tbsp.	chopped Thai chili	25 mL

To make slaw, heat vinegar, sugar, salt, pepper and oil in a small saucepan over low heat until sugar is dissolved. Chill.

In a large bowl, toss dressing with cabbage and scallions. If not using immediately, refrigerate in a covered container. Makes about 2 cups (500 mL).

To make spice mixture, combine all ingredients in a small dish. Set aside.

To make barbecue sauce, mix all ingredients together in a small saucepan over medium heat, and simmer for 8 minutes. Remove from heat, and set aside. (Extra sauce can be stored in refrigerator in a covered container for up to 1 month.) Makes about 2 cups (500 mL).

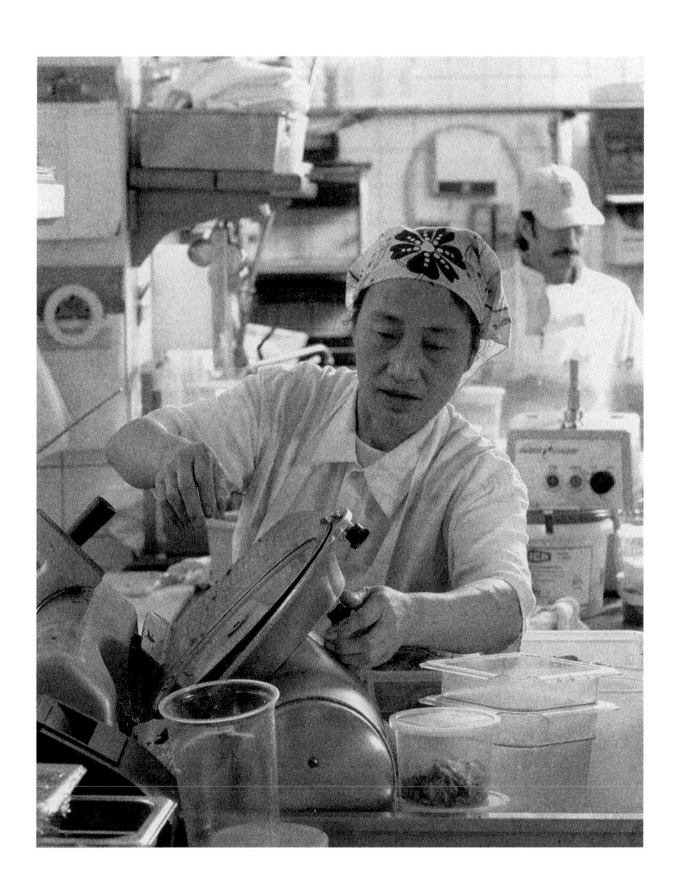

pulled pork

$1\frac{1}{2}$ lb.	boned pork shoulder	680 g
	Spice mixture	
$\frac{1}{4}$ cup	extra-virgin olive oil	50 mL
$\frac{1}{2}$ cup	Ly's barbecue sauce	125 mL
	Sea salt (optional)	
	Freshly ground black pepper (optional)	

sandwich

4–6 Calabrese buns, sliced
Pulled pork
Apple cider slaw

To prepare pork, preheat oven to 325°F (160°C). Rub outside of pork liberally with spice mixture. In a Dutch oven just big enough to hold pork, sear pork in olive oil over medium-high heat until browned on all sides, 3 to 5 minutes total.

Add enough water to cover three-quarters of the pork. Bring to a boil, transfer to oven and braise, covered, for 1 to $1\frac{1}{2}$ hours, until meat is fall-apart tender. Check pot from time to time, and add water as needed.

Remove pork from liquid, and shred, discarding fat. Keep warm. Skim fat off liquid, and strain. If necessary, reduce liquid over medium-high heat to about $\frac{1}{2}$ cup (125 mL). Stir liquid into barbecue sauce, and toss with pork. Taste, and add salt and pepper, if needed.

Sandwich assembly: bun bottom, pork, slaw, bun top.

Makes 4-6 sandwiches

shropshire sage scone with ham, old cheddar + roasted tomatoes

A little British influence at brunch — or high tea, if you prefer. Its pale orange colour sets Shropshire blue cheese apart.

roasted tomatoes

2	large tomatoes, sliced 1/2 inch (1 cm) thick	2
1 Tbsp.	extra-virgin olive oil	15 mL
1 Tbsp.	red-wine vinegar	15 mL
	Sea salt	
	Freshly ground black pepper	

shropshire sage scones

2 1/2 cups	all-purpose flour	625 mL
2 Tbsp.	baking powder	25 mL
1 tsp.	sea salt	5 mL
1/2 cup	cold unsalted butter	125 mL
1/2 cup	crumbled Shropshire blue cheese	125 mL
1/2 cup	sliced scallions	125 mL
1/2 cup	chopped fresh sage	125 mL
1 cup	buttermilk	250 mL
1	large egg	1
1 Tbsp.	10% M.F. cream	15 mL

sandwich

6 Shropshire sage scones
Dijon mustard
Shaved Black Forest ham
Old Cheddar cheese, sliced
Roasted tomatoes

To make roasted tomatoes, preheat oven to 325°F (160°C) and line a baking sheet with parchment paper. Place tomato slices on baking sheet, drizzle with olive oil and vinegar, and season with salt and pepper. Bake for 15 to 20 minutes.

To make scones, preheat oven to 425°F (220°C) and line a baking sheet with parchment paper. In a large bowl, thoroughly mix together flour, baking powder and salt. Cut butter into flour mixture until tiny butter pieces are coated with flour. Place in refrigerator until mixture is completely chilled, 10 to 15 minutes.

Stir in cheese, scallions and sage. With a spatula, fold in buttermilk and work dough until it just holds together. Place dough on a lightly floured surface, and roll to a thickness of 2 inches (5 cm). Push dough into a rectangular shape, and cut into 6 equal squares. Using a spatula, gently place each scone on baking sheet. Refrigerate to chill scones completely, about 10 minutes.

Meanwhile, in a small bowl, whisk together egg and cream to make egg wash. Brush top of each scone lightly with egg wash, and bake for 15 to 20 minutes, until a toothpick inserted in centre of scone comes out clean. Place scones on a wire rack until cool enough to slice in half. Makes 6 scones.

Sandwich assembly: scone bottom, mustard, ham, cheese, tomatoes, scone top. Place on a baking sheet in a 350°F (180°C) oven for 5 to 7 minutes. Serve immediately.

Makes 6 sandwiches

calabrese sandwich

An all-Italian extravaganza and a cinch to prepare: It's a whole lotta meat on a whole lotta bread.

garlic parmesan oil

2 Tbsp.	finely minced garlic	25 mL
2 Tbsp.	freshly grated Parmigiano-Reggiano (see note)	25 mL
1/3 cup	extra-virgin olive oil	75 mL
	Pinch sea salt	
	Pinch freshly ground black pepper	

sandwich

4 Calabrese buns, sliced
Garlic Parmesan oil
16 slices hot Calabrese sausage
16 slices hot cappicola
16 slices Genoa salami
4 thin slices prosciutto
8 slices provolone cheese
Olive + Caper Relish (see page 223)

To make garlic oil, mix all ingredients together in a small bowl. Set aside.

note

Parmesan should be very finely grated, so be sure to use a microplane or rasp.

Sandwich assembly: bun bottom, a drizzle of garlic oil, 4 slices each of sausage, cappicola and salami, 1 slice prosciutto, 2 slices cheese, about 2 Tbsp. (25 mL) relish, bun top.

Makes 4 sandwiches

cumin-spiced lamb pita with aegean sauce, green olives, watercress + onion piyazi

Pan Chancho's signature sandwich. One taste, and there's no going back.

spiced lamb

2 lb.	boned lamb shoulder	900 g
1/4 cup	extra-virgin olive oil	50 mL
1	carrot, small dice	1
1	cooking onion, small dice	1
1	stalk celery, small dice	1
1	28 oz. (796 mL) can whole tomatoes, with juice	1
1/4	Preserved Lemon (see page 216)	1/4
1	1-inch (2.5 cm) stick cinnamon	1
1 Tbsp.	cumin seed	15 mL
2	cloves garlic, thinly sliced	2
1 tsp.	freshly ground black pepper	5 mL
1 tsp.	sea salt	5 mL
1 cup	lamb stock or Chicken Stock (see page 60)	250 mL

aegean sauce

1 cup	chopped trimmed watercress	250 mL
6	pitted green olives, chopped	6
1/4 cup	crumbled cow's milk feta	50 mL
2 Tbsp.	white-wine vinegar	25 mL
1/4 cup	extra-virgin olive oil	50 mL
	Pinch sea salt	
	Pinch freshly ground black pepper	

To prepare lamb, preheat oven to 350°F (180°C). In a large, heavy-bottomed ovenproof pot over medium heat, brown lamb in olive oil on all sides. Add carrot, onion and celery, and cook, stirring, for 5 minutes. Break up whole tomatoes, and add to lamb along with remaining ingredients. Cover, and braise in oven for 1 1/2 to 2 hours, until meat is falling apart.

Remove lamb from liquid, and shred, discarding fat. Skim fat off liquid, and strain. If necessary, reduce liquid over medium-high heat to 1 cup (250 mL). Stir liquid into lamb, and keep warm.

To make sauce, combine watercress, olives, feta and vinegar in a food processor. While processor is running, slowly drizzle in olive oil, and add salt and pepper. Refrigerate until ready to use. (Extra sauce can be stored in refrigerator in a covered container for up to 2 days.) Makes 1 cup (125 mL).

onion piyazi

1	medium red onion, sliced into 1/2-inch (1 cm) half rounds	1
2	pinches sea salt	2
	Pinch ground sumac	
	Pinch cayenne	
2 Tbsp.	coarsely chopped fresh Italian parsley	25 mL
1 tsp.	lemon juice	5 mL

sandwich

4–6 Pitas (see page 19)
Extra-virgin olive oil
Za'atar (see page 90)
Aegean sauce
Spiced lamb
Green olives, sliced lengthwise into sixths
Onion piyazi
Watercress

To make onion piyazi, place onion in a medium bowl, and sprinkle with salt. Gently squeeze between your fingers for 15 to 30 seconds to release juices. Add remaining ingredients, and toss to combine.

Sandwich assembly: Brush both sides of pita lightly with olive oil, and sprinkle both sides with za'atar. Place pita in a dry frying pan over medium heat, and lightly brown on each side, turning with tongs. Remove, and top with sauce to taste, lamb, olives, onions and watercress. Fold pita tightly, and secure with a wooden skewer. Serve immediately.

Makes 4-6 sandwiches

lamb burger with feta-dill mayonnaise

In our neck of the woods, Kingston's annual sheepdog trials are a much-anticipated early-August ritual. And this is the perennially popular burger that Pan Chancho baa-baa-cues on site.

feta-dill mayonnaise

1/4 tsp.	Dijon mustard	1 mL
1 tsp.	lemon juice	5 mL
1 tsp.	red-wine vinegar	5 mL
	Pinch sea salt	
1/4 tsp.	freshly ground black pepper	1 mL
1	large egg	1
1 cup	canola oil	250 mL
2 tsp.	chopped fresh dill	10 mL
1/3 cup	crumbled cow's milk feta	75 mL

lamb burgers

2 lb.	lean ground lamb	900 g
2	scallions, thinly sliced	2
1	cooking onion, finely diced	1
1/2 cup	chopped fresh mint	125 mL
1 Tbsp.	lemon juice	15 mL
1 tsp.	ground cumin	5 mL
1 tsp.	ground cinnamon	5 mL
1/2 tsp.	ground coriander seed	2 mL
1/2 tsp.	crushed dried chilies	2 mL
2	large eggs	2
1 tsp.	sea salt	5 mL
1 tsp.	freshly ground black pepper	5 mL

burger

6 sesame buns, sliced
6 lamb burgers
Dill pickles, sliced
Tomato slices
Red onion slices
Feta-dill mayonnaise

To make mayonnaise, place mustard, lemon juice, vinegar, salt and pepper in a blender, and purée. Add egg, and purée. While blender is running, slowly drizzle in oil until a thick mayonnaise forms. Stir in dill and feta by hand. Taste, and add more salt and pepper, if needed. Refrigerate until ready to use. (Extra mayonnaise can be stored in refrigerator in a covered container for up to 4 days.) Makes about 1 cup (250 mL).

To make burgers, combine all ingredients in a large bowl, and mix well. Form into 6 patties, and grill on the barbecue on both sides until cooked through, about 20 minutes total.

Burger assembly: bun bottom, burger, pickles, tomato, onion, mayonnaise to taste, bun top.

Makes 6 burgers

meaty meat burger

Bursting with fresh herb flavours, this scrumptious burger is a standard on our menu. But because Zal liked everything "mo' better," we also serve a variation that features Stilton pâté and crispy pancetta as garnishes.

meaty burgers

2 lb.	medium ground beef	900 g
2	large eggs	2
2	scallions, thinly sliced	2
1/2 tsp.	chopped fresh rosemary	2 mL
1/2 tsp.	chopped fresh thyme	2 mL
1 tsp.	tomato paste	5 mL
1 tsp.	Dijon mustard	5 mL
1 tsp.	Worcestershire sauce	5 mL
1 tsp.	fine breadcrumbs	5 mL
1 tsp.	sea salt	5 mL
1 tsp.	freshly ground black pepper	5 mL

burger

4 sesame buns, sliced
Fresh baby greens
4 meaty burgers
Dill pickles, sliced
Tomato slices
Red onion slices
Chive Aïoli (see page 111)

To make burgers, combine all ingredients in a large bowl, and mix well. Form into 4 patties. Grill or fry on both sides until cooked to your liking.

Burger assembly: bun bottom, greens, burger, pickles, tomato, onion, bun top. Serve aïoli on the side.

Makes 4 burgers

zalman's mo' better burger

In a frying pan over medium-high heat, fry cubed pancetta (enough to garnish each burger) until crispy. Spread some Stilton pâté on the grilled burgers, and top with pancetta. Mmmm, now isn't that mo' better?

savouries + sides

quiche lorraine, page 145

savouries

macaroni + cheese bleu

This version of mac 'n' cheese is for blue-cheese lovers everywhere, and there is a wealth of blue cheese available — from France's Roquefort Papillon Noir and Bleu d'Auvergne to Italy's Gorgonzola Piccante and Spain's Valdeón.

2 Tbsp.	butter	25 mL
1½ Tbsp.	all-purpose flour	20 mL
1¼ cups	2% milk	300 mL
⅓ cup	crumbled blue cheese	75 mL
1 tsp.	Worcestershire sauce	5 mL
1½ tsp.	Dijon mustard	7 mL
	Tabasco sauce	
	Pinch ground nutmeg	
	Sea salt	
	Freshly ground black pepper	
2 cups	penne or rigatoni	500 mL
1 lb.	baby spinach	450 g
4	scallions, sliced	4
½ cup	breadcrumbs	125 mL
2 tsp.	extra-virgin olive oil	10 mL
2 tsp.	chopped fresh Italian parsley	10 mL

Preheat oven to 350°F (180°C). In a small saucepan over low heat, melt butter. Stir in flour, and cook for 4 to 5 minutes, being careful not to brown the mixture. Increase heat to medium-low, and gradually add milk, stirring constantly until thickened slightly, about 5 minutes. Add cheese, Worcestershire, mustard, 2 drops of Tabasco, nutmeg, ½ tsp. (2 mL) salt and ¼ tsp. (1 mL) pepper. Set aside.

Cook pasta in boiling salted water until al dente. Drain pasta, and place in a large bowl. Add cheese sauce, spinach and scallions, and toss. Spoon pasta mixture into a casserole dish.

In a small bowl, mix breadcrumbs with olive oil, parsley and a pinch of salt and pepper. Sprinkle over pasta. Bake for 20 to 30 minutes, uncovered, until breadcrumbs are browned.

Serves 4-6

spicy italian sausage lasagne

Here's why we told you to make such a big batch of Italian Sausage Ragù alla Bolognese on page 174!

3½ cups	grated mozzarella cheese	875 mL
4 cups	freshly grated Parmigiano-Reggiano	1 L
1	10 oz. (285 g) pkg. spinach, washed + picked	1
1¼ cups	ricotta cheese	300 mL
	Pinch ground nutmeg	
	Sea salt	
	Freshly ground black pepper	
6 cups	Italian Sausage Ragù alla Bolognese (see page 174)	1.5 L
1	2 lb. (900 g) pkg. fresh lasagne noodles	1

Preheat oven to 350°F (180°C). In a large bowl, mix together mozzarella and 3½ cups (875 mL) of the Parmesan. Set aside.

Blanch spinach by immersing briefly in boiling salted water, then drain and plunge into cold water. Drain again, squeeze dry, and chop. In a medium bowl, stir together spinach and ricotta. Add remaining ½ cup (125 mL) Parmesan, nutmeg and salt and pepper to taste. Stir, and set aside.

To assemble lasagne, spoon some meat sauce into the bottom of a deep 11-by-16-inch (4 L) baking dish. Top with a layer of lasagne noodles, more meat sauce, half of the mozzarella mixture, a layer of lasagne noodles, meat sauce, another layer of lasagne noodles, ricotta mixture, final layer of lasagne noodles and remaining meat sauce.

Bake, uncovered, for 30 to 40 minutes. During the last 5 to 10 minutes, top with remaining mozzarella mixture, and continue baking until cheese is melted and lightly browned.

Serves 8–10

roasted vegetable lasagne

You can't beat the taste of roasted vegetables — for a smokier, richer flavour, grill vegetables on the barbecue.

tomato sauce

3	medium cooking onions, finely diced	3
2 Tbsp.	minced garlic	25 mL
1/4 cup	extra-virgin olive oil	50 mL
2 tsp.	dried basil	10 mL
2 tsp.	dried thyme	10 mL
2 tsp.	dried oregano	10 mL
1/2 tsp.	fennel seed	2 mL
1/2 tsp.	crushed dried chilies	2 mL
3	28 oz. (796 mL) cans crushed tomatoes	3
1 tsp.	sea salt	5 mL
1 tsp.	freshly ground black pepper	5 mL
2 Tbsp.	brown sugar (optional)	25 mL

lasagne

3 1/2 cups	grated mozzarella cheese	875 mL
4 cups	freshly grated Parmigiano-Reggiano	1 L
1	10 oz. (285 g) pkg. spinach, washed + picked	1
1 1/4 cups	ricotta cheese	300 mL
	Pinch ground nutmeg	
	Sea salt	
	Freshly ground black pepper	
1	medium eggplant, large dice	1
	Extra-virgin olive oil	
	Balsamic vinegar	
1	red bell pepper, large dice	1
1	red onion, sliced into 1/2-inch-thick (1 cm) rings	1
1	medium zucchini, large dice	1
	Tomato sauce	
1	2 lb. (900 g) pkg. fresh lasagne noodles	1

To make tomato sauce, cook onions and garlic in olive oil in a large saucepan over low heat until onions are soft, about 10 minutes. Add basil, thyme, oregano, fennel, dried chilies and tomatoes, and bring to a simmer. Cook, uncovered, stirring occasionally, for 40 to 50 minutes. Add salt, pepper and sugar, if using. (To use this sauce as a pizza sauce, quarter the recipe.) Makes about 6 cups (1.5 L).

To make lasagne, mix together in a large bowl mozzarella and 3 1/2 cups (875 mL) of the Parmesan. Set aside.

Preheat oven to 350°F (180°C). Blanch spinach by immersing briefly in boiling salted water, then drain and plunge into cold water. Drain again, squeeze dry, and chop. In a medium bowl, stir together spinach and ricotta. Add remaining 1/2 cup (125 mL) Parmesan, nutmeg and salt and pepper to taste. Stir, and set aside.

In a medium bowl, drizzle eggplant with olive oil and vinegar, and sprinkle with salt and pepper. Toss to coat, and spread on a large baking sheet. Roast for 20 minutes. Dress red pepper and onion likewise, and add to baking sheet to roast for 15 minutes. Dress zucchini likewise, and add to baking sheet to roast for 10 minutes. Set aside to cool. In a large bowl, toss roasted vegetables with 2 cups (500 mL) of the tomato sauce.

To assemble lasagne, spoon some tomato sauce into the bottom of a deep 11-by-16-inch (4 L) baking dish. Top with a layer of lasagne noodles, more tomato sauce, half of the mozzarella mixture, a layer of lasagne noodles, tomato sauce, roasted vegetables, another layer of lasagne noodles, ricotta mixture, final layer of lasagne noodles and remaining tomato sauce.

Bake, uncovered, for 30 to 40 minutes. During the last 5 to 10 minutes, top with remaining mozzarella mixture, and continue baking until cheese is melted and lightly browned.

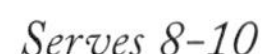

Serves 8-10

baked pasta with prosciutto

The rich combination of prosciutto, chèvre and cream has made this one of our most popular baked-pasta dishes.

4 oz.	chèvre	115 g
2¼ cups	35% M.F. cream	550 mL
2	medium cooking onions, small dice	2
¼ cup	minced garlic (about 10 cloves)	50 mL
3	fresh rosemary sprigs, minced	3
2 Tbsp.	extra-virgin olive oil	25 mL
¼ cup	dry white wine	50 mL
1	1 lb. (450 g) pkg. penne or other short pasta	1
2½ oz.	shaved prosciutto	70 g
½ cup	freshly grated Parmigiano-Reggiano	125 mL
4 cups	loosely packed baby spinach	1 L
	Sea salt	
	Freshly ground black pepper	
1 cup	breadcrumbs	250 mL
	Extra-virgin olive oil	
1 Tbsp.	chopped fresh Italian parsley	15 mL

Crumble chèvre into a large bowl. Stir in cream, then cover with plastic wrap, and allow mixture to come to room temperature, about 1 hour, stirring occasionally to eliminate lumps and combine.

Meanwhile, cook onions, garlic and rosemary in olive oil in a frying pan over low heat until onions are soft. Add wine, increase heat to medium, and reduce liquid by half. Cool, then stir onion mixture into chèvre and cream.

Preheat oven to 350°F (180°C). Cook pasta in boiling salted water until al dente. Drain pasta, and toss with chèvre mixture. Stir in prosciutto, Parmesan and spinach. Add salt and pepper to taste. Spoon pasta into a baking dish.

In a small bowl, mix breadcrumbs with a drizzle of olive oil to moisten, and add parsley and a pinch of salt and pepper. Sprinkle over pasta. Bake for 20 to 30 minutes, uncovered, until piping hot and golden brown on top.

Serves 4

spinach ravioli stuffed with artichoke hearts + chèvre

This spinach pasta is a beautiful deep green colour, and making it is a soul-satisfying labour of love.

filling

4	14 oz. (398 mL) cans artichoke hearts, drained + rinsed	4
1/4 lb.	chèvre, room temperature	115 g
1/4 tsp.	sea salt	1 mL
1/4 tsp.	freshly ground black pepper	1 mL
1/4 tsp.	dried thyme	1 mL
2 Tbsp.	extra-virgin olive oil	25 mL

spinach pasta

1	10 oz. (285 g) pkg. frozen chopped spinach, thawed + squeezed dry	1
2	large eggs	2
1 tsp.	sea salt	5 mL
2 cups	all-purpose flour	500 mL

Milk or water for brushing dough
Unsalted butter or extra-virgin olive oil
Freshly grated Parmigiano-Reggiano

Preheat oven to 350°F (180°C). Place artichokes in cheesecloth, and twist tightly to remove as much liquid as possible. Spread artichokes evenly on a baking sheet. Cover tightly with aluminum foil, and bake for 10 minutes. Reduce heat to 225°F (110°C), remove foil, and bake for 20 to 25 minutes, until fairly dry.

Place artichokes in a food processor, and blend on high until puréed. Add chèvre, salt, pepper and thyme, and blend. While processor is running, pour in olive oil to bind the mixture together. Wrap artichoke filling in plastic wrap, and refrigerate overnight.

food processor method

To make pasta in a food processor, purée together spinach, eggs and salt. Add only as much flour as you need to form a smooth ball, blending for 10 to 15 seconds. Do not knead the dough; wrap tightly in plastic wrap, and let rest at room temperature for 30 minutes.

blender/hand method

To make pasta in a blender, purée together spinach, eggs and salt at medium speed. Place spinach mixture in a large bowl, and use a wooden spoon to stir in flour until it forms a stiff dough. On a well-floured surface, knead dough until smooth but not sticky, about 20 times. Wrap dough in plastic wrap, and let rest at room temperature for 30 minutes.

Roll dough, by hand or machine, into two very thin rectangular sheets, roughly 12 inches (30 cm) by 3 inches (7.5 cm). (If rolling by hand, work on a floured surface.) As you work on each sheet, keep remaining dough covered with a damp cloth to prevent it from drying out. On one of the sheets, place portions of filling (about 1 tsp./5 mL each) in two horizontal rows lengthwise, leaving about 2 inches (5 cm) between each portion. Brush sheet with milk or water along edges and between rows of filling to help pastry edges stick together after ravioli are cut.

Place second sheet of dough over the first, pressing down gently all over to prevent air pockets from forming and along edges and between rows. Using a fluted pastry wheel, cut along edges and then between rows to form small squares with the filling in the centre. Repeat this process until dough and filling are used up.

Place ravioli on a lightly floured surface, and allow to dry for 30 minutes. Turn them over occasionally to let both sides dry. (If desired, ravioli can now be frozen for later use. Spread ravioli on a lightly floured baking sheet, and place in freezer. When frozen, place ravioli in freezer bags. Can be stored in freezer for up to 6 months.)

Bring a large pot of salted water to a boil, and drop in ravioli. Stir frequently until water returns to a boil. Cook for 4 to 5 minutes. As ravioli float to the surface, remove with a slotted spoon and place in a large serving bowl. Toss with butter or olive oil, sprinkle with Parmesan, and serve immediately. (Can also be served with your favourite sauce.)

Serves 6

slow-baked beans with molasses

Serve these hearty beans on their own or with our delectable Marsala + Orange Braised Pork Roast *(see page 173)*.

$2\frac{1}{2}$ cups	Great Northern beans	625 mL
1	medium cooking onion, diced	1
3–4	cloves garlic, minced	3–4
$\frac{1}{2}$ cup	tomato paste	125 mL
$\frac{1}{4}$ cup	dry mustard	50 mL
$\frac{1}{4}$ cup	maple syrup	50 mL
$\frac{1}{2}$ cup	dark molasses	125 mL
$\frac{1}{2}$ lb.	salt pork, medium dice	225 g
2	bay leaves	2
$\frac{1}{4}$ cup	cider vinegar	50 mL
	Pinch sea salt	
	Pinch freshly ground black pepper	

Preheat oven to 300°F (150°C). Sort through beans, discarding any stones or broken beans, then rinse and drain. Place beans in a large pot, and cover with cold water. Place over high heat, and bring to a boil. Reduce heat to low, and simmer, uncovered, for 1 to $1\frac{1}{2}$ hours, until beans are soft. (You may have to add more water to keep the beans covered as they cook.)

Drain beans, reserving liquid, and return to pot. Mix remaining ingredients with beans, and spoon into a large casserole dish. Pour in enough of the reserved liquid just to cover beans (add water if there is not enough liquid). Bake, covered, for 3 to 4 hours. Before serving, taste, and add salt and pepper, if needed.

Serves 8

smoked vegetable chili

Make it a party, and spend a late-summer afternoon slow-cooking fresh vegetables on the barbecue over mesquite chips. Then freeze portions, and you can enjoy the smoky taste of summer in the middle of winter.

4 cups	mesquite chips (see box below)	1 L
2	28 oz. (796 mL) cans diced tomatoes, with juice	2
	Extra-virgin olive oil	
$\frac{1}{4}$ cup	dry red wine	50 mL
	Sea salt	
	Freshly ground black pepper	
2 Tbsp.	dried oregano	25 mL
$1\frac{1}{2}$ Tbsp.	minced fresh rosemary	20 mL
7	cloves garlic, peeled	7
1 Tbsp.	chopped chipotle chili in adobo sauce	15 mL
	Cocoa powder	
1	3-inch (7.5 cm) stick cinnamon	1
1 Tbsp.	smoked paprika	15 mL
1 Tbsp.	ground cumin	15 mL
$1\frac{1}{2}$ cups	diced red bell pepper	375 mL
$1\frac{1}{2}$ cups	diced green bell pepper	375 mL
1 cup	diced cooking onion	250 mL
$1\frac{1}{2}$ cups	diced zucchini	375 mL
$1\frac{1}{2}$ cups	diced eggplant	375 mL
3 cups	quartered white mushrooms	750 mL
1	19 oz. (540 mL) can chickpeas, drained + rinsed	1
1 tsp.	white sugar (optional)	5 mL

smokin'!

Soak mesquite chips in water for 10 minutes, then drain. Sprinkle damp mesquite chips directly on the barbecue rocks, or wrap damp chips in heavy-duty aluminum foil, poke holes in the foil to allow smoke to escape, and place directly on the rocks.

Bring barbecue to high heat, and add mesquite chips. Spread tomatoes in a deep roasting pan that will fit on the barbecue with the lid closed. Stir in 2 Tbsp. (25 mL) olive oil, wine, 1 tsp. (5 mL) salt, $\frac{1}{2}$ tsp. (2 mL) pepper, oregano, rosemary, garlic, chipotle, 2 pinches of cocoa powder, cinnamon, paprika and cumin. Place pan on barbecue grill, close lid, and smoke tomato mixture for 30 to 40 minutes.

Toss red and green peppers with $\frac{1}{2}$ Tbsp. (7 mL) olive oil and a few pinches of salt and pepper. Spread peppers in a roasting pan large enough to hold all the vegetables. Place pan on barbecue grill, close lid, and smoke peppers for 20 minutes. Add onion, zucchini, eggplant and 2 to 3 Tbsp. (25-40 mL) olive oil to peppers. Toss well, sprinkle with salt and pepper to taste, and smoke for 15 to 20 minutes, until all the vegetables are tender.

Meanwhile, preheat oven to 325°F (160°C). While vegetables are smoking, place pan with smoked tomato mixture in oven for 1 to $1\frac{1}{2}$ hours, until tomatoes are caramelized and thick but not too dry. (If left on the barbecue any longer, tomatoes will taste far too smoky.)

In a frying pan on the stove over medium heat, cook mushrooms in 2 Tbsp. (25 mL) olive oil seasoned with salt and pepper for 6 to 7 minutes, until tender.

Combine caramelized tomatoes, smoked vegetables and mushrooms in a large pot, add chickpeas, and season with salt and pepper. If chili is a little acidic, add sugar.

Serves 6–8

bread pudding with gorgonzola, wild mushrooms + rosemary

Bread pudding is a natural at Pan Chancho, where we always have lots of bread. Developed for a holiday menu, this recipe makes an excellent side dish. You'll find dried wild-mushroom mixes of all descriptions at most grocery stores.

2 tsp.	melted unsalted butter	10 mL
6	large eggs	6
2	large egg yolks	2
3 cups	2% milk	750 mL
1 cup	35% M.F. cream	250 mL
1 tsp.	sea salt	5 mL
	Pinch freshly ground black pepper	
1 lb.	sourdough bread, crusts removed, cut into 3/4-inch (2 cm) cubes	450 g
5 1/2 oz.	Gorgonzola cheese, crumbled	155 g
1 cup	dried wild-mushroom mix	250 mL
2 Tbsp.	unsalted butter, plus more for topping	25 mL
3	leeks, thinly sliced + rinsed	3
2 Tbsp.	minced garlic	25 mL
2 Tbsp.	minced fresh rosemary	25 mL
1/4 cup	dry white wine	50 mL

Grease a shallow 9-by-13-inch (3 L) baking dish or six 8-ounce (225 g) ramekins with melted butter. In a large bowl, whisk together eggs and egg yolks. Add milk, cream, salt, pepper and bread cubes, and stir to coat bread. Stir in cheese, cover with plastic wrap, and let sit at room temperature for 30 minutes to allow bread to soak up egg mixture.

Meanwhile, rehydrate mushrooms in a small bowl in about 1/2 cup (125 mL) boiling water. Drain, discard liquid, and set mushrooms aside.

In a large frying pan over low heat, melt butter. Add leeks, garlic and rosemary, and cook until leeks are softened but not browned. Add mushrooms and wine, and continue cooking until most of the liquid has evaporated. Remove from heat, and allow mixture to cool.

Preheat oven to 350°F (180°C). Stir cooled mushroom mixture into bread mixture. Spoon into baking dish or ramekins, dot with butter, and place in a roasting pan. Pour hot water into pan until it reaches the midway point on the baking dish or ramekins. Bake for 30 to 45 minutes, until a toothpick inserted in centre of pudding comes out clean. Serve warm.

Serves 6

Variation

Substitute Rougette de Brigham, a Québec cheese with an apple-cider-washed rind, for the Gorgonzola, and sage for the rosemary; omit the mushrooms. Instead of sourdough, use our Apple + Cider Bread (see page 32).

laura's cheddar spoon bread

This spoon bread makes a delightful snack or can be served with any chunky-tomato-based dish or with stewed chicken. Either way, everyone will be very happy.

2¼ cups	water	550 mL
½ tsp.	sea salt	2 mL
1 cup	fine cornmeal	250 mL
	Freshly ground black pepper	
2 Tbsp.	unsalted butter	25 mL
1 cup	2% milk	250 mL
4	large eggs, beaten	4
1½ cups	grated old Cheddar cheese	375 mL
2 Tbsp.	thinly sliced scallions	25 mL

Preheat oven to 400°F (200°C). Grease a medium casserole dish, and set aside.

In a large saucepan, bring water to a boil. Add salt, reduce heat, and slowly add cornmeal while stirring with a whisk to prevent lumps from forming. Cook, stirring constantly, for 1 to 2 minutes.

Remove pan from heat, and add a pinch of pepper. Stir in butter, then milk, and continue stirring until smooth and well mixed. Beat in eggs until smooth. Stir in cheese and scallions.

Pour mixture into casserole dish, and bake, uncovered, for 50 to 60 minutes, until a toothpick inserted in centre comes out clean. Serve warm.

Serves 6

coconut lime rice

This rice dish goes well with any Asian cuisine, whether Thai, Vietnamese, Malaysian, Indian or Chinese.

2 cups	jasmine rice	500 mL
1 cup	unsweetened coconut milk	250 mL
2 cups	water	500 mL
4–5	fresh or frozen kaffir lime leaves	4–5
1 Tbsp.	unsweetened dried coconut	15 mL
3/4 tsp.	lime zest	4 mL
1/2 tsp.	sea salt	2 mL
2 tsp.	butter	10 mL

Place rice in a medium bowl, and rinse under cold running water, stirring constantly with your hand, until water is clear. Drain in a colander.

In a medium saucepan over medium heat, bring rice and remaining ingredients to a boil. Stir once, reduce heat to low, and cover. Cook for 10 to 15 minutes, until rice is tender.

Serves 6

note

If using a rice cooker, place rinsed rice and remaining ingredients in cooker, stir, and set rice to cook.

ping's five-jewel rice

At Pan Chancho, this rice is so popular, it doesn't last five minutes "in the case." It's beautiful, it's addictive, and it's perfect as a meal on its own or as a side dish. You'll find Chinese sausage at any Asian market.

1 cup	jasmine rice	250 mL
1¼ cups	water	300 mL
2 Tbsp.	dried shrimp	25 mL
6	pieces dried Chinese black mushrooms	6
1 Tbsp.	chopped garlic	15 mL
2 Tbsp.	canola oil	25 mL
1	piece double-smoked bacon, thinly sliced	1
1	Chinese sausage (lop chong), thinly sliced	1
6	large raw shrimp, cut in half lengthwise	6
1 Tbsp.	oyster sauce	15 mL
3 Tbsp.	Kung Fu soy sauce	40 mL
1 Tbsp.	chopped cilantro	15 mL
2 Tbsp.	thinly sliced scallions	25 mL
	Sea salt	
	Freshly ground black pepper	

Place rice in a medium bowl, and rinse under cold running water, stirring constantly with your hand, until water is clear. Drain in a colander.

In a medium saucepan over medium heat, bring rice and water to a boil. Stir once, reduce heat to low, and cover. Cook for 10 to 15 minutes, until rice is tender.

Meanwhile, in a small bowl, cover dried shrimp with hot water, and soak for 5 minutes. Drain, discard liquid, and set aside. Repeat the same process with dried mushrooms.

In a large frying pan over medium heat, cook garlic in oil for 1 to 2 minutes. Add bacon, and cook for 4 to 5 minutes. Add sausage, and cook for 4 to 5 minutes more. Add mushrooms, rehydrated and fresh shrimp, oyster sauce and soy sauce. Continue to cook until fresh shrimp turn pink (be careful not to overcook shrimp). Stir in cilantro and scallions.

In a large bowl, combine the warm rice with the "jewels." Add salt and pepper to taste and more soy sauce, if desired. Serve warm.

Serves 4-6

pilao rice

Studded with colourful vegetables and whole spices, this Indian pilaf is just as pleasing to the eye as it is to the palate.

2 cups	basmati rice	500 mL
1/2 cup	finely diced cooking onion	125 mL
1/2 cup	finely diced carrot	125 mL
1/2 cup	finely diced celery	125 mL
1/4 cup	ghee or clarified butter	50 mL
1	1-inch (2.5 cm) stick cinnamon	1
1	bay leaf	1
7	green or white cardamom pods, cracked	7
4	whole cloves	4
7	black peppercorns	7
1/8 tsp.	cumin seed, toasted	0.5 mL
1/8 tsp.	black mustard seed, toasted	0.5 mL
1/4 tsp.	sea salt	1 mL
3 1/2 cups	water	875 mL
1/2 cup	fresh green peas	125 mL
1/2 cup	cashew pieces, toasted	125 mL

Place rice in a large bowl, and rinse under cold running water, stirring constantly with your hand, until water is clear. Drain in a colander for 5 minutes (the rice should be dry).

In a large saucepan over medium heat, cook onion, carrot and celery in ghee or clarified butter until vegetables are tender, 3 to 4 minutes. Add cinnamon, bay leaf, cardamom pods, cloves, peppercorns, cumin seed, mustard seed, salt, rice and water, and stir. Increase heat to medium-high, and bring to a boil. Reduce heat to low, cover, and cook for 10 to 12 minutes, until rice is tender.

Stir in peas and cashews, and serve.

Serves 6–8

savoury porcini + spinach cheesecake

This cheesecake is a great summer meal. Make it early in the day, and serve it for supper with a fresh garden salad. It's excellent topped with Chez Piggy Chili Sauce *(see page 225).*

1 Tbsp.	melted unsalted butter	15 mL
1/2 cup	breadcrumbs seasoned with sea salt + freshly ground black pepper	125 mL
2 Tbsp.	freshly grated Parmigiano-Reggiano	25 mL
1/2 cup	dried porcini mushrooms	125 mL
1/2 cup	dry white wine	125 mL
1	10 oz. (285 g) pkg. spinach, washed + picked	1
1	large cooking onion, diced	1
2 Tbsp.	unsalted butter	25 mL
4 cups	sliced fresh shiitake mushrooms	1 L
1/2 lb.	ricotta cheese	225 g
1/2 lb.	chèvre	225 g
4	large eggs	4
1 tsp.	sea salt	5 mL
1/2 tsp.	freshly ground black pepper	2 mL
1/2 tsp.	ground nutmeg	2 mL

Preheat oven to 350°F (180°C). In a small bowl, mix together melted butter, breadcrumbs and Parmesan. Press into a 9-inch (2.5 L) springform pan lined with parchment paper, and bake for 10 minutes. Set aside, and reduce oven temperature to 300°F (150°C).

Meanwhile, in a small saucepan over medium heat, simmer porcini mushrooms in wine until mushrooms are soft, 5 to 10 minutes. Remove mushrooms with a slotted spoon, and coarsely chop. Strain wine through a coffee filter into a small bowl to remove any grit. Set mushrooms and wine aside.

Blanch spinach by immersing briefly in boiling salted water, then drain and plunge into cold water. Drain again, squeezing out as much water as possible. Chop coarsely, and set aside.

In a large frying pan over medium heat, sauté onion in butter for 1 to 2 minutes. Add shiitake mushrooms, and cook for 4 minutes, until mushrooms are soft. Add reserved porcini mushrooms and wine, and cook for 3 minutes, until wine is reduced by half. Set aside to cool.

Blend ricotta and chèvre in a food processor, add eggs, salt, pepper and nutmeg, and liquefy. In a large bowl, stir spinach and mushroom mixture together, then stir in ricotta mixture. Pour onto crust in springform pan, and bake until set, about 1 1/2 hours.

Remove from oven, allow to cool, then refrigerate. Serve cold.

Serves 6-8

debris-free

Dried mushrooms are almost always sandy. If your recipe calls for the liquid in which the mushrooms were rehydrated, be sure to strain it before using. We recommend using a coffee filter for this — it's quick and easy and does the trick.

traditional tourtière

In Québec, every family has its own tourtière recipe, each different in its own way. This is ours.

4	medium cooking onions, finely diced	4
3	stalks celery, finely diced	3
1/4 cup	extra-virgin olive oil	50 mL
2 lb.	lean ground pork	900 g
3 lb.	lean ground beef	1.4 kg
3/4 cup	hot water	175 mL
1 tsp.	ground sage	5 mL
1 tsp.	dried marjoram	5 mL
1 tsp.	ground cloves	5 mL
1 tsp.	ground cinnamon	5 mL
1 1/2 tsp.	sea salt	7 mL
1 tsp.	freshly ground black pepper	5 mL
2 cups	breadcrumbs	500 mL
	Sour Cream Pastry (double recipe on page 203)	
1	large egg	1
1 Tbsp.	10% M.F. cream	15 mL

In a large heavy-bottomed saucepan over medium heat, cook onions and celery in olive oil until soft, 5 to 7 minutes. Add pork and beef, and continue to cook until meat is no longer pink, stirring frequently to break apart any lumps. Add water, and simmer, uncovered, for 30 minutes. Skim off as much fat as is your preference, but keep in mind that the fat contributes moistness and a lot of flavour. (We usually skim off about half the fat.) Stir in sage, marjoram, cloves, cinnamon, salt and pepper, then stir in breadcrumbs. Taste, and add more salt and pepper, if needed. Remove from heat, spread mixture on a baking sheet, and allow to cool.

Preheat oven to 450°F (230°C). Roll out 4 pie-crust rounds, and line two 9-inch (23 cm) pie plates with pastry. In a small bowl, whisk together egg and cream to make egg wash. Brush the edge of each bottom crust with egg wash, and divide filling between the two pie shells. Place a round of pastry on top of each pie, and crimp edges to seal. Brush tops with egg wash, and cut a small hole in centre of each pie to allow steam to escape.

Bake for 10 minutes, then reduce heat to 325°F (160°C), and bake for 35 to 45 minutes more, until crust is golden brown. Let tourtière rest for 10 minutes before cutting. Serve warm or at room temperature.

Makes two 9-inch (23 cm) pies; each pie serves 6

vegetarian tourtière

Vegetarian comfort food for people who've given up eating traditional tourtière, this recipe was developed to imitate the taste and texture of the original meat-based savoury pie. Even meat eaters will be fooled.

4 lb.	white mushrooms	1.8 kg
1	large cooking onion, finely diced	1
3	cloves garlic, finely minced	3
2 Tbsp.	extra-virgin olive oil	25 mL
1 1/4 cups	raw organic millet	300 mL
1 1/4 cups	organic rolled oats	300 mL
1 1/2 tsp.	dried sage	7 mL
1 tsp.	dried marjoram	5 mL
1/2 tsp.	ground cloves	2 mL
1/8 tsp.	ground cinnamon	0.5 mL
1/4 cup	Japanese soy sauce	50 mL
2 tsp.	sea salt	10 mL
1 1/2 tsp.	freshly ground black pepper	7 mL
	Sour Cream Pastry (double recipe on page 203)	
1	large egg	1
1 Tbsp.	10% M.F. cream	15 mL

In a food processor, pulse mushrooms to a mealy consistency. Set aside.

In a large heavy-bottomed saucepan over low heat, cook onion and garlic in olive oil until soft but not browned, 8 to 10 minutes. Increase heat to medium, and stir in mushrooms. Simmer until mushrooms are cooked and have released their liquid, 20 to 25 minutes.

Transfer mushroom mixture to a colander placed over a bowl. Put a weight on top of the mixture (e.g., a plate with a can of soup on top) to extract as much liquid as possible. Allow to drain for 30 minutes. Measure mushroom broth, and add water, if needed, to make a total of 5 1/2 cups (1.4 L). Reserve mushroom mixture.

In a small pot, bring 3 1/2 cups (875 mL) of the broth to a boil, and add millet. Cook, stirring frequently, until millet is soft and broth is completely absorbed, 15 to 20 minutes. Cook rolled oats in remaining 2 cups (500 mL) broth for 8 to 10 minutes. In a large bowl, combine mushroom mixture, millet, oats, sage, marjoram, cloves and cinnamon. Stir in soy sauce, salt and pepper. Spread mixture on a baking sheet to cool.

In a small bowl, whisk together egg and cream to make egg wash. To assemble and bake pies, proceed as directed in Traditional Tourtière (see facing page).

Makes two 9-inch (23 cm) pies; each pie serves 6

florentine torte

A rustic Italian savoury pie, the torte was traditionally about 24 inches (60 cm) wide and was baked in the village hearth.

4	medium cooking onions, thinly sliced	4
1/4 cup	minced garlic (about 10 cloves)	50 mL
1/4 cup	extra-virgin olive oil	50 mL
1/2 tsp.	sea salt	2 mL
1/4 tsp.	Freshly ground black pepper	1 mL
1/4 tsp.	ground nutmeg	1 mL
1	10 oz. (285 g) pkg. baby spinach, washed	1
2 cups	grated Asiago cheese	500 mL
	Sour Cream Pastry (see page 203)	
1	large egg	1
1 Tbsp.	10% M.F. cream	15 mL
	Coarse sea salt	

In a large frying pan over low heat, cook onions and garlic in olive oil until onions are completely soft but not browned, 25 to 30 minutes. Stir in 1/2 tsp. (2 mL) salt, pepper and nutmeg. Increase heat to medium, add spinach, cover, and cook, stirring occasionally, until spinach is just wilted. Drain in a colander to remove excess liquid, and allow to cool. In a medium bowl, combine spinach mixture with cheese.

Preheat oven to 400°F (200°C), and line a baking sheet with parchment paper. Divide pastry into 6 pieces, and roll each into a thin 8-inch (20 cm) round. Place equal amounts of spinach mixture in centre of each round, leaving about a 2-inch (5 cm) border.

In a small bowl, whisk together egg and cream to make egg wash. Brush border of each pastry round with egg wash, and fold edges toward centre, making 5 or 6 pleats. As you complete each fold, brush top of pleat with egg wash. The centre portion of the spinach filling should remain uncovered.

Brush top of pastry with egg wash, and sprinkle lightly with coarse salt. Place tortes on baking sheet, and bake for 20 to 25 minutes, until golden brown. Serve warm or at room temperature.

Serves 6

note

If you'd prefer one large torte, roll pastry into a thin 14-inch (35 cm) round, transfer to a baking sheet lined with parchment paper, and fill, leaving a 3-inch (7.5 cm) border. Fold in edges, as with individual tortes, brush pastry with egg wash, sprinkle lightly with coarse salt, and bake.

quiche lorraine

At Pan Chancho, quiche is the comeback kid, and it's largely due to Mariela Santamaria, our gifted go-to quiche baker.

2	large eggs	2
2	large egg yolks	2
1½ cups	half-and-half cream	375 mL
	Pinch freshly ground black pepper	
½ tsp.	sea salt	2 mL
¼ lb.	double-smoked bacon, rind removed, diced	115 g
1	medium cooking onion, diced	1
1	blind-baked Sour Cream Pastry shell (see page 203)	1
½ cup	grated Gruyère cheese	125 mL

Preheat oven to 325°F (160°C). In a large bowl, whisk together eggs, egg yolks, cream, pepper and salt. Set aside.

In a cast-iron frying pan over medium heat, fry bacon until fat is rendered. Reduce heat to low, add onion, and cook with bacon until onion is soft, 15 to 20 minutes. If you are using regular bacon, you may have too much bacon fat, in which case you should drain off some before frying the onion.

Spoon bacon pieces and onion into pie shell, then top with cheese. Pour egg mixture into pie shell, and bake for 45 to 60 minutes, until custard is set and top is golden brown. Serve warm or at room temperature.

Serves 4-6

variations

Fillings change, but everything else — the pie shell, custard recipe, oven temperature and number of servings — remains the same for each variation presented on the following pages.

smoked salmon quiche with dill

3–4	slices smoked salmon, roughly chopped	3–4
2	scallions, thinly sliced	2
1 tsp.	chopped fresh dill	5 mL
1/2 cup	coarsely grated Parmigiano-Reggiano	125 mL

Layer salmon, scallions and dill into pie shell, then top with cheese. Pour egg mixture into pie shell, and bake for 45 to 60 minutes, until custard is set and top is golden brown. Serve warm or at room temperature. (See page 145 for detailed instructions.)

broccoli + cheddar quiche with caramelized onions + chives

1/4 cup	Caramelized Onions (see page 226)	50 mL
1/2 cup	blanched broccoli florets	125 mL
1/2 cup	grated old Cheddar cheese	125 mL
1 tsp.	chopped fresh chives	5 mL

Layer onions, broccoli, cheese and chives into shell. Pour egg mixture into pie shell, and bake for 45 to 60 minutes, until custard is set and top is golden brown. Serve warm or at room temperature. (See page 145 for detailed instructions.)

shiitake + kale quiche

2 Tbsp.	sliced shallots	25 mL
1 Tbsp.	extra-virgin olive oil	15 mL
1 tsp.	chopped garlic	5 mL
1/4 cup	sliced shiitake mushrooms	50 mL
1/2 cup	loosely packed chopped green kale	125 mL
1 Tbsp.	chopped fresh chives	15 mL
1/2 cup	coarsely grated Parmigiano-Reggiano	125 mL

In a frying pan over medium heat, cook shallots in olive oil until soft. Add garlic, and cook for 1 minute. Remove from pan, and set aside. Sauté mushrooms in pan until soft. Remove, and set aside. Add kale to pan, and cook until just wilted.

Layer shallot mixture, mushrooms, kale and chives into pie shell, and top with cheese. Pour egg mixture into pie shell, and bake for 45 to 60 minutes, until custard is set and top is golden brown. Serve warm or at room temperature. (See page 145 for detailed instructions.)

shrimp, brie + arugula quiche

1 cup	coarsely chopped cooked shrimp	250 mL
1/2 cup	loosely packed, coarsely chopped arugula	125 mL
1/2 – 3/4 cup	diced Brie cheese	125–175 mL

Layer shrimp and arugula into pie shell, and top with cheese. Pour egg mixture into pie shell, and bake for 45 to 60 minutes, until custard is set and top is golden brown. Serve warm or at room temperature. (See page 145 for detailed instructions.)

fish + seafood

salade diablo, page 153

fish

halibut à la provençal

This dish is delicious with Warm Potato Salad with Sherry Vinegar + Crispy Leeks *(see page 95).*

	Sea salt	
	Pinch cayenne	
4	6 oz. (170 g) halibut fillets	4
2	scallions, sliced thinly on the diagonal	2
4	fresh Italian parsley sprigs	4
4	fresh thyme sprigs, plus extra for garnish	4
8	slices of lemon	8
3 Tbsp.	extra-virgin olive oil	40 mL
1 cup	dry white wine	250 mL
1–1½ lb.	mussels, scrubbed + debearded	450–680 g
½ cup	cold unsalted butter, cut into ½-inch (1 cm) cubes	125 mL
20	cherry tomatoes	20
20	niçoise olives, pitted	20
1 Tbsp.	drained capers	15 mL

Preheat oven to 400°F (200°C). Sprinkle salt and cayenne sparingly on flesh side only of halibut fillets. In a cast-iron frying pan coated with olive oil, sear fillets, skin side down, over high heat for 1 minute. Place in a casserole dish in a single layer, and top with scallions, parsley, thyme and lemon slices. Drizzle with olive oil and ¼ cup (50 mL) of the wine. Bake, uncovered, for 12 to 15 minutes, until flaky but not dry.

Meanwhile, place a large saucepan over high heat. Add mussels, a pinch of salt and remaining ¾ cup (175 mL) wine, and cook, covered, for 3 to 4 minutes, until mussels open. Stir them or shake pan to make sure all the mussels are cooked. Discard any that do not open. Remove mussels with a slotted spoon, and keep warm.

Over high heat, reduce liquid in pan by half. Remove from heat, and add butter cubes 3 or 4 at a time, whisking constantly. Stir in tomatoes, olives and capers.

To serve, spoon tomato mixture onto each plate, top with fish, and drizzle with pan juices. Garnish with lemon, mussels and thyme sprigs.

Serves 4

canuck cooks

We may be famous for our hockey, but citizens the world over also like us for the "Canadian cooking theory," formulated long ago in an Ottawa test kitchen at the Department of Fisheries. It's a handy little formula that fish lovers still rely on when cooking fish in any form. Simply put, measure your fish at its thickest point, and allow 10 minutes' cooking time for every 1 inch (2.5 cm). The low-fat-fish exceptions to the rule are tilapia and wild salmon, which will be far too dry if not served rare or medium-rare. And that's really the most critical rule in fish cookery: Do not overcook!

green curried haddock steamed in banana leaves

Banana leaves provide a tropical "green" fragrance to this dish. Sold in Asian markets, they are packaged as folded whole leaves, but you'll need to cut them into smaller segments for use here.

green curry paste

1	lemon	1
2	small green Thai chilies, minced	2
1/4 cup	chopped cilantro	50 mL
1	medium cooking onion, finely chopped	1
1/2 tsp.	minced fresh ginger	2 mL
1	clove garlic, minced	1
1/2 tsp.	ground cumin	2 mL
1/4 tsp.	ground fenugreek	1 mL
1/4 cup	desiccated coconut	50 mL
1 Tbsp.	ghee or clarified butter	15 mL
	Pinch sea salt	
1 tsp.	garam masala	5 mL
4	6 oz. (170 g) haddock fillets	4
	Sea salt	
4	sections of banana leaves, washed (about 10 x 10 inches/25 x 25 cm)	4

Segment lemon, and discard rind, membrane and seeds. In a blender or food processor, purée lemon and juice, chilies, cilantro, half of the onion, ginger, garlic, cumin and fenugreek. Add coconut, and pulse to combine.

In a small saucepan, heat ghee or clarified butter over medium heat. Add remaining onion, and fry until soft and golden in colour. Add puréed lemon mixture, and cook, stirring frequently, for 6 to 7 minutes. Stir in salt and garam masala. Taste, and add more salt, if needed.

Season both sides of haddock fillets with salt, and place 1 fillet in centre of a banana-leaf section. Coat fillet with green curry paste, then wrap with leaf to form a snug package. Secure with butcher's twine or a strip of banana leaf. Repeat with remaining fillets.

Place fish packages in a steamer or colander over simmering water, cover and steam for 25 to 30 minutes. To serve, remove fish from cooked banana leaf and place on a fresh banana leaf. Serve with steamed rice.

Serves 4

note

Banana leaves should be thoroughly washed under cold running water before being cut into sections, but be very gentle, as they have a tendency to tear if handled roughly.

chilled stuffed lobster + orzo salad with vanilla + chive crème fraîche

For a relaxed celebration of a special occasion, prepare the components of this elegant dinner ahead of time.

	Sea salt	
3	3/4 -lb. (340 g) whole fresh lobsters	3
1	1 lb. (450 g) pkg. orzo	1
2 Tbsp.	canola oil	25 mL
2 cups	Crème Fraîche (see page 230)	500 mL
3 Tbsp.	finely chopped fresh chives	40 mL
	Zest of 1 orange	
1/2	vanilla bean	1/2
	Fresh chive sprigs for garnish	

Fill a large stockpot with cold salted water, and place over high heat. When water comes to a boil, drop lobsters in headfirst. When water returns to a boil, reduce heat to a simmer, and cook, uncovered, for 7 minutes. Remove lobsters, and set aside until cool enough to handle.

Pull off claws, and break them to free the meat. Leave claw meat intact as a garnish. Gather any other bits from claws, and set aside. Cut lobsters in half lengthwise. Pull out tail meat, chop, and set aside. Wash and dry shells, and set aside. If you're serving the dish later in the day, refrigerate until needed.

note

The black mass behind the lobster's eyes is the stomach. Remove and discard. The green tomalley, or liver, is delicious when stirred into the cooked pasta. If any red coral, or lobster roe, is present, add to the cooked pasta as well.

Cook pasta in boiling salted water until al dente, drain, place in a large bowl and immediately mix with oil. Allow to cool, then stir in crème fraîche, chives and orange zest. Scrape seeds from vanilla bean, and stir them into the pasta along with the chopped lobster and bits from claws, tomalley and any coral.

Stuff lobster shells with pasta salad, and garnish with claw meat and chive sprigs. Chill before serving.

Serves 6

salade diablo

It's a hard combination to beat: our spicy Diablo Hot Sauce with the intense flavour of spicy glazed mushrooms counterbalanced by buttery Bibb lettuce, cool blue cheese dressing and crunchy scallions. This is one of our favourites. The mushrooms can also be served at room temperature as an appetizer.

shrimp

1/4 cup	extra-virgin olive oil	50 mL
1/4 tsp.	crushed dried chilies	1 mL
1/4 tsp.	yellow mustard seed	1 mL
	Sea salt	
1/2 cup	dry white wine	125 mL
3 cups	water	750 mL
6	black peppercorns	6
2	large celery leaves	2
1/2	lemon	1/2
30–36	large shrimp, peeled + deveined	30–36

In a small pan over low heat, mix together olive oil, dried chilies, mustard seed and a pinch of salt. Cook, stirring, for 1 to 2 minutes. Set aside.

In a large pot, mix together wine, water, peppercorns, celery leaves, lemon and 1/2 tsp. (2 mL) salt. Place over high heat, and bring to a boil. Reduce heat to medium, and add shrimp. Poach shrimp for 3 to 4 minutes, uncovered, until pink throughout. Remove shrimp with a slotted spoon, place in a large bowl, and set aside to cool. Pour olive oil mixture over cooled shrimp, and toss to coat. Chill in refrigerator.

spicy glazed mushrooms

2 Tbsp.	unsalted butter	25 mL
8 oz.	white button mushrooms	225 g
1/4 cup	Worcestershire sauce	50 mL
4	shakes Tabasco sauce	4
	Pinch sea salt	
	Pinch freshly ground black pepper	

To glaze mushrooms, melt butter in a cast-iron frying pan, and add mushrooms, Worcestershire, Tabasco, salt and pepper. Stir to coat mushrooms completely. Cook, covered, over medium-low heat, stirring frequently, until mushrooms are shiny and deep brown in colour and butter separates from Worcestershire, 15 to 20 minutes. Remove from heat, and allow to cool.

2	heads Bibb lettuce	2
	Highland Blue Cheese Dressing (see page 232)	
6	scallions, cut into 1/2-inch (1 cm) pieces	6
	Diablo Hot Sauce (see page 224)	

To serve, divide lettuce among 6 salad plates, drizzle with dressing, mound shrimp in centre and scatter mushrooms and scallions on top. Then drizzle with hot sauce.

Serves 6

saigon shrimp cakes

These seafood cakes don't rely on a flour-and-egg filler to hold them together. The fish and shrimp stand alone. Serve with Dragon Noodles (see page 87) and a grilled slice of fresh pineapple.

14–16	large shrimp, peeled, deveined + coarsely chopped	14–16
1 Tbsp.	finely chopped garlic	15 mL
1 Tbsp.	minced Thai chilies	15 mL
1 Tbsp.	minced fresh ginger	15 mL
1¼ lb.	tilapia or other white fish, cut into medium dice	570 g
1 tsp.	sea salt	5 mL
¼ tsp.	freshly ground black pepper	1 mL
2 Tbsp.	finely sliced scallions	25 mL
3 Tbsp.	red bell pepper, small dice	40 mL
3 Tbsp.	finely chopped cilantro	40 mL

Preheat oven to 350°F (180°C). In a food processor, purée shrimp, garlic, chilies and ginger together. Add half of the fish, and pulse, scraping down sides to mix thoroughly. Add remaining fish, salt and pepper, and pulse briefly to combine. Leave mixture chunky. Remove to a large bowl, and fold in scallions, red pepper and cilantro.

Form into 8 patties, and place on an oiled baking sheet. Bake for 12 to 15 minutes, until cooked through.

Serves 8

camarones à la flamenca

The tender flower stalks of young garlic plants are known as scapes, garlic scapes or green garlic. Sweeter than mature garlic, scapes are available only in early spring, so keep an eye out for them at your local farmers' market. Look for puréed garlic scape in specialty food shops, or make it yourself by food-processing scapes, olive oil, salt and pepper.

½ cup	extra-virgin olive oil	125 mL
¼ tsp.	sea salt	1 mL
28	large shrimp, peeled + deveined	28
½	red bell pepper, finely julienned	½
½	yellow bell pepper, finely julienned	½
¼ cup	dry sherry	50 mL
2 Tbsp.	sherry vinegar	25 mL
2 Tbsp.	lime juice	25 mL
½ cup	puréed garlic scape	125 mL

Chopped fresh Italian parsley for garnish
Crusty bread

In a large cast-iron frying pan, heat olive oil and salt over very high heat. When oil is almost smoking, add shrimp, and cook on one side for 1 to 2 minutes. Turn shrimp, and add peppers. Fry for 1 to 2 minutes, until shrimp just changes colour. Add sherry, vinegar, lime juice and garlic scape. Remove from heat, and stir to combine.

Spoon onto plates, garnish with parsley, and serve immediately, passing bread at the table to sop up the juice.

Serves 4-6 as an appetizer

curried mussels with india pale ale

Serve as an appetizer with lots of crusty bread or as an aromatic main course with steamed basmati rice on the side.

3 1/2 Tbsp.	ghee or clarified butter	45 mL
2 cups	chopped scallions	500 mL
4	cloves garlic, minced	4
3 Tbsp.	minced fresh ginger	40 mL
3	Thai chilies, minced	3
1/8 tsp.	turmeric	0.5 mL
3 tsp.	ground coriander seed	15 mL
1/8 tsp.	chili powder	0.5 mL
1/4 tsp.	sea salt	1 mL
1 cup	East India Pale or British ale	250 mL
2 lb.	mussels, scrubbed + debearded	900 g
1/4 cup	chopped cilantro	50 mL
1	lime, cut into 4 wedges	1

In a medium bowl, combine ghee or clarified butter, scallions, garlic, ginger, chilies, turmeric, coriander, chili powder and salt.

In a saucepan large enough to hold mussels no more than 2 layers deep, heat scallion mixture over low heat. Add ale, increase heat to medium-high, and bring to a boil. Boil for 6 to 8 minutes to reduce slightly. Add mussels, and cook, covered, for 3 to 4 minutes, until mussels open. Stir them or shake pan to make sure all the mussels are cooked evenly. Discard any that do not open.

Pour mussels and cooking liquid into a large serving bowl or 4 individual serving bowls, and garnish with cilantro. Serve lime wedges on the side, or squeeze lime juice over mussels.

Serves 4

thai red curry scallops

Versatile red curry paste can be your secret ingredient in any number of dishes. Use it with any kind of braised beef, with shrimp or mussels or in soups and stews for a little extra oomph. And, of course, with these scallops.

red curry paste

1 Tbsp.	coriander seed	15 mL
2 tsp.	cumin seed	10 mL
1 tsp.	black peppercorns	5 mL
2 tsp.	dried shrimp paste	10 mL
10	red Thai chilies	10
1/2 cup	chopped shallots	125 mL
1 Tbsp.	chopped garlic	15 mL
1/4 cup	chopped fresh lemongrass	50 mL
1 Tbsp.	chopped fresh galangal	15 mL
1 Tbsp.	chopped fresh coriander roots or stems	15 mL
4	fresh or frozen kaffir lime leaves, stem removed, minced	4
1 tsp.	lime zest	5 mL
3 Tbsp.	canola oil	40 mL
2 tsp.	paprika	10 mL
1 tsp.	turmeric	5 mL

scallops

1	14 oz. (398 mL) can unsweetened coconut milk	1
1/3 cup	red curry paste	75 mL
12	fresh kaffir lime leaves	12
3 Tbsp.	fish sauce	40 mL
3 Tbsp.	brown sugar	40 mL
1 1/2 lb.	sea scallops	680 g
	Thai basil leaves for garnish	

To make curry paste, toast coriander, cumin and peppercorns in a small frying pan over medium heat until fragrant, being careful not to burn them. Cool and grind in a spice grinder or with a mortar and pestle, and set aside.

Wrap shrimp paste in a double layer of aluminum foil, and heat in a frying pan over medium heat for 2 to 3 minutes on each side until fragrant. Unwrap and cool.

In a blender or food processor, purée chilies, shallots, garlic, lemongrass, galangal, coriander, lime leaves, lime zest and oil into a smooth paste. Add paprika, turmeric, ground spices and shrimp paste, and process until smooth. Curry paste can be stored in refrigerator in a covered container for up to 1 week or in freezer for up to 2 months. Makes 1 cup (250 mL).

To prepare scallops, heat coconut milk, curry paste and lime leaves in a large frying pan over medium-low heat. Whisk until smooth, bring to a simmer, and cook for 10 minutes. Add fish sauce and brown sugar, and cook for about 2 minutes. Add scallops, and poach until they are done, 5 to 10 minutes, depending on size of scallops and your preference.

To serve, spoon scallops and sauce onto plates piled with steaming rice, and garnish with basil.

Serves 4–6

pickled sardines with salsa verde

For sardine lovers — this method produces a cleaner flavour than either grilling or frying.

2 cups	white vinegar	500 mL
1/4 cup	sea salt	50 mL
12	whole frozen sardines, partially thawed	12

marinade

1 cup	extra-virgin olive oil	250 mL
3	cloves garlic, sliced	3
1 Tbsp.	chopped fresh Italian parsley	15 mL

salsa verde

10 oz.	fresh spinach, washed + picked	285 g
3	cloves garlic, minced	3
3 cups	fresh Italian parsley leaves	750 mL
1	2 oz. (60 g) can anchovies	1
1 cup	drained capers	250 mL
1/2 cup	extra-virgin olive oil	125 mL
	Freshly ground black pepper	

Black olives

Mix vinegar and salt in a container that will hold the sardines. Set brine aside.

If there are any scales on the sardines, scrape them off with the dull side of a knife blade. Remove heads, and slit sardines open at belly. Press sardines open, leaving tail portion intact. Remove and discard insides. Grasp backbone at top, and pull it away from the fish. This removes side bones as well. Rinse, pat dry, and place in brine to cover sardines completely. Refrigerate, covered, for 12 hours.

To make marinade, combine olive oil, garlic and parsley in a covered container that will hold sardines. Remove sardines from brine, discarding brine, and transfer to marinade, making sure sardines are covered by the oil. Store in refrigerator for up to 2 weeks.

To make salsa verde, blanch spinach by immersing briefly in boiling salted water, then drain and plunge into cold water. Drain again, and squeeze out excess water. Place spinach in a food processor with garlic, parsley, anchovies and capers, and coarsely chop. While still processing, drizzle in olive oil, and process until smooth. Season to taste with pepper. You can make this ahead and store in refrigerator in a covered container for 4 to 5 days.

To serve, remove sardines from marinade and arrange on a plate. Pass salsa verde and olives at the table.

Serves 4-12

tuna confit

Our version of "canned" tuna taken to a whole new level. At Pan Chancho, we use only sushi-quality albacore tuna, and one of the many ways we serve it is with grilled radicchio, roasted baby potatoes and crispy golden onion rings. It also makes a terrific tuna salad.

3 cups	extra-virgin olive oil	750 mL
1	medium cooking onion, thinly sliced	1
2	fresh rosemary sprigs	2
6	fresh thyme sprigs	6
1	bay leaf	1
3 Tbsp.	sea salt	40 mL
1 tsp.	black peppercorns, coarsely cracked	5 mL
	Zest of 1 lemon	
2 lb.	fresh tuna loin	900 g

Place olive oil, onion, rosemary, thyme, bay leaf, salt, peppercorns and lemon zest in a heavy-bottomed sauté pan over medium heat. The oil should reach a temperature of 150°F (65°C). Remove pan from heat, and let oil cool and flavours infuse for 30 minutes (oil should be just warm to the touch).

Return pan to stove over medium-low heat, add tuna, making sure it is completely covered with oil. Gradually increase heat to bring temperature of oil back to 150°F (65°C). Remove pan from heat, and let tuna cook in hot oil until it is firm but still pinkish and starting to flake inside. Remove tuna with a slotted spoon. Place tuna and oil in separate storage containers, and allow to cool.

Strain cooled oil, and pour over tuna to preserve it. (Tuna should be covered with oil, so add more olive oil if necessary.) Cover and refrigerate for up to 2 weeks.

Makes 2 lb. (900 g)

turkish fish stew

A purplish lemon-flavoured berry, sumac is ground to a powder or used in its dried-berry form. It is a popular addition to boost the lemon flavour in Middle Eastern dishes that feature fish, meat or vegetables.

1 cup	marinated artichoke hearts	250 mL
1	small cooking onion, chopped	1
1	green bell pepper, chopped	1
2 Tbsp.	extra-virgin olive oil	25 mL
2	cloves garlic, minced	2
1 tsp.	drained capers	5 mL
12	small green olives, pitted	12
1	14 oz. (398 mL) can diced tomatoes, with juice	1
2 Tbsp.	dry white wine	25 mL
1 Tbsp.	lemon juice	15 mL
1 cup	water	250 mL
2 tsp.	ground sumac	10 mL
1½ tsp.	crushed dried chilies	7 mL
1 tsp.	dried basil	5 mL
1 tsp.	ground cumin	5 mL
1 tsp.	minced fresh ginger	5 mL
½ tsp.	sea salt	2 mL
¼ tsp.	freshly ground black pepper	1 mL
2 lb.	tilapia or other white fish, cut into 1-inch (2.5 cm) cubes	900 g

Drain artichokes, reserving oil, and cut into quarters. Set aside.

In a large pot over medium-high heat, sauté onion and green pepper in olive oil until soft, about 10 minutes. Add garlic, and cook for 2 minutes. Add artichokes and reserved oil, capers, olives, tomatoes, wine, lemon juice and water. Bring to a simmer, and add sumac, dried chilies, basil, cumin, ginger, salt and pepper.

Increase heat to bring stew to a slow boil, and add fish. Reduce heat, and simmer, uncovered, for 8 to 10 minutes, until fish is tender.

Serve over couscous or plain rice.

Serves 4-6

haddock with tomato, sweet pepper + chorizo sauce

The cornmeal crust gives the haddock a nice crunch, while the smoky chorizo sauce will leave your guests begging for more.

chorizo sauce

8 oz.	chorizo sausage, small dice	225 g
1/4 cup	extra-virgin olive oil	50 mL
1	medium cooking onion, small dice	1
1	yellow bell pepper, small dice	1
1	red bell pepper, small dice	1
1	green bell pepper, small dice	1
3	cloves garlic, minced	3
2 Tbsp.	dry sherry	25 mL
2	medium tomatoes, small dice	2
1 Tbsp.	chopped fresh Italian parsley	15 mL
	Sea salt	
	Freshly ground black pepper	

haddock

3/4 cup	stone-ground cornmeal	175 mL
1 Tbsp.	all-purpose flour	15 mL
	Pinch cayenne	
1/2 tsp.	cumin seed, toasted	2 mL
6	8 oz. (225 g) portions haddock fillets	6
	Extra-virgin olive oil for frying	
	Chopped fresh Italian parsley for garnish	

To make sauce, sauté chorizo in a cast-iron frying pan over medium heat until browned and some of the fat is rendered. Remove chorizo, and set aside.

Add just enough of the olive oil to pan to cook onion and peppers. Add onion, and cook over medium heat for 2 minutes. Add peppers, and cook until soft, about 10 minutes. Stir in garlic, sherry and tomatoes, and cook for 4 minutes. Turn off heat, and stir in parsley. Add chorizo, and season with salt and pepper. Keep warm.

To prepare haddock, mix together cornmeal, flour, cayenne and cumin seed in a shallow dish. Dredge fillets in mixture to coat both sides.

Heat about 1/4 inch (6 mm) olive oil in a cast-iron or heavy-bottomed frying pan until almost smoking. Place fillets in pan, and cook for about 4 minutes, turn and cook on the other side for another 4 minutes. (The cooking time will vary depending on thickness of fillets. For more, see "Canuck Cooks," page 150.) Test with a fork to make sure flesh is flaky.

To serve, place one portion of haddock on each plate, spoon sauce on top, and garnish with parsley.

Serves 6

fish tacos with salsa fresca

There's a little bit of Mexico, by way of the Golden State, in this dish developed by former Californian Christyne Flynn.

fish

3 Tbsp.	lime juice	40 mL
$\frac{1}{2}$ tsp.	ground cumin	2 mL
$\frac{1}{2}$ tsp.	chili powder	2 mL
$\frac{1}{4}$ tsp.	dried oregano	1 mL
	Pinch sea salt	
	Pinch freshly ground black pepper	
$1\frac{1}{2}$–2 lb.	haddock, cod or tilapia fillets	680–900 g

salsa fresca

4	medium tomatoes, seeded + finely diced	4
1	small cooking onion, finely diced (about $\frac{1}{4}$ cup/50 mL)	1
1–2	cloves garlic, minced	1–2
1–2	Thai chilies, minced	1–2
$\frac{1}{2}$ cup	coarsely chopped cilantro	125 mL
$\frac{1}{4}$ cup	lime juice	50 mL
	Sea salt	

6	8-inch (20 cm) flour tortillas	6
1–$1\frac{1}{2}$ cups	Lime-Cilantro Coleslaw (see page 91)	250–375 mL
	Sour cream for garnish	
2 cups	Guacamole (see page 230)	500 mL

Preheat oven to 400°F (200°C), and line a baking sheet with parchment paper. To prepare fish, mix lime juice and spices, and rub over fillets. Place on baking sheet, and bake for 10 to 15 minutes. Allow to cool, and flake fish with fork.

To make salsa, combine all ingredients, and set aside.

Warm tortillas in a dry frying pan, one at a time, turning once, and place on a plate. On one half of each tortilla, place a portion of fish, 3 heaping Tbsp. (40 mL) coleslaw and 2 Tbsp. (25 mL) salsa. Fold tortilla over filling. Garnish with sour cream, and serve with guacamole on the side.

Serves 6

wild salmon with yogurt, honey + wehani + wild rice pilaf

A honey dip you won't soon forget: Black peppercorns give it a bite, cardamom adds a warm, spicy flavour, and the honey brings home the sweetness. For a special treat, use this as a dipping sauce with your favourite fried-chicken recipe.

pepper-infused honey

1/2 cup	liquid honey	125 mL
2	black cardamom pods, cracked open	2
1 tsp.	cracked black peppercorns	5 mL

pilaf

1/2 cup	Wehani rice	125 mL
1/2 cup	wild rice	125 mL
1	small yam, peeled + diced	1
	Sea salt	
1	large red onion, diced	1
2	cloves garlic, minced	2
1 Tbsp.	chopped fresh rosemary	15 mL
2 Tbsp.	extra-virgin olive oil	25 mL
1/4 cup	balsamic vinegar	50 mL
	Freshly ground black pepper	

salmon

6	6 oz. (170 g) portions of wild salmon fillets	6
	Sea salt	
	Freshly ground black pepper	
	Extra-virgin olive oil	
	10% M.F. yogurt for garnish	

To infuse honey, combine ingredients in a small saucepan over low heat, and warm gently for 5 to 10 minutes. Store, covered, at room temperature for up to 2 days. Before serving, remove cardamom pods.

To clean Wehani and wild rices, place each in a medium bowl and run under cold running water, stirring with your hand, until water is clear. Place each rice in a separate saucepan with 4 cups (1 L) cold salted water. Bring to a rolling boil, reduce heat to medium-low, and simmer, uncovered, until rice grains split open and rice is tender — 35 to 45 minutes for wild rice, 30 to 40 minutes for Wehani. Drain well, then stir together in a large bowl.

Meanwhile, in a medium saucepan, cook yam in boiling salted water, uncovered, until just tender, about 10 minutes. Drain, and add to rice mixture.

In a medium skillet over low heat, soften onion, garlic and rosemary in olive oil, about 10 minutes. Add vinegar, and simmer until vinegar is reduced to about 1 Tbsp. (15 mL). Stir into rice mixture. Season with salt and pepper. Keep warm.

To prepare salmon, preheat oven to 400°F (200°C), and sprinkle flesh side of salmon fillets with salt and pepper. In a cast-iron frying pan coated with olive oil, sear fillets, skin side down, for 1 minute over high heat. Drizzle with olive oil, transfer to oven, and bake for 5 to 7 minutes, until fish is firm. Place one portion of salmon on each plate, top with a dollop of yogurt, and drizzle with honey. Serve with pilaf.

Serves 6

wild salmon with caramelized shallots + green-peppercorn sour cream

If you're feeling extravagant, indulge yourself by garnishing this dish with caviar.

caramelized shallots

6–10	shallots	6–10
2 Tbsp.	extra-virgin olive oil	25 mL
2 Tbsp.	vodka	25 mL
2	fresh thyme sprigs	2
	Pinch sea salt	
	Pinch freshly ground black pepper	
1 Tbsp.	clarified butter	15 mL

peppercorn sour cream

1 1/4 tsp.	canned green peppercorns in brine, drained	6 mL
3/4 cup	sour cream	175 mL
	Sea salt	

salmon

6	6 oz. (170 g) portions of wild salmon fillets	6
	Sea salt	
	Freshly ground black pepper	
	Extra-virgin olive oil	

spinach

1/4 cup	clarified butter	50 mL
2	10 oz. (285 g) pkg. spinach, washed + picked	2
	Sea salt	
	Freshly ground black pepper	

Preheat oven to 375°F (190°C). Peel shallots, leaving stem end intact so that they do not fall apart while cooking. If small, use whole shallot. If big, separate into lobes. Wrap shallots, olive oil, vodka, thyme, salt and pepper in parchment paper. Wrap parchment-paper packet in aluminum foil, and steam in oven for 35 to 45 minutes.

To caramelize shallots, open packet and drain liquid. Place clarified butter in a small frying pan over high heat, and brown shallots until golden brown and glazed. Keep warm.

To prepare sour cream, rough-chop peppercorns, and stir into sour cream. Add salt to taste, and refrigerate until ready to use.

Increase oven temperature to 400°F (200°C). Sprinkle flesh side of salmon fillets with salt and pepper. In a cast-iron frying pan coated with olive oil, sear fillets, skin side down, for 1 minute over high heat. Drizzle with olive oil, transfer to oven, and bake for 5 to 7 minutes, until fish is firm.

When salmon is almost ready to serve, place clarified butter in a large pan over medium-high heat. Toss in spinach, and cook, stirring, until just wilted. Add salt and pepper to taste.

To serve, divide warm spinach among 6 plates, top each serving with a portion of salmon, garnish with shallots and a dollop of sour cream.

Serves 6

wild salmon with blueberry-rhubarb compote, rosemary crème fraîche + wild rice + corn fritters

We developed this recipe as part of a special Native American dinner, but the fritters and compote are lovely on their own. In fact, the sweet corn flavour and satisfying crunch of these fritters make them a perfect foil for smoked salmon.

compote

2 cups	blueberries, frozen or fresh	500 mL
2 cups	chopped rhubarb, frozen or fresh	500 mL
1/4 cup	apple cider vinegar	50 mL
1/3 cup	maple syrup	75 mL
3	juniper berries, ground	3
1/8 tsp.	ground cinnamon	0.5 mL
3	allspice berries, ground	3
3	whole cloves, ground	3
	Pinch crushed dried chilies	

rosemary crème fraîche

1 tsp.	chopped fresh rosemary	5 mL
2 tsp.	clarified butter	10 mL
3/4 cup	Crème Fraîche (see page 230)	175 mL
	Pinch sea salt	
	Pinch freshly ground black pepper	

To make compote, combine all ingredients in a heavy-bottomed pan, and simmer over medium heat, stirring occasionally, for 30 to 40 minutes. Makes 2 cups (500 mL). You will need about 1/2 cup (125 mL) for this recipe. Compote can be stored in refrigerator for up to 2 weeks.

To make créme fraîche, gently warm rosemary in butter in a small pan over low heat to mellow flavour. Remove from heat, and allow to cool. In a small bowl, mix together crème fraîche, salt, pepper and rosemary. Set aside. This can be stored in refrigerator for up to 2 days.

fritters

1/4 cup	wild rice	50 mL
1/2 cup	masa harina	125 mL
1 cup	stone-ground cornmeal	250 mL
1/2 cup	fresh or frozen corn kernels	125 mL
1/2 Tbsp.	white sugar	7 mL
3/4 tsp.	sea salt	4 mL
1 tsp.	chopped fresh Italian parsley	5 mL
1	scallion, thinly sliced	1
2	large eggs	2
3/4 cup	buttermilk	175 mL
	Canola oil for frying	

salmon

6	6 oz. (170 g) portions of wild salmon fillets	6
	Sea salt	
	Freshly ground black pepper	
	Extra-virgin olive oil	

To clean wild rice, place in a medium bowl under cold running water, stirring with your hand, until water is clear. In a small saucepan, generously cover rice with cold salted water. Bring to a rolling boil, reduce heat to medium-low, and simmer, uncovered, until rice grains split open and rice is tender, 35 to 45 minutes. Drain well, and cool.

To make fritters, mix together masa harina, cornmeal, corn, sugar, salt, parsley, scallion and wild rice in a large bowl. In a separate bowl, whisk eggs together with buttermilk, then add to rice mixture, and combine well.

In a cast-iron frying pan, add canola oil to a depth of 1 inch (2.5 cm), and place over medium-high heat. When a small drop of batter sizzles when dropped into oil, start cooking the fritters. Gently drop 1/4 cup (50 mL) batter into hot oil for each fritter, and cook for 5 to 6 minutes, turning once, until golden brown. Makes 12 fritters.

Meanwhile, preheat oven to 400°F (200°C). Sprinkle flesh side of salmon fillets with salt and pepper. In a cast-iron frying pan coated with olive oil, sear fillets, skin side down, for 1 minute over high heat. Drizzle with olive oil, transfer to oven, and bake for 5 to 7 minutes, until fish is firm.

To serve, place one portion of salmon on each plate, spoon on some compote, and top with a dollop of crème fraîche. Serve fritters on the side.

Serves 6

braised lamb shanks

An old favourite that always satisfies. Serve over creamy polenta or buttery mashed potatoes.

4	lamb shanks	4
1/4 cup	extra-virgin olive oil	50 mL
1	medium cooking onion, finely diced	1
1	stalk celery, finely diced	1
1	large carrot, finely diced	1
4	cloves garlic	4
2	fresh rosemary sprigs	2
2 Tbsp.	tomato paste	25 mL
3/4 cup	dry red wine	175 mL
2 cups	canned diced tomatoes, with juice	500 mL
2 cups	lamb stock	500 mL

(if unavailable, substitute Chicken Stock or Brown Stock, see pages 60 and 61)

Sea salt

Freshly ground black pepper

Preheat oven to 350°F (180°C). On stovetop, in a large, heavy-bottomed ovenproof pan over high heat, brown lamb shanks, two at a time, in olive oil. Remove shanks, and set aside.

Reduce heat to medium, and add onion, celery, carrot and garlic. Cook, stirring, until vegetables are tender, 8 to 10 minutes. Add rosemary, and stir in tomato paste. Cook for 2 to 3 minutes to caramelize tomato paste, then add wine and cook for 2 to 3 minutes more to reduce the wine. Return lamb shanks to pan, add tomatoes and enough stock to cover shanks, and bring to a boil. Cover, and place in oven.

Braise for 2 hours, turning shanks once or twice to ensure that they are covered with liquid as they cook. When meat is very tender and pulls easily away from the bone, remove shanks from sauce, and season with salt and pepper. Remove and discard rosemary sprigs, and skim excess fat from sauce.

If sauce is too thin, bring to a boil on stovetop and reduce to a thicker consistency. Pour sauce over shanks, and serve.

Serves 4

tuscan pork tenderloin

Serve this hearty dish with white rice or polenta. If you're unable to find Taggiasche olives, any good-quality small black olive can be substituted.

2	pork tenderloins (2 lb./900 g total)	2
6–8	sun-dried tomatoes	6–8
1/4 cup	minced garlic	50 mL
3 Tbsp.	drained + rinsed capers	40 mL
1/2 cup	pitted Taggiasche olives	125 mL
3 Tbsp. + 2 Tbsp.	extra-virgin olive oil	40 mL + 25 mL
1/2 cup	dry white wine	125 mL
1/4 cup	coarsely chopped fresh Italian parsley	50 mL
2 Tbsp.	chopped fresh thyme	25 mL
6	anchovies, minced	6
6	canned artichoke hearts, rinsed, drained + quartered	6
1 cup	Chicken Stock or Brown Stock (see pages 60 and 61)	250 mL
	Sea salt	
	Freshly ground black pepper	

Slice pork into 1/2-inch (1 cm) medallions, and set aside. Place sun-dried tomatoes in a small bowl, and add hot water to cover. Allow to soak for up to 20 minutes, until tomatoes are soft, then drain and julienne.

In a large bowl, mix tomatoes, garlic, capers, olives, 3 Tbsp. (40 mL) olive oil, wine, parsley, thyme, anchovies and artichokes. Add pork, cover, and marinate in refrigerator for 4 to 6 hours, stirring occasionally.

Remove pork from marinade, and reserve marinade. In a large frying pan over high heat, heat 2 Tbsp. (25 mL) olive oil, and place pork medallions in a single layer in pan. Cook on one side to brown, 1 to 2 minutes, turn, and brown the other side for 1 to 2 minutes. Remove pork from pan, and set aside. Reduce heat to medium-low, and stir in stock and reserved marinade. Continue to simmer until liquid reaches a saucy consistency, 8 to 10 minutes. Season with salt and pepper.

Return pork to pan to warm through, then serve.

Serves 4-6

marsala + orange braised pork roast

Pan Chancho's own version of pork and beans. We serve these individual little pork roasts with our Slow-Baked Beans with Molasses (see page 134). To add extra richness to this dish, make your ham broth with a smoked ham hock.

2 lb.	boned pork butt, cut into four 1/2-lb. (225 g) roasts	900 g
3 Tbsp.	extra-virgin olive oil	40 mL
1	head garlic, cut in half crosswise	1
1 cup	Marsala	250 mL
2 Tbsp.	yellow mustard seed	25 mL
	Zest + juice of 4 oranges	
1 Tbsp.	black peppercorns	15 mL
4 cups	Ham Broth or Chicken Stock (see pages 75 and 60)	1 L

Preheat oven to 350°F (180°C). In a cast-iron frying pan over high heat, brown pork in olive oil on all sides. Place roasts in a heavy-bottomed ovenproof pan that is just big enough to hold them. Add garlic, Marsala, mustard seed, orange zest and juice, peppercorns, pan juices and enough stock to cover meat.

Bring to a boil over high heat. Cover, place in oven, and braise until pork is very tender, 1 1/2 to 2 hours. Turn roasts once, and check liquid levels occasionally, adding a little more stock if needed. Remove pork from liquid, and set aside.

On stovetop, in a separate pan, bring liquid to a boil to reduce. When sauce is consistency of gravy, strain and drizzle over pork.

Serves 4-6

italian sausage ragù alla bolognese

Ragù recipes often call for cooking times of only 2 to 3 hours, but here, an extended simmering time allows the flavours to evolve and deepen. To compensate for the extra effort, we've made this recipe extra large so that you'll have some to freeze and enjoy later, perhaps in our Spicy Italian Sausage Lasagne *(see page 129)*.

3	medium cooking onions, finely diced	3
3 Tbsp.	minced garlic (about 8 cloves)	40 mL
1 Tbsp.	dried basil	15 mL
2 tsp.	dried thyme	10 mL
2 tsp.	dried oregano	10 mL
1	bay leaf	1
2–3 tsp.	crushed dried chilies	10–15 mL
1	½-inch (1 cm) stick cinnamon	1
2 Tbsp.	extra-virgin olive oil	25 mL
1½ lb.	pork butt, cut into ¾-inch (2 cm) cubes	680 g
1 lb.	ground pork	450 g
1½ lb.	medium ground beef	680 g
3	28 oz. (796 mL) cans diced tomatoes, with juice	3
1	28 oz. (796 mL) can crushed tomatoes	1
¾ lb.	sliced white mushrooms	340 g
1	red bell pepper, medium dice	1
1 lb.	hot Italian sausages (about 4 sausages)	450 g
	Sea salt	
	Freshly ground black pepper	

In a large stockpot over low heat, cook onions, garlic, basil, thyme, oregano, bay leaf, dried chilies and cinnamon in olive oil, stirring frequently, until onions are soft and sweet, 25 to 30 minutes.

Increase heat to medium, and add pork butt. Brown pork, stirring. Add ground pork, and cook, stirring, until no longer pink, then stir in ground beef. When beef is cooked through, add diced and crushed tomatoes, reduce heat to low, and simmer, uncovered. Add mushrooms after 2 hours, and continue simmering for 2 more hours, stirring occasionally.

Add red pepper. Cover, and cook over very low heat for 1 to 3 more hours, stirring frequently to avoid burning.

Meanwhile, in a large frying pan over medium heat, brown sausages on all sides until cooked through. Remove sausages from pan, and cut into ¼-inch (6 mm) slices. Add to ragù for the last hour of cooking. Season with salt and pepper, and serve piping hot in bowls over your favourite pasta.

Serves 8-10

smokin' wilburs

Smoky, spicy, sweet and scrumptious — that's some pig!

$^{1}/_{2}$ cup	water	125 mL
$^{1}/_{2}$ tsp.	sea salt	2 mL
$^{1}/_{4}$ tsp.	freshly ground black pepper	1 mL
$^{1}/_{4}$ cup	lemon juice	50 mL
2	racks pork ribs (about $3^{1}/_{2}$ lb./1.6 kg), cut into 4-rib pieces	2
$^{1}/_{3}$ cup	Mexican Chili Paste (see page 228)	75 mL
$^{3}/_{4}$ cup	canned pineapple tidbits + juice, puréed	175 mL
1 Tbsp.	lime juice	15 mL
2 Tbsp.	brown sugar	25 mL
$^{1}/_{2}$ cup	Chicken Stock, Brown Stock or Ham Broth (see pages 60, 61 and 75)	125 mL

Preheat oven to 300°F (150°C). In a small bowl, mix together water, salt, pepper and lemon juice. Place ribs in a roasting pan, and brush generously with lemon water. Bake, uncovered, for 1 hour, then turn ribs, brush generously with lemon water, and return to oven for $1^{1}/_{2}$ to 2 hours more, until meat pulls easily away from bone.

Meanwhile, in a medium bowl, mix together chili paste, pineapple, lime juice, brown sugar and stock. When ribs have finished cooking, use tongs to dip each section of ribs into pineapple mixture to coat completely. Return ribs to oven for 30 minutes, or finish on the barbecue.

Serves 4–6

juniper apple chicken ragoût

The word ragoût generally suggests a heavy, complex meat dish, but this is a light and aromatic chicken stew. Our apple liqueur of choice is Berentzen's Apfelkorn, which has the double benefit of being inexpensive and very flavourful. A savoury brioche is the perfect complement to this delicious meal.

1	medium leek	1
1	small cooking onion, finely diced	1
1	clove garlic, minced	1
1 Tbsp.	chicken fat or unsalted butter	15 mL
1½ Tbsp.	all-purpose flour	20 mL
3 Tbsp.	gin	40 mL
2	juniper berries, crushed	2
½ Tbsp.	chopped fresh thyme	7 mL
1	bay leaf	1
2½ cups	Chicken Stock (see page 60)	625 mL
3½–5 lb.	whole roasted chicken, torn into large pieces, skin + bone discarded	1.6–2.3 kg
½ cup	pearl onions, parboiled + peeled	125 mL
1 tsp.	sea salt	5 mL
¼ tsp.	freshly ground black pepper	1 mL
½	medium celeriac, peeled, ½-inch (1 cm) dice	½
2	medium red apples	2
½ cup + 2 Tbsp.	apple liqueur	125 mL + 25 mL
1 Tbsp.	coarsely chopped fresh Italian parsley	15 mL
1	medium red onion, ½-inch (1 cm) dice	1
1 Tbsp.	unsalted butter	15 mL
1 Tbsp.	finely chopped fresh chives for garnish	15 mL

Trim leek, and discard green leaves. Quarter lengthwise, then cut into ¾-inch (2 cm) pieces. Rinse thoroughly, dry, and set aside.

In a large heavy-bottomed pot over low heat, cook onion and garlic in chicken fat or butter until soft, about 20 minutes. Sprinkle with flour, and cook for 2 minutes, stirring constantly. Stir in gin, juniper berries, thyme, bay leaf and stock. Increase heat to bring to a boil, then reduce heat to medium-low and simmer for 6 to 8 minutes. Add chicken and pearl onions, and warm through. Add salt and pepper.

Meanwhile, in separate pots over high heat, blanch leek and celeriac in boiling salted water until leek is tender, 3 to 4 minutes, and celeriac is soft, 4 to 5 minutes. Drain, and set aside.

Peel and grate 1 apple, and cook with ½ cup (125 mL) liqueur in a small heavy-bottomed pot over medium-high heat until very soft, 5 to 6 minutes. Sprinkle parsley over top, and set aside.

Peel remaining apple, and cut into ½-inch (1 cm) dice. Toss with 2 Tbsp. (25 mL) liqueur. In a medium heavy-bottomed pot over medium-high heat, cook diced apple and red onion in butter until soft, stirring occasionally. Stir in leek, celeriac and grated-apple mixture, and heat through.

To serve, ladle ragoût into shallow bowls, top with apple-vegetable mixture and garnish with chives.

Serves 4–6

white chili

Great Northern beans are the dried seeds of green beans, and we like them because they are more flavourful than traditional navy beans. They also do a superb job of taking on the flavours of other foods, as in this inspired variation on conventional tomato-based chili — a recipe that took the Most Original Chili award at Kingston's 2000 Chilifest.

2 lb.	Great Northern beans	900 g
1	large cooking onion, diced	1
2 Tbsp.	extra-virgin olive oil	25 mL
6	cloves garlic, minced	6
2	jalapeños, seeded + finely diced	2
1 tsp.	ground cumin	5 mL
1 tsp.	dried oregano	5 mL
6 cups	Chicken Stock (see page 60)	1.5 L
1/2 cup	lightly packed, coarsely chopped cilantro	125 mL
3–4	boneless, skinless chicken breasts, cooked + shredded or cubed	3–4
1	yellow bell pepper, diced	1
	Sea salt	
	Freshly ground black pepper	
1 lb.	Monterey Jack cheese, grated	450 g
	Sour cream for garnish	

Sort beans, discarding any stones and broken beans, and place in a large pot. Cover with cold water, and bring to a rolling boil over high heat. Turn off heat, cover, and let beans soak for 1 hour. Drain before using.

In a large pot over medium heat, cook onion in olive oil until soft. Add garlic, jalapeños, cumin and oregano, and cook, stirring, for 3 to 4 minutes. Add stock, beans, and 1/4 cup (50 mL) of the cilantro. Bring to a boil, then reduce heat, and simmer uncovered, stirring occasionally, for 1 1/2 hours.

Stir in chicken and yellow pepper, and continue to simmer until beans are soft, 45 to 60 minutes. This should be a thick stew. Add salt and pepper to taste.

Just before serving, stir in half of the cheese and garnish with remaining 1/4 cup (50 mL) cilantro, remaining cheese and sour cream.

Serves 4-6

italian chicken fricassee with olives + kale

A simple chicken dish with tomatoes and kale to give it brightness, this fricassee received a "10" for colour, flavour and texture from Rose.

$3\frac{1}{2}$ lb.	chicken, cut into 8 pieces	1.6 kg
	Sea salt	
	Freshly ground black pepper	
	Pinch cayenne	
2 tsp.	minced fresh rosemary	10 mL
1 Tbsp.	extra-virgin olive oil	15 mL
5	cloves garlic, peeled	5
1 cup	dry white wine	250 mL
5	kale leaves, ribs removed, coarsely chopped	5
24	cherry or grape tomatoes	24
12	kalamata olives, pitted	12

Preheat oven to 400°F (200°C). Season chicken, skin side up, with salt, pepper, cayenne and rosemary. Heat olive oil in a large, heavy-bottomed ovenproof frying pan over medium-high heat. Place chicken pieces in pan, skin side down, and brown until chicken turns golden brown, about 5 minutes. As chicken cooks, season the other side in the same way. Then turn chicken skin side up, gently stir in garlic and wine, and place pan in oven. Cook, uncovered, for 20 minutes.

Remove pan from oven, and gently stir in kale to wilt. Stir in tomatoes and olives, and serve immediately.

Serves 4

poulet au vinaigre

A traditional French dish is given a Canadian spin, thanks to apples, apple cider vinegar and maple syrup.

2	apples, peeled + cut into 8 wedges each	2
1 Tbsp.	maple syrup	15 mL
2	leeks	2
$3^1/_2$–5 lb.	chicken, cut into 8 pieces	1.6-2.3 kg
	Sea salt	
	Freshly ground black pepper	
2 Tbsp.	extra-virgin olive oil	25 mL
2 Tbsp.	unsalted butter	25 mL
2 Tbsp.	minced garlic	25 mL
7	fresh thyme sprigs	7
$^1/_2$ cup	apple cider vinegar	125 mL
$^1/_2$ cup	Chicken Stock (see page 60)	125 mL
	Chopped fresh thyme for garnish	

Preheat oven to 400°F (200°C). In a medium bowl, toss apple wedges in maple syrup to coat, and set aside. Trim leeks of outer green leaves, cut into $^1/_2$-inch (1 cm) rounds, wash thoroughly, and set aside.

Sprinkle chicken pieces with salt and pepper. In a heavy-bottomed ovenproof pan large enough to hold chicken in a single layer, heat olive oil and 1 Tbsp. (15 mL) of the butter over high heat until butter begins to sputter. Add chicken to pan, skin side down, and brown until chicken is a deep golden colour, 4 to 5 minutes. Turn chicken pieces, and repeat.

Remove chicken from pan, and set aside. Drain excess fat from pan, and add leeks and garlic. Cook over medium-high heat to soften, 8 to 10 minutes. Add thyme sprigs and vinegar, and simmer until vinegar is reduced by half, scraping up any brown bits from bottom and sides of pan with a wooden spoon. Stir in stock, and return chicken to pan, turning to coat with liquid. Place pan in oven, uncovered, for 20 to 25 minutes, until chicken is tender.

Meanwhile, in a heavy-bottomed frying pan, heat remaining 1 Tbsp. (15 mL) butter over medium-low heat, and add apples. Stir gently to caramelize.

Garnish chicken with apples and thyme, and serve.

Serves 4

rosalita's pollo en pepitoria

Classic Spanish ingredients — chorizo, saffron and sherry — come together in a dish named for Rose, who loved it all.

½ lb.	chorizo sausage, sliced	225 g
¼ cup	extra-virgin olive oil	50 mL
1	small cooking onion, sliced	1
1	small fennel bulb, thinly sliced	1
3	cloves garlic, minced	3
	Small pinch saffron threads	
6	chicken legs	6
6	chicken thighs	6
	Sea salt	
	Freshly ground black pepper	
½ cup	dry white wine	125 mL
¼ cup	dry sherry	50 mL
1 cup	Chicken Stock (see page 60)	250 mL
3–4	canned piquillo peppers, cut into thick strips	3–4

Preheat oven to 350°F (180°C). In an ovenproof frying pan large enough to hold chicken pieces in a single layer, cook chorizo in olive oil over medium heat for about 5 minutes, turning once to brown both sides. Remove chorizo, and set aside, but leave fat in pan.

Add onion, fennel, garlic and saffron to pan, and cook over medium heat, scraping up any brown bits from bottom of pan, until vegetables are softened, about 10 minutes. Remove vegetables, and set aside.

Add chicken to pan, skin side down, and brown over high heat until a deep golden colour, about 5 minutes. Season with a pinch of salt and pepper. Turn chicken skin side up. Return vegetables and chorizo to pan, and add wine, sherry and stock. Stir and bring to a boil, then place pan, uncovered, in oven for 25 to 30 minutes, until chicken is almost cooked through. Layer peppers across chicken, and return to oven for 10 minutes. Serve with rice or Laura's Cheddar Spoon Bread (see page 137).

Serves 6

pomegranate-glazed chicken breast with honey-toasted walnuts

Shining like little rubies, the seeds of the pomegranate are a beautiful garnish for this chicken dish. Pomegranate-based condiments such as the molasses in this recipe are now available from any well-stocked supermarket. It's also very simple to make your own pomegranate molasses.

spice mixture

2 tsp.	anise seed	10 mL
1/4 tsp.	cumin seed	1 mL
1/8 tsp.	freshly ground black pepper	0.5 mL
1/8 tsp.	sea salt	0.5 mL

pomegranate molasses

1 1/2 cups	pomegranate juice	375 mL
1/4 cup	white sugar	50 mL
2 Tbsp.	lime juice	25 mL
2 Tbsp.	lemon juice	25 mL

honey-toasted walnuts

6 Tbsp.	walnut pieces	75 mL
	Pinch cayenne	
1 Tbsp.	honey	15 mL

1/4 cup	lemon juice	50 mL
1 tsp.	extra-virgin olive oil	5 mL
3	whole chicken breasts, split, skin on, bone in	3
1/2 cup	pomegranate molasses	125 mL
	10% M.F. yogurt for garnish	
	Pomegranate seeds for garnish	

In a shallow baking dish, stir together lemon juice and olive oil. Add chicken, and turn to coat with marinade. Cover, and marinate in refrigerator for up to 2 hours, turning occasionally.

To prepare spice mixture, toast anise seed in a small, dry frying pan over medium-low heat, shaking pan, until seeds are fragrant. Remove from pan, and allow to cool. Repeat process with cumin seed. Coarsely grind both seeds in a spice grinder or using a mortar and pestle. In a small bowl, combine anise, cumin, pepper and salt, then set aside.

To make molasses, stir ingredients together in a small heavy-bottomed saucepan over medium heat. Bring to a low boil, and cook, stirring occasionally, until liquid is reduced to 1/2 cup (125 mL). Watch carefully to prevent burning. Remove from heat, and set aside.

To make honey-toasted walnuts, preheat oven to 350°F (180°C). In a small bowl, combine walnuts, cayenne and honey. Transfer to a small ovenproof pan, and toast in oven for 5 minutes, stirring occasionally. Set aside.

Increase oven temperature to 400°F (200°C). Remove chicken from marinade, and place on a baking sheet, skin side up. Sprinkle with spice mixture. Bake for 20 minutes, then brush chicken with pomegranate molasses, and bake for 10 minutes. Brush with molasses again, and return to oven for 5 minutes more.

Arrange chicken on a serving platter, and garnish with yogurt, walnuts and pomegranate seeds. Drizzle with remaining molasses, and serve.

Serves 6

prosciutto-wrapped chicken breast stuffed with asiago cheese, caramelized onions + spinach

The sharpness of the Asiago cheese and the saltiness of the prosciutto offset the caramelized onions' sweetness in this great-looking, easy-to-make dish developed by one of Pan Chancho's early chefs, Stev George.

10 oz.	fresh spinach, washed + picked	285 g
6	boneless, skinless chicken breasts	6
6–12	slices prosciutto	6–12
	Sea salt	
	Freshly ground black pepper	
1/2 cup	Caramelized Onions (see page 226)	125 mL
1/2 cup	grated Asiago cheese	125 mL
3/4 cup	Chicken Stock (see page 60)	175 mL
1/4 cup	brandy	50 mL

Preheat oven to 375°F (190°C). Blanch spinach by immersing briefly in boiling salted water, then drain and plunge into cold water. Drain again, and squeeze dry into a loaf shape. Divide loaf into 6 equal portions, and set aside.

Between pieces of plastic wrap, pound each chicken breast to a uniform thickness of about 1/2 inch (1 cm). On clean plastic wrap, place 1 slice of prosciutto. Lay 1 chicken breast on top, and sprinkle with salt and pepper. Place a portion of spinach across width of breast, followed by a portion of onions and cheese. Roll breast around filling, with prosciutto on the outside. Repeat with other breasts, adding prosciutto if necessary. Place breasts, seam side down, in a 9-by-13-inch (3 L) baking dish. Add stock and brandy, and bake for 30 to 45 minutes, until chicken is cooked through.

Strain cooking juices into a small saucepan, and place over medium-high heat. Bring to a boil, and reduce to a caramel-like consistency, about 20 minutes. Brush chicken rolls with sauce to glaze, and serve.

Serves 6

turkey breast stuffed with chestnuts + dried fruit chutney with rum-orange glaze

In addition to being a great accompaniment to poultry, this warm, spicy chutney really perks up a Cheddar cheese sandwich. And the mild-flavoured chestnuts, whether canned, individually quick-frozen or roasted over an open fire, add a toothsome texture to this dish.

dried fruit chutney

1/2 lb.	dried apricots, small dice	250 g
1/2 lb.	dried peaches, small dice	250 g
1/2 lb.	pitted dates, small dice	250 g
1/2 lb.	seedless raisins, coarsely chopped	250 g
2 cups	finely diced cooking onion	500 mL
1 1/2 cups	apple cider vinegar	375 mL
1/2 cup	water	125 mL
1 cup	white sugar	250 mL
1 Tbsp.	minced garlic	15 mL
1 Tbsp.	mustard seeds, crushed	15 mL
1 Tbsp.	ground ginger	15 mL
1 Tbsp.	ground coriander	15 mL
1 tsp.	ground cinnamon	5 mL
1 tsp.	cayenne	5 mL
1 Tbsp.	sea salt	15 mL

turkey breast

1/2 cup	dark rum	125 mL
1 cup	orange juice	250 mL
1/2 cup	Chicken Stock (see page 60)	125 mL
1 cup	dried fruit chutney	250 mL
1/3 cup	chopped chestnuts	75 mL
3 lb.	turkey breast, skin on	1.5 kg
	Sea salt	
	Freshly ground black pepper	

Preheat oven to 325°F (160°C). To make chutney, mix all ingredients together in a large bowl (see "So Long, Sulphur" on page 114). Transfer mixture to a covered baking dish, and bake for 30 to 45 minutes, stirring every 10 minutes. When chutney is ready, it will be fragrant and just beginning to thicken. Remove from oven, and allow to cool. Store in refrigerator in a covered container for up to 1 month. Makes 5 cups (1.25 L).

To make glaze, combine rum, orange juice and stock in a small saucepan. Bring to a boil over high heat, and reduce to about 1/3 cup (75 mL). Set aside.

In a small bowl, stir together chutney and chestnuts. Along the thickest part of the turkey breast, cut a deep slit to create a pocket. Carefully stuff chutney mixture into pocket, spreading it over as much of the breast as possible. Sprinkle with salt and pepper to taste.

Increase oven temperature to 400°F (200°C). Place breast, skin side up, in a roasting pan. Bake for 1 to 1 1/4 hours, brushing with glaze several times in the last 15 minutes until glaze is used up. Remove turkey from oven, and allow to sit for 5 minutes before slicing.

Serves 4–6

desserts

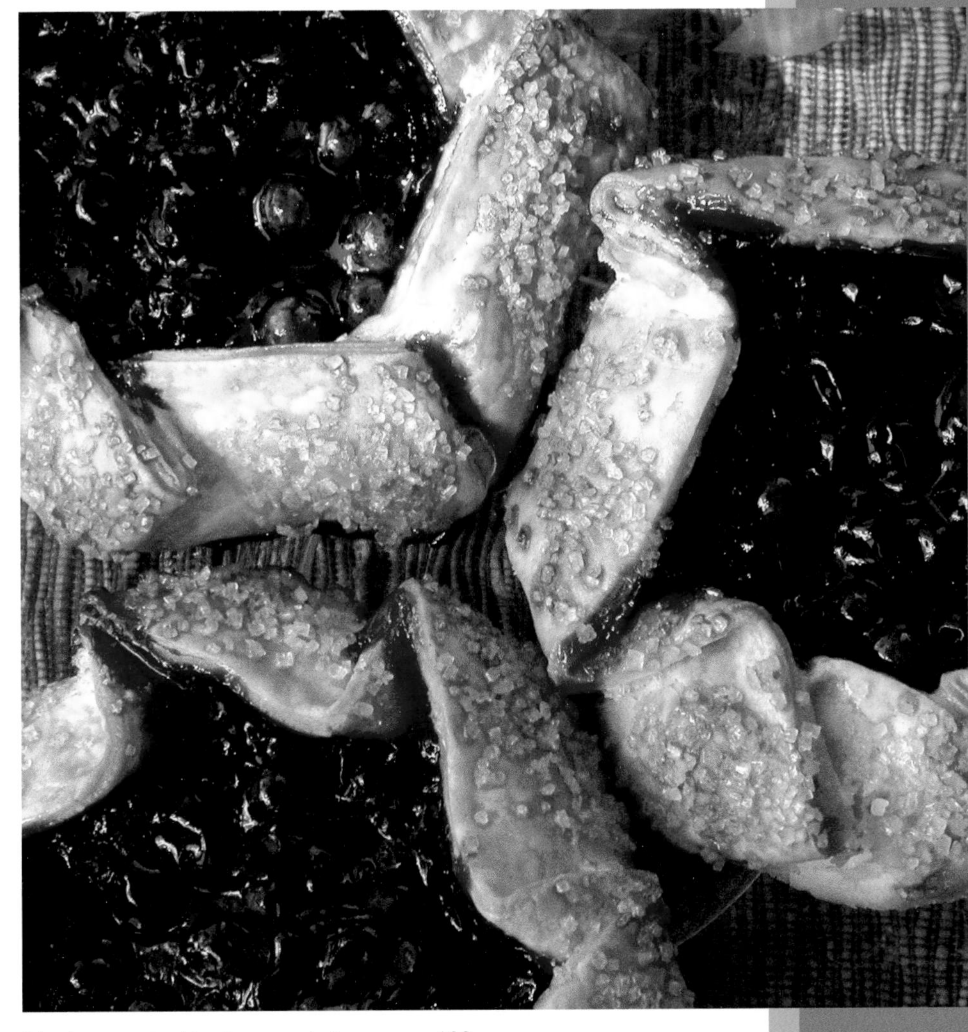

blackcurrant + blueberry galettes, page 199

desserts

vanilla crème brûlée

It tastes as though it's made with all cream, but a little milk lightens this luscious custard and brings out the vanilla.

1/2 cup	2% milk	125 mL
1/3 cup + 4 tsp.	white sugar	75 mL + 20 mL
1/2	vanilla bean	1/2
6	large egg yolks	6
1/2 tsp.	vanilla extract	2 mL
1 1/2 cups	35% M.F. cream	375 mL

Preheat oven to 300°F (150°C), and place four 8-ounce (225 g) ramekins in a deep baking pan.

In a small saucepan, combine milk and 1/3 cup (75 mL) sugar. Scrape seeds from vanilla bean into milk, then add pod. Bring milk to a boil over medium-high heat, stirring occasionally to dissolve sugar.

Meanwhile, in a medium bowl, whisk together egg yolks and vanilla extract. When milk reaches a boil, pour it over yolks in a slow, steady stream while whisking constantly. Whisk in cream, then strain custard through a fine-mesh sieve to remove vanilla pod and any cooked yolk.

Divide custard among ramekins. Fill baking pan with hot water to midway point on ramekins. Cover pan with aluminum foil, and bake for 30 minutes or until centre of custard is jiggly.

Remove pan from oven, and allow custard to cool in pan for 15 to 20 minutes. Remove ramekins from pan, and place on a baking sheet. Turn on broiler, sprinkle each custard with 1 tsp. (5 mL) sugar, and broil for 3 to 7 minutes, until sugar has caramelized into a golden crust. Serve immediately.

Serves 4

caramel pot de crème

Close your eyes and appreciate the smooth-as-silk texture of this creamy custard.

1	large egg	1
5	large egg yolks	5
1 cup	2% milk	250 mL
2 cups	35% M.F. cream	500 mL
1 cup	white sugar	250 mL
1/4 cup	water	50 mL
	Dark chocolate, melted (optional)	

Preheat oven to 300°F (150°C), and place six 8-ounce (225 g) ramekins in a deep baking pan.

In a medium bowl, whisk together egg and egg yolks, and set aside. In a small saucepan, combine milk and cream, and bring to a simmer over medium heat.

While milk mixture is heating, combine sugar and water in a medium saucepan. Mix until sugar is just wet, then cover, and bring to a boil over medium-high heat to caramelize. Check every couple of minutes, but do not stir. When syrup begins to colour, remove lid and continue cooking until caramel turns a deep amber colour.

Slowly and carefully (it will sputter and froth), add hot milk mixture to caramel. Reduce heat to medium-low, and continue cooking, stirring until caramel has melted and mixture is uniform in colour. Slowly pour hot caramel mixture into eggs, whisking constantly. Strain custard through a fine-mesh sieve, and divide among ramekins.

Fill baking pan with hot water to midway point on ramekins. Cover pan with aluminum foil, and bake for 50 to 60 minutes, until custard is wobbly but set. Chill for 6 hours before serving. Drizzle with chocolate, if desired.

Serves 6

maple mousse with maple-glazed walnuts

A simple, delicious way of cooking with maple syrup. Pair this mousse with any seasonal fruit for a fresh burst of flavour.

glazed walnuts

1/3 cup	maple syrup	75 mL
1/4 cup	packed brown sugar	50 mL
1 cup	walnut pieces	250 mL

mousse

2 tsp.	gelatin powder	10 mL
2 Tbsp.	cold water	25 mL
2	large egg yolks	2
2/3 cup	maple syrup	150 mL
1 1/3 cups	35% M.F. cream	325 mL

Preheat oven to 350°F (180°C), and line a baking sheet with parchment paper.

To glaze walnuts, combine maple syrup and brown sugar in a small saucepan, and bring to a boil over medium-high heat. Reduce heat to low, and gently simmer for 2 minutes. Remove from heat, and add walnuts, stirring to coat completely.

Spread walnut mixture evenly over baking sheet. Bake for 12 to 15 minutes, until mixture is bubbling. Remove from oven, and allow to cool. Break walnuts apart, and set aside. (If walnut pieces are freshly shelled, they can be stored at room temperature in an airtight container for 2 to 3 weeks.)

To make mousse, sprinkle gelatin powder over water in a small dish, and allow to stand until powder is completely moistened. Do not stir. Meanwhile, whisk egg yolks and 1/3 cup (75 mL) of the maple syrup in a double boiler over simmering water until mixture is hot to the touch, about 2 minutes. Stir gelatin into egg mixture until gelatin is dissolved. Stir in remaining 1/3 cup (75 mL) maple syrup, and pour into a small bowl. Place bowl in refrigerator until mixture is cool, not cold, to the touch. Do not allow it to set.

Whip cream into soft peaks, and fold into cooled maple-syrup mixture. Divide mousse among martini glasses or containers of your choice, and place in refrigerator to set, about 3 hours. Before serving, sprinkle with glazed walnuts.

Serves 4–6

sticky toffee pudding with caramel rum sauce

Sweet, homey and comforting, this dessert hits the spot on a blustery winter's day.

pudding

3/4 cup	pitted dates (about 30)	175 mL
3/4 tsp.	baking soda	4 mL
3/4 cup	boiling water	175 mL
3 Tbsp.	unsalted butter	40 mL
1/2 cup	packed brown sugar	125 mL
1	large egg	1
1	large egg white	1
3/4 cup + 2 Tbsp.	all-purpose flour	200 mL
3/4 tsp.	baking powder	4 mL

sauce

1 cup	packed brown sugar	250 mL
1/2 cup	water	125 mL
1/4 cup	unsalted butter	50 mL
1/2 cup	35% M.F. cream	125 mL
3 Tbsp.	dark rum	40 mL
1/2 tsp.	vanilla extract	2 mL

Preheat oven to 350°F (180°C), and grease six 8-ounce (225 g) ramekins. To make pudding, place dates and baking soda in a small bowl. Add water, cover, and allow to cool. Place cooled date mixture in blender, and purée until smooth. Set aside.

Cream butter and brown sugar together until light and fluffy. Beat in egg and egg white. Combine flour and baking powder, and stir into egg mixture, then add date purée, and stir until just combined. Divide batter evenly among ramekins, and bake for 20 to 25 minutes, until top of cake springs back when lightly pressed.

To make sauce, combine brown sugar, water, butter and cream in a saucepan over low heat, and simmer for 8 to 10 minutes. Remove from heat, and add rum and vanilla. Let cool, then brush sauce over slightly cooled cakes. Serve at room temperature with extra sauce.

Serves 6

apple berry crisp

9 cups	sliced peeled apples (preferably Ida Red or Granny Smith)	2.25 L
3/4 cup	fresh or frozen raspberries	175 mL
3/4 cup	fresh or frozen blueberries	175 mL
1 Tbsp.	lemon juice	15 mL
1 Tbsp.	brandy	15 mL
3 Tbsp.	white sugar, or to taste	40 mL
1/3 cup	all-purpose flour	75 mL
1/2 tsp.	ground cinnamon	2 mL
1/3 cup	rolled oats	75 mL
1/3 cup	packed brown sugar	75 mL
1/4 cup	unsalted butter, chilled	50 mL

Preheat oven to 350°F (180°C). In a large bowl, gently toss together apples, raspberries, blueberries, lemon juice, brandy and white sugar. Spread mixture in an 8-inch-square (2 L) baking dish.

In a small bowl, combine flour, cinnamon, rolled oats and brown sugar. Cut in butter until mixture forms coarse crumbs. Sprinkle evenly over fruit, and bake until apples are soft and topping is browned, about 45 minutes.

Serves 6–8

chocolate banana bread pudding

Everybody loves the classic combination of banana and chocolate, but the light, buttery croissants that stand in for the traditional day-old bread in this pudding raise it to a whole new level.

4	Croissants (see page 30), cut into 1-inch (2.5 cm) cubes (about 6 cups/1.5 L)	4
2	ripe bananas	2
	Crème Fraîche (see page 230)	

ganache

1/2 cup	35% M.F. cream	125 mL
5 oz.	bittersweet chocolate, coarsely chopped	140 g

custard

2 cups	2% milk	500 mL
2 Tbsp. + 1 tsp.	unsalted butter	30 mL
3/4 cup	white sugar	175 mL
3	large eggs	3
2	large egg yolks	2
1 tsp.	vanilla extract	5 mL
	Pinch salt	

Preheat oven to 350°F (180°C). Place croissant cubes on a baking sheet, and toast for about 10 minutes, until they are browned and dry. Place cubes in an 8-inch-square (2 L) baking pan, and set aside.

To make ganache, place cream in a small saucepan over medium-high heat, and bring to a boil. Place chocolate in a small bowl, and add hot cream. Stir until chocolate is completely melted and ganache is uniform in colour. Drizzle half of the ganache over croissant cubes, and refrigerate remaining ganache.

Break bananas into 1/2-inch (1 cm) pieces, and toss with croissant cubes until mixture is coated with ganache. Settle mixture evenly in the baking pan.

To make custard, place milk and butter in a saucepan over medium-high heat, and bring to a boil. In a large bowl, whisk together sugar, eggs and egg yolks. Slowly whisk in hot milk mixture. Stir in vanilla and salt. Strain mixture through a fine-mesh sieve, then pour evenly over bananas and croissant cubes.

Top with remaining ganache, dotting it in small, evenly spaced lumps, and bake for 30 minutes or until bread pudding is puffed up and a small knife inserted in centre comes out clean. Serve with crème fraîche.

Serves 6–8

chocolate mousse profiteroles

You can't go wrong with the versatile profiterole. From sweet to savoury, the fillings are limited only by your imagination.

mousse

6 oz.	bittersweet chocolate, coarsely chopped (preferably Lindt or Callebaut)	170 g
1 1/2 cups	35% M.F. cream	375 mL
4	large egg yolks	4
2 Tbsp.	white sugar	25 mL
2 tsp.	brandy	10 mL

choux paste

1/4 tsp.	salt	1 mL
1 Tbsp.	white sugar	15 mL
1/2 cup	all-purpose flour	125 mL
1/2 cup	water	125 mL
1/4 cup	unsalted butter	50 mL
3	medium eggs	3

White and/or dark chocolate, melted, or icing sugar

To make mousse, place chocolate in a small bowl. In a small saucepan over medium-high heat, bring 1/2 cup (125 mL) of the cream to a boil. Pour over chocolate, and stir until chocolate is completely melted. In a double boiler over simmering water, whisk egg yolks, sugar and brandy together for about 5 minutes, until mixture is pale and slightly thickened. Fold into chocolate mixture. Whip remaining 1 cup (250 mL) cream until soft peaks form. Fold into chocolate mixture until completely incorporated. Refrigerate mousse for at least 4 hours.

To make choux paste, mix salt, sugar and flour together in a small bowl, and set aside. In a small heavy-bottomed saucepan, heat water and butter over low heat until butter is melted. Increase heat to medium-high, bring to a boil, and add flour mixture all at once. Stir vigorously with a wooden spoon until batter pulls away from sides of pan. Continue to cook, stirring, for 30 seconds. Remove from heat, and transfer batter to a large bowl. Stir for 1 minute to cool, then add eggs, one at a time, mixing well after each addition. If using an electric mixer, use paddle attachment. (Batter should be thick and rather sticky and drop slowly from a spoon. If batter seems too stiff, add 1 egg white.) Smooth plastic wrap over top of batter, and refrigerate for at least 1 hour, or overnight.

Preheat oven to 400°F (200°C), and line a baking sheet with parchment paper. Drop large dollops of batter onto baking sheet, 3 inches (7.5 cm) apart. With a pastry brush lightly dipped in water, brush each mound to smooth any edges. Bake for 10 minutes, then reduce oven temperature to 375°F (190°C), and continue baking for 20 to 25 minutes, until profiteroles are an even deep brown colour.

Allow profiteroles to cool. Using a serrated knife, slice off top third of each pastry, and set aside. Spoon mousse into pastry, or use a piping bag with a large, round tip to fill pastry. Replace top, drizzle with chocolate or sprinkle with icing sugar, and serve.

Makes 8-10

lemon curd tart

The lively tartness of lemon is a perfect foil for the buttery tart shell. The lemon curd itself is a keeper — have it on hand for last-minute desserts. It's a great topping for sponge cake and is an ideal filling for mini tart shells.

1 cup less 1 Tbsp.	lemon juice	235 mL
1 cup	white sugar	250 mL
12	large egg yolks	12
$1^3/_4$ cups	unsalted butter, room temperature, cut into pea-sized pieces	425 mL
	10-inch (25 cm) prebaked tart shell (see Tart Dough, page 198)	

Combine lemon juice, sugar and egg yolks in a double boiler over simmering water. Whisk until thoroughly mixed. Then, using a spatula, stir continuously until mixture has thickened and is hot to the touch. Do not bring to a boil. Strain immediately into a large bowl, and begin whisking in butter, a little bit at a time. When butter has been combined, pour curd into tart shell and refrigerate for about 2 hours.

Drizzle with Raspberry Sauce (see below), or garnish with fresh berries before serving.

Serves 10

raspberry sauce

Drizzle this delightful sauce over our Lemon Curd Tart, ice cream or anything chocolatey. Be sure your raspberries have not been frozen in syrup, or the sauce will be far too sweet. For a fuller flavour, use a fruity wine.

1 lb.	frozen unsweetened raspberries	450 g
$3^1/_2$ Tbsp.	white sugar	45 mL
$^1/_3$ cup + 2 Tbsp.	dry white wine	100 mL
2 Tbsp.	lemon juice	25 mL

Place raspberries in a medium saucepan over medium heat. When liquid begins to boil, remove from heat, and allow to cool for 5 minutes. Purée raspberries in a blender, then strain into a small bowl through a fine-mesh sieve or one lined with cheesecloth, pressing on the solids until there is 1 cup (250 mL) purée.

Return purée to saucepan over medium-high heat, stir in sugar, wine and lemon juice, and bring to a boil. Cook, stirring, until sugar is dissolved. Allow to cool before using.

Makes $1^1/_3$ cups (325 mL)

raspberry-rhubarb custard tart

This beautiful tart was assistant pastry chef Joy McBride's dessert solution in a hot, hot kitchen one sweltering July day and is delicious with any fresh fruit in season. Simple and quick, the crust does not have to be chilled or rolled.

crust

3 Tbsp.	ground almonds	40 mL
1 cup	all-purpose flour	250 mL
6 Tbsp.	white sugar	75 mL
1 Tbsp.	brown sugar	15 mL
1/8 tsp.	salt	0.5 mL
1/4 tsp.	vanilla extract	1 mL
1/2 cup + 1 Tbsp.	unsalted butter, chilled	140 mL

custard

1/2 cup	35% M.F. cream	125 mL
2	large eggs	2
1/2 cup	white sugar	125 mL
1/4 cup	all-purpose flour	50 mL
2 Tbsp.	ground almonds	25 mL
2 Tbsp.	brandy	25 mL
3/4 tsp.	vanilla extract	4 mL
1/2 tsp.	salt	2 mL
1 1/2 cups	1/2-inch-thick (1 cm) slices fresh rhubarb	375 mL
1 1/2 cups	fresh raspberries	375 mL
2 Tbsp.	sliced almonds	25 mL

Preheat oven to 325°F (160°C), and line a 10-inch (25 cm) tart pan with parchment paper. Combine almonds, flour, white and brown sugar, salt and vanilla, and cut in butter until mixture forms coarse crumbs. Press dough into tart pan, using as much of the crumble as you need to form a 1/4-inch-thick (6 mm) shell. Reserve remaining crumble. Bake shell for 10 to 15 minutes, until lightly browned. Allow to cool.

To make custard, whisk together cream, eggs and sugar in a medium bowl, then stir in flour, almonds and brandy. Add vanilla and salt, and whisk until smooth.

Spoon rhubarb and raspberries into tart crust, and pour custard over fruit. Scatter remaining crumble over top, and sprinkle with almonds. Bake until custard is slightly puffed and fruit is bubbling around edge, 30 to 35 minutes. Allow to cool, and serve at room temperature.

Serves 10

apple frangipane tart

For sheer good looks, this tart sets a very high standard. And with its creamy almond filling and sweet or tart apples, it's the ideal late-summer dessert. Serve it slightly warm with a scoop of real vanilla ice cream.

filling

2 Tbsp.	all-purpose flour	25 mL
1 cup	ground almonds	250 mL
1/2 cup less 1 Tbsp.	unsalted butter, room temperature	110 mL
1/2 cup	white sugar	125 mL
2	large eggs	2

10-inch (25 cm) partially baked tart shell
(see Tart Dough, page 198)

2	apples (preferably Ida Red or Granny Smith)	2
1 tsp.	ground cinnamon	5 mL

glaze

2/3 cup	apricot jam	150 mL
3 Tbsp.	water	40 mL

Preheat oven to 350°F (180°C). To make filling, combine flour and almonds in a small bowl, and set aside. Cream butter and sugar together in a medium bowl until light and fluffy. Beat in eggs, one at a time. Add flour mixture, and blend together. Spoon filling into tart shell, and smooth top.

Peel and core apples, then cut in half. Cut each half into thin slices. Layer slices on top of filling, working from the outside in. Sprinkle with cinnamon, and bake for 30 minutes or until filling is firm but still moist. Allow to cool.

To make glaze, heat jam and water in a small saucepan over medium-low heat, stirring until incorporated. Strain, then return to pan, and bring to a boil. While glaze is still hot, brush over cooled tart.

Serves 8-10

chocolate truffle tart

Some alcohols are stronger than others, so when making this truffle tart, be sure to choose yours judiciously. Grand Marnier is a perennial favourite, port adds a wonderful depth, but pastry chef Stefanie Killen prefers crème de menthe, which makes a wintry statement.

crust

6 Tbsp.	unsalted butter	75 mL
$\frac{1}{2}$ cup	white sugar	125 mL
	Pinch salt	
$\frac{3}{4}$ tsp.	vanilla extract	4 mL
5 Tbsp.	unsweetened cocoa	65 mL
$\frac{1}{2}$ cup	all-purpose flour	125 mL

filling

$8\frac{1}{2}$ oz.	bittersweet chocolate, coarsely chopped	240 g
$2\frac{1}{2}$ Tbsp.	unsalted butter, room temperature	35 mL
$\frac{3}{4}$ cup	35% M.F. cream	175 mL
3 Tbsp.	liqueur, or to taste	40 mL

To make crust, cream butter and sugar together in a small bowl until light and fluffy. Add salt and vanilla. Sift cocoa and flour together, add to butter mixture, and mix until well combined. Press dough into a 9-inch (23 cm) tart pan or five $4\frac{1}{2}$-inch (11 cm) tart pans with removable bottoms. Place in freezer for 2 to 4 hours.

Meanwhile, preheat oven to 375°F (190°C). Bake tart shell(s) for 12 to 15 minutes, until dough has stopped bubbling. Remove from oven, and allow to cool.

To make filling, place chocolate and butter in a small bowl. In a small saucepan over medium-high heat, bring cream to a boil, then pour over chocolate and butter. Stir until chocolate is melted and mixture is uniform in colour. Add liqueur, and stir until it is completely incorporated.

Pour filling into tart shell(s), and refrigerate for 4 hours or until set. To make small truffle triangles, cut each $4\frac{1}{2}$-inch (11 cm) tart into 6 pieces.

Makes one 9-inch (23 cm) tart or 30 triangles

pear + chocolate tart

Rose loved this tart for its full pear flavour and the taste of dark chocolate, which gets an extra boost from the cocoa.

4 tsp.	unsweetened cocoa	20 mL
2 oz.	bittersweet chocolate, chopped into pea-sized pieces	60 g
	9-inch (23 cm) partially baked tart shell (see Tart Dough, page 198)	
2	large, ripe pears (preferably Flemish Beauty), or 5 to 6 ripe sugar pears, peeled + cut into 1/4-inch (6 mm) slices	2
2	large eggs	2
4 1/2 Tbsp.	white sugar	60 mL
1/2 cup	35% M.F. cream	125 mL
1 1/2 tsp.	Poire Williams or brandy	7 mL
3/4 tsp.	vanilla extract	4 mL
	Pinch salt	

Preheat oven to 375°F (190°C). In a small bowl, toss cocoa with chocolate. Reserve 1 Tbsp. (15 mL) of this mixture, and spread the rest evenly over tart shell. Top with pears.

In a small bowl, whisk together eggs, sugar, cream, Poire Williams or brandy, vanilla and salt. Spoon over pears, and sprinkle with reserved chocolate mixture.

Bake for 25 to 30 minutes, until custard filling is set but still has a little movement in centre. Allow to cool, then refrigerate until chilled before serving.

Serves 8

walnut turtle tart

Sweet caramel, brown-butter-infused chocolate ganache and the earthy flavour of walnuts make this tart hard to beat.

1 1/2 cups	walnut halves	375 mL
	10-inch (25 cm) prebaked tart shell	

caramel

2/3 cup	white sugar	150 mL
3 Tbsp.	orange juice	40 mL
2 1/2 Tbsp.	unsalted butter	35 mL
4 1/2 Tbsp.	35% M.F. cream	60 mL
1/4 cup	coarsely chopped white chocolate	50 mL

ganache

6 Tbsp.	unsalted butter	75 mL
generous 1/2 cup	coarsely chopped milk chocolate	125 mL
generous 1/2 cup	coarsely chopped bittersweet chocolate	125 mL
scant 1/2 cup	35% M.F. cream	125 mL
2 1/2 Tbsp.	glucose	35 mL

Place walnuts in a large, dry frying pan over medium-low heat, and toast, shaking pan, until golden brown and fragrant. Set aside.

To make caramel, place sugar and orange juice in a small covered saucepan over medium-high heat, and cook, without stirring, until liquid begins to turn amber, 5 to 8 minutes. Remove lid, and continue to cook until caramel is a uniform deep amber colour. Add butter and cream (the caramel will sputter at this point; be careful not to burn yourself), and stir until mixture is smooth. Remove saucepan from heat, and add chocolate, stirring until it has completely melted. Pour caramel into tart shell, spreading it evenly. Scatter walnuts over caramel to form a single, flat layer. Refrigerate.

To make ganache, place butter in a small saucepan over medium-high heat. When it comes to a boil, reduce heat and simmer, without stirring, until milk solids have separated and browned (at this point, butter will have a nutty aroma and be golden in colour). Pour through a sieve lined with a paper napkin, discard solids, and set aside.

Place milk chocolate and bittersweet chocolate in a medium bowl. In a small saucepan over medium-high heat, bring cream and glucose to a boil. Pour over chocolate, and stir until chocolate is completely melted. Add browned butter, and stir until mixture is incorporated. Pour ganache over tart, spreading to cover walnuts evenly. Refrigerate for a few hours, until chocolate is set.

Serves 8–10

sweeten up

Found in health- and bulk-food stores, glucose is known as an "invert sugar," which means that it is sweeter than an equivalent sucrose solution by weight and thus can be used in recipes to reduce the quantity of sugar needed. For this tart, corn syrup can be substituted for the slightly thicker glucose.

tart dough

Buttery and slightly sweet, this tart dough works beautifully with a wide range of fillings.

1/2 cup	unsalted butter	125 mL
1/4 cup	white sugar	50 mL
1	large egg yolk	1
2 Tbsp.	35% M.F. cream	25 mL
1 1/2 cups	all-purpose flour, sifted	375 mL
	Pinch salt	
1	large egg white, lightly beaten	1

In a small bowl, cream butter and sugar together until mixture is light and fluffy. In a separate bowl, mix egg yolk and cream together, then add to butter mixture in thirds, scraping the sides of the bowl after each addition. Add flour and salt, mixing just until incorporated. If using an electric mixer, use paddle attachment. Chill dough for 1 hour before rolling out tart shell.

To partially bake tart shell, preheat oven to 400°F (200°C). Line a 10-inch (25 cm) tart pan with dough, and place in refrigerator for 20 minutes. Bake for 10 to 12 minutes, until crust is light golden in colour. (To fully bake tart shell, leave in oven until shell is a dark golden brown in colour.) Remove from oven, allow to cool for a few minutes, then brush bottom and sides with a little egg white. Allow to cool completely before filling.

Makes one 10-inch (25 cm) tart shell

blackcurrant + blueberry galettes

This is one of our most popular galettes, both for its marvellous taste and its magnificent colour. Use wild blueberries, if possible, because their sweetness nicely balances the tartness of the blackcurrants. Mashing the blackcurrants to break down their tough skin helps the berries absorb the sugar.

5 Tbsp.	cornstarch	65 mL
$1^1/2$ cups	white sugar, or to taste	375 mL
	Salt	
1 tsp.	lemon juice	5 mL
$2^1/2$ cups	fresh blackcurrants, partially mashed	625 mL
$2^1/2$ cups	fresh blueberries	625 mL
1	large egg	1
1 tsp.	water	5 mL
6	7-inch (18 cm) rounds of Sour Cream Pastry (see page 203)	6
	Turbinado sugar	

In a large bowl, stir together cornstarch, white sugar and a pinch of salt. Add lemon juice, blackcurrants and blueberries, and toss.

In a small bowl, lightly beat egg with water and a pinch of salt. Brush a 1-inch (2.5 cm) band of egg wash around edge of each pastry round. Reserve remaining egg wash.

Divide berry mixture among pastry rounds, mounding berries in centre. Fold edges of pastry toward the middle, leaving a small circle of berries exposed in the centre. Refrigerate galettes for 1 hour.

Preheat oven to 400°F (200°C). Brush pastry with remaining egg wash, and sprinkle with turbinado sugar. Bake for 25 to 30 minutes, until fruit is bubbling thickly and pastry is well browned.

Makes 6 galettes

rhubarb-apple-raspberry pie

A perfect summer pie. Apples mellow the tartness of the fresh rhubarb, while raspberries and lemon give it a nice kick.

4 cups	1/2-inch (1 cm) slices fresh rhubarb	1 L
2 cups	sliced peeled apples (preferably Ida Red or Granny Smith)	500 mL
1 1/3 cups	fresh raspberries	325 mL
3/4 cup	white sugar	175 mL
1 1/2 Tbsp.	cornstarch	20 mL
1 tsp.	lemon zest	5 mL
3 Tbsp. + 1 tsp.	all-purpose flour	45 mL
generous 1/4 cup	sour cream	50 mL
	Pastry for 9-inch (23 cm) double pie crust (see Sour Cream Pastry, page 203)	
1	large egg	1
	Pinch salt	
1 Tbsp.	water	15 mL
	Turbinado sugar	

In a large bowl, toss together rhubarb, apples, raspberries, white sugar, cornstarch, lemon zest, flour and sour cream, and allow to sit for 10 minutes.

Place a round of pie crust in a 9-inch (23 cm) pie plate, then mound fruit filling in pie shell. In a small bowl, whisk egg with salt and water. Brush edges of both pastry rounds with egg wash. Reserve remaining egg wash. Lay top crust over filling, egg-washed side down. Tuck overhang under bottom-crust edge. Crimp edges to seal pastry, cut vents in top, and place pie in refrigerator for 1 hour.

Preheat oven to 425°F (220°C). Before baking, brush top with remaining egg wash and sprinkle with turbinado sugar. Bake for 45 to 50 minutes, until fruit is soft and juices are bubbling thickly from vents. (If top or edges brown too quickly, protect with strips of aluminum foil.) Remove from oven, and allow to cool.

Serves 6-8

peach caramel pie

Joy McBride's favourite childhood pie — the sweet flavour of fresh peaches is unbeatable.

6 cups	sliced fresh peaches	1.5 L
1 Tbsp.	lemon juice	15 mL
1/2 cup	packed brown sugar	125 mL
	Salt	
1/8 tsp.	ground cinnamon	0.5 mL
	Pinch ground nutmeg	
5 tsp.	cornstarch	25 mL
	Pastry for 9-inch (23 cm) double pie crust (see Sour Cream Pastry, page 203)	
1	large egg	1
1 Tbsp.	water	15 mL
2 Tbsp.	brown sugar	25 mL
1 Tbsp.	all-purpose flour	15 mL
1 Tbsp.	unsalted butter, softened	15 mL
2 Tbsp.	corn syrup	25 mL

In a large bowl, toss peaches with lemon juice and brown sugar. Set aside for at least 30 minutes. Drain juice into a small saucepan. Over low heat, reduce juice until it has the consistency of syrup. Pour over peaches. Add a pinch of salt, cinnamon, nutmeg and cornstarch, and toss thoroughly.

Place a round of pie crust in a 9-inch (23 cm) pie plate, then mound peaches in pie shell. In a small bowl, whisk egg with water and a pinch of salt. Brush edges of both pastry rounds with egg wash. Lay top crust over filling, egg-washed side down. Tuck overhang under bottom-crust edge. Crimp edges to seal pastry, cut vents in top, and place pie in refrigerator for 1 hour.

Meanwhile, thoroughly cream brown sugar, flour, butter and corn syrup in a small bowl. Set aside.

Preheat oven to 400°F (200°C). Bake pie for 40 to 50 minutes, until juices are bubbling through vents. Remove from oven, and spread brown-sugar mixture over hot crust. Bake for a few more minutes, until topping is bubbling. Allow to cool for a few hours.

Serves 6–8

chocolate bourbon pecan pie

For adults only. Boozy, gooey, nutty and chocolatey — one piece is never enough.

1 cup	whole pecans	250 mL
1/3 cup	semisweet chocolate chips	75 mL
	9-inch (23 cm) partially blind-baked single pie shell (see Sour Cream Pastry, page 203)	
4	large egg yolks	4
1/3 cup	corn syrup	75 mL
1/2 cup	packed brown sugar	125 mL
1/4 cup	unsalted butter	50 mL
1/4 cup	35% M.F. cream	50 mL
1/8 tsp.	salt	0.5 mL
1 1/2 tsp.	vanilla extract	7 mL
4 tsp.	bourbon	20 mL

Preheat oven to 350°F (180°C). Scatter pecans and chocolate chips over bottom of pie shell, and set aside.

In a small saucepan over medium heat, mix together egg yolks, corn syrup, brown sugar, butter, cream and salt. Stir occasionally; do not bring to a boil. When butter has melted and mixture has thickened slightly, remove from heat, and stir in vanilla and bourbon.

Pour filling over pecans and chocolate chips in pie shell. Bake for 20 to 30 minutes, until filling is bubbling. Allow to cool, then chill before serving.

Serves 6-8

maple walnut pie

Follow recipe above, substituting maple syrup for corn syrup; Calvados or any nut liqueur, such as amaretto or Frangelico, for bourbon; and 1 1/2 cups (375 mL) walnut halves for pecans and chocolate chips.

sour cream pastry

Following our technique, this pastry rises like a rich, crisp puff pastry. Sour cream helps turn the crust a golden brown as it bakes, and butter gives it its deep full flavour. (Hats off to Rose Levy Beranbaum for the idea of separating the butter.)

1 3/4 cups	all-purpose flour	425 mL
	Pinch salt	
1/2 cup + 2 Tbsp.	unsalted butter, chilled + cut into 1/2-inch (1 cm) cubes	150 mL
2 Tbsp.	beaten egg	25 mL
5 Tbsp.	sour cream	65 mL
1	large egg white, beaten	1

sticky dough

Outside humidity can affect the moisture content of your flour, which in turn affects how much liquid you'll need to make your pastry. On very humid days, start by adding only three-quarters of the liquid. If the crumbs won't come together, add liquid, as needed, until a dough forms.

In a large bowl, mix together flour and salt. Add two-thirds of the butter cubes, and toss to coat with flour. Refrigerate flour mixture and remaining butter cubes for at least 1 hour.

Either by hand or with an electric mixer fitted with a whisk attachment, cut butter into flour until mixture is light and powdery, with no discernible butter chunks. Flatten remaining butter cubes by hand, leaving them intact, and toss with flour mixture. Refrigerate for another hour.

In a small bowl, stir together egg and sour cream. Add to flour mixture, and toss, either by hand or with an electric mixer fitted with a paddle attachment, until crumbs are evenly moistened. Knead dough by hand until it comes together, then divide into equal portions (two for pie crusts or six for galettes). Flatten into 1/2-inch-thick (1 cm) rounds, wrap in plastic wrap, and refrigerate for 30 minutes before rolling out.

Preheat oven to 400°F (200°C). To partially blind bake pie shells, line pie shells with aluminum foil, then fill with dried beans or pie weights. Bake for 10 to 15 minutes, until edges are golden brown. Remove from oven, remove foil and beans or weights, and prick bottom and sides of shell with a fork. (To blind bake fully, return pie shell to oven for 5 to 10 minutes, until inside of shell is a dark golden brown. Cover edges with strips of aluminum foil to prevent them from burning.) Allow to sit for a few minutes. Brush bottom of shell with a little egg white.

Makes two 9-inch (23 cm) crusts or 6 individual galettes

sacher torte

Rich and chocolatey, this classic Viennese cake is destined to become one of your favourites. For a lively change, substitute Grand Marnier for the crème de framboise.

ganache

17 oz.	bittersweet chocolate (preferably Callebaut), coarsely chopped	480 g
1 3/4 cups	35% M.F. cream	425 mL
3 Tbsp.	crème de framboise	40 mL

framboise syrup

1/4 cup	white sugar	50 mL
3 Tbsp.	water	40 mL
1 Tbsp.	crème de framboise	15 mL

cake

8 oz.	bittersweet chocolate (preferably Callebaut), coarsely chopped	225 g
1 cup	unsalted butter	250 mL
1 cup + 2 Tbsp.	white sugar	275 mL
8	large eggs, separated	8
3/4 cup	all-purpose flour	175 mL

To make ganache, place chocolate in a large bowl. In a small saucepan over medium-high heat, bring cream to a boil, then pour over chocolate. Stir until chocolate is melted and mixture is smooth and uniform in colour. Add liqueur, and stir until well combined. Cover bowl, and allow to sit at room temperature overnight. (The ganache may also be chilled quickly in the refrigerator. Just be sure to remove it as soon as it reaches a spreadable consistency.)

To make syrup, combine sugar and water in a small saucepan over medium heat, and bring to a boil. Cook just until sugar is dissolved. Remove from heat, stir in liqueur, and allow to cool.

Preheat oven to 350°F (180°C), and line bottoms and sides of two 9-inch (2.5 L) springform pans with parchment paper. To make cake, melt chocolate in a double boiler over simmering water, and keep warm. In a large bowl, cream together butter and sugar until light and fluffy. Add egg yolks, one at a time, scraping down sides of bowl after each addition until yolks have been incorporated. Add chocolate, and mix just until combined. If using an electric mixer, use paddle attachment. Set aside.

Whip egg whites until stiff peaks form, then fold into chocolate mixture, alternating with flour, beginning and ending with flour. Divide batter between prepared pans, and smooth tops. Bake for 20 to 30 minutes, until cake springs back when lightly tapped and a small knife inserted in centre comes out clean, with a few moist crumbs attached. Allow to cool on wire rack, and unmould.

To assemble cake, use a serrated knife to level tops of cake rounds, then brush surface of each with syrup. Place one cake round, cut side up, on a baking sheet. Spread cut side with a 1/2-inch (1 cm) layer of ganache, then top with second cake round, cut side down. Spread a very thin layer of ganache over top and sides of cake (you should be able to see cake through the ganache), then refrigerate until ganache is set.

Heat remaining ganache until it liquefies. Pour over chilled cake to cover top and sides completely. Refrigerate until ganache is set. Bring to room temperature before serving.

Serves 12-16

chocolate pâté

Who but a chocolate lover could have created this decadent pâté? Use only the very best chocolate.

1/2 cup	unsalted butter	125 mL
6 oz.	bittersweet chocolate (preferably Lindt or Callebaut), coarsely chopped	170 g
3	large eggs	3
1/4 cup	white sugar	50 mL
1 1/2 tsp.	coffee extract	7 mL

Preheat oven to 325°F (160°F). Lightly grease a 9-by-5-inch (2 L) loaf pan, and line bottom and sides with parchment paper.

Combine butter and chocolate in a double boiler over simmering water, stirring occasionally. When chocolate has melted, set aside. In a small bowl, whisk eggs, sugar and coffee extract together until frothy, then immediately strain and add to chocolate, stirring to combine thoroughly. Pour into loaf pan, and place in a roasting pan. Pour hot water into roasting pan to come midway up loaf pan. Cover both pans with aluminum foil, and bake for 1 hour 45 minutes. Pâté should be soft yet set in the middle. Remove pan from water, and refrigerate 6 hours before unmoulding.

Makes 1 pound (450 g)

chocolate hazelnut mousse cake

For a lovely contrast, serve this cake in a pool of Orange Sauce (see page 207). Be sure to use fresh hazelnuts.

1/3 cup	pastry flour	75 mL
1/2 cup	unsweetened cocoa	125 mL
1/2 cup	ground hazelnuts	125 mL
2/3 cup	unsalted butter	150 mL
1/2 cup + 1/3 cup	white sugar	125 mL + 75 mL
7	large eggs, separated	7

mousse

6 oz.	bittersweet chocolate, coarsely chopped	170 g
1 1/2 cups	35% M.F. cream	375 mL
4	large egg yolks	4
2 Tbsp.	white sugar	25 mL
2 tsp.	brandy	10 mL

ganache

6 oz.	bittersweet chocolate, coarsely chopped	170 g
2/3 cup	35% M.F. cream	150 mL

Preheat oven to 375°F (190°C). Sift flour and cocoa together in a small bowl, stir in hazelnuts, and set aside. In a medium bowl, cream butter and 1/2 cup (125 mL) sugar until light and fluffy. Beat in egg yolks, one or two at a time. In a separate bowl, whip egg whites until they form ribbons, then slowly add 1/3 cup (75 mL) sugar. Continue whipping until soft peaks form. Alternating with dry ingredients, fold egg whites into butter mixture, starting and ending with egg whites. Pour into ungreased 9-inch (2.5 L) springform pan, and bake for 30 to 45 minutes. Allow cake to cool completely, then unmould. If necessary, trim top to make cake even, then slice in half to create two layers.

To make mousse, place chocolate in a small bowl. Bring 1/2 cup (125 mL) of the cream to a boil over medium-high heat. Pour over chocolate, stirring until chocolate is completely melted. In a double boiler over simmering water, whisk egg yolks, sugar and brandy for about 5 minutes, until mixture is pale and slightly thickened. Fold into chocolate. Whip remaining 1 cup (250 mL) cream until soft peaks form, then fold into chocolate until completely incorporated.

To assemble cake, place one layer in a springform pan. Pour mousse evenly over cake, shaking pan slightly to settle it. Add second layer, and gently press down. Wrap pan with plastic wrap or aluminum foil, and chill in refrigerator for 8 hours or in freezer for 3 hours.

To make ganache, place chocolate in a small bowl. In a small saucepan over medium-high heat, bring cream to a boil. Pour over chocolate, whisking until chocolate is melted and mixture is smooth. Unmould cake, and smooth sides. Pour ganache over top, spreading it to cover sides as well. Refrigerate until ganache sets, then serve. If cake has been frozen, leave in refrigerator for a few hours before covering with ganache.

Serves 10–12

pumpkin cheesecake

This subtly spiced cheesecake is light and mousselike in texture. Don't wait for a holiday to serve this tasty dessert.

crust

1 cup	graham cracker crumbs	250 mL
3 Tbsp.	unsalted butter, melted	40 mL
1/2 tsp.	icing sugar	2 mL

filling

28 oz.	cream cheese, room temperature	800 g
2/3 cup	packed brown sugar	150 mL
8	large eggs, separated	8
3/4 cup	pumpkin purée	175 mL
4 tsp.	maple syrup	20 mL
4 tsp.	light rum	20 mL
1/2 tsp.	ground cinnamon	2 mL
1/2 tsp.	ground ginger	2 mL
	Pinch ground nutmeg	
	Pinch ground cloves	
2 tsp.	vanilla extract	10 mL
2 Tbsp.	white sugar	25 mL

Preheat oven to 375°F (190°C), and line a 9-inch (2.5 L) springform pan with parchment paper. To make crust, stir together graham crumbs, butter and icing sugar until well mixed. Press into pan, and set aside.

To make filling, cream the cream cheese in a large bowl until smooth, regularly scraping down sides of bowl and beater. If using an electric mixer, use paddle attachment. Add brown sugar, and mix until combined, scraping bowl and beater. Add egg yolks one at a time, beating after each addition and scraping sides of bowl until just mixed. Add pumpkin purée, maple syrup, rum, spices and vanilla, and beat until just mixed.

In a separate bowl, beat egg whites until soft peaks form, add white sugar, and beat until stiff. Fold one-third of whites into batter, then fold in remaining whites. Pour over crust, smoothing the top. Place pan in oven, and reduce temperature to 275°F (140°C). Bake for 60 to 90 minutes, until cheesecake is set. Chill for about 2 hours before serving.

Serves 10

orange sauce

1 1/2 tsp.	arrowroot	5 mL
2 cups	orange juice	500 mL
6 Tbsp.	white sugar	75 mL
1 1/2 tsp.	lemon juice	7 mL
1/2 tsp.	lemon zest	2 mL
1 tsp.	orange zest	5 mL

Dissolve arrowroot in 1 tsp. (5 mL) water. In a saucepan over medium-high heat, bring orange juice to a boil. Reduce heat, and simmer until reduced by half. Stir in sugar and arrowroot, and simmer for 1 minute. Remove from heat, and let cool. Stir in lemon juice and zest.

Makes about 1 cup (250 mL)

peach upside-down cakes

These charming little cakes get their extraordinary flavour from fresh peaches, vanilla and crème fraîche, but feel free to substitute or add seasonal fruit — from rhubarb in spring to cranberries in winter.

3 Tbsp. + 1/4 cup	unsalted butter	40 mL + 50 mL
generous 1/4 cup	packed brown sugar	50 mL
1 1/2 tsp.	bourbon	7 mL
2–3	fresh peaches, peeled + sliced	2–3
1/2 cup	white sugar	125 mL
1	large egg	1
3/4 cup + 2 Tbsp.	all-purpose flour	200 mL
1 tsp.	baking powder	5 mL
1/2 tsp.	salt	2 mL
1/2 cup	Crème Fraîche (see page 230)	125 mL
1 tsp.	vanilla extract	5 mL

Preheat oven to 350°F (180°C). Grease five 8-ounce (225 g) ramekins, and set aside.

In a small saucepan over medium heat, bring 3 Tbsp. (40 mL) butter and brown sugar to a boil. Add bourbon, and stir thoroughly. Pour caramel into ramekins, and arrange peaches in one layer on top. Set aside.

In a medium bowl, cream 1/4 cup (50 mL) butter. Add sugar, and beat until light and fluffy. Beat in egg until combined. In a separate bowl, mix together flour, baking powder and salt. Gradually add dry ingredients to egg mixture, alternating with crème fraîche, beginning and ending with dry ingredients. Stir in vanilla, mixing until just combined.

Scoop 1/3 cup (75 mL) batter into each ramekin, mounding batter toward edge and leaving an indentation at centre. Fruit in centre should be covered with only a thin layer of batter (this will create a flat surface when cakes are unmoulded).

Bake for 15 to 20 minutes. Cake tester should come out clean, with a few moist crumbs attached, and cakes should bounce back when lightly pressed. Allow cakes to cool until you can safely handle the ramekins, then turn cakes out onto wire rack to finish cooling. Serve at room temperature.

Serves 5

note

To make a single large cake, use a 12-inch (30 cm) cast-iron frying pan, and double the recipe to serve 10.

mixed berry oat squares

Thanks to the widespread availability of tasty frozen berries, you can make these scrumptious squares all year round. To lower the sugar level, substitute sugar-free jam.

1/4 cup	unsalted butter, room temperature	50 mL
3/4 cup	all-purpose flour	175 mL
1/4 tsp.	salt	1 mL
2	large eggs	2
1/2 cup	white sugar	125 mL
1/2 tsp.	vanilla extract	2 mL

fruit layer

1 cup	frozen raspberries	250 mL
1 cup	frozen blueberries	250 mL
1 cup	frozen cranberries	250 mL
1/4 cup	white sugar	50 mL
1/2 cup	raspberry jam	125 mL

topping

1/3 cup	all-purpose flour	75 mL
1/2 tsp.	ground cinnamon	2 mL
1/3 cup	rolled oats	75 mL
1/2 cup	packed brown sugar	125 mL
1/4 cup	unsalted butter, chilled	50 mL

Preheat oven to 350°F (180°C), and grease and flour an 8-inch-square (2 L) cake pan. With an electric mixer, beat together butter, flour and salt for about 5 minutes. In a small bowl, beat eggs, then stir in sugar and vanilla. Gradually add egg mixture to flour mixture, stirring until well combined. Pour into cake pan, and spread flat. Cover with plastic wrap, and place in refrigerator.

To prepare fruit layer, toss frozen berries with sugar, and place in an 8-inch-square (2 L) pan in a single layer. Bake for 15 minutes. Remove from oven, and allow to cool. Drain and discard excess liquid.

Remove cake pan from refrigerator. Stir jam to soften, and spread over batter. Then spread fruit over jam.

To make topping, toss flour, cinnamon, rolled oats and brown sugar together, making sure there are no sugar lumps. Cut butter into 1/2-inch (1 cm) cubes, and mix with dry ingredients. Sprinkle evenly over fruit layer. Bake for 50 minutes or until topping is light golden brown. Let cool, then chill to set.

Makes 12-16 squares

chocolate hazelnut cherry bar

Moist and chewy, this is a brownie with ambition. With dense chocolate, cherries, hazelnuts and a rich ganache topping, it pushes the boundaries of the conventional brownie.

2/3 cup	dried cherries	150 mL
	Kirsch to soak cherries	
1 cup	hazelnuts, skinned (see box)	250 mL
3/4 cup	all-purpose flour	175 mL
1/2 cup	white sugar	125 mL
1/2 tsp.	salt	2 mL
1/4 cup	unsalted butter	50 mL
6 oz.	bittersweet chocolate, coarsely chopped	170 g
2	large eggs	2

ganache

1/2 cup	35% M.F. cream	125 mL
	Pinch salt	
1	large egg yolk	1
6 oz.	bittersweet chocolate, coarsely chopped	170 g

Preheat oven to 350°F (180°C), and line a 9-by-13-inch (3 L) cake pan with parchment paper. Place dried cherries in a small bowl, cover with kirsch, and soak until needed.

Blend hazelnuts, flour, sugar and salt in a food processor until fine. Set aside. In a double boiler over simmering water, melt butter and chocolate, whisking until well combined. Remove from heat, and add eggs one at a time, whisking until smooth. Stir in flour mixture. Drain cherries, reserving kirsch, and fold into batter. Spread batter in pan, and bake for 15 minutes or until firm and dry on top. Cake tester should come out clean, with moist crumbs attached. Place pan on wire rack to cool.

To make ganache, place cream and salt in a small saucepan over medium-high heat, and bring to a boil. Remove from heat. Slowly add hot cream to egg yolk, whisking constantly. Return mixture to saucepan over medium-low heat, stirring constantly until custard has thickened, 1 to 2 minutes. Do not boil. Whisk in chocolate until smooth. Add 1 1/2 tsp. (7 mL) of the reserved kirsch, and whisk. Pour ganache over cake in pan, and refrigerate until ganache is set, 4 to 6 hours. Cut into squares.

Makes about 24 squares

the skinny

To remove the bitter skin of hazelnuts, toast nuts in a 350°F (180°C) oven until skin turns black and cracks, about 10 minutes. While nuts are still warm, gently rub them together in a tea towel to loosen skin. Allow to cool completely before grinding.

triple chocolate almond biscotti

Stefanie Killen has been using this recipe for seven years, and it has stood the test of time. "Biscotti" means double-baked, and that's what gives these cookies their crisp, dense texture. As always, for best results, use good-quality chocolate.

1 cup	slivered almonds	250 mL
1/4 cup	unsalted butter	50 mL
2/3 cup	packed brown sugar	150 mL
1	large egg	1
1/4 cup	bittersweet chocolate chips	50 mL
1/4 cup	milk chocolate chips	50 mL
1/4 cup	white chocolate chips	50 mL
1 1/4 cups	all-purpose flour	300 mL

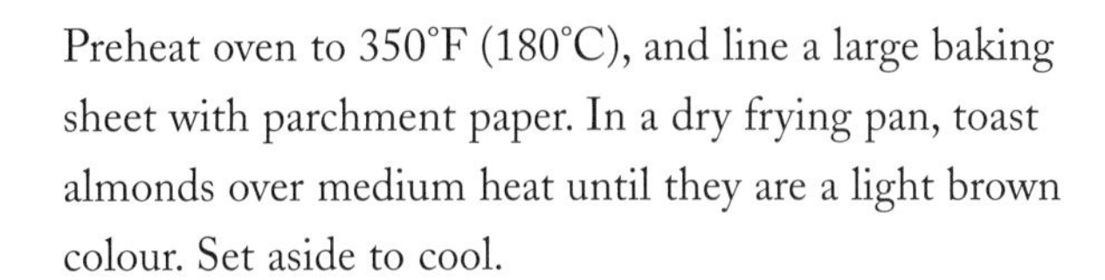

Preheat oven to 350°F (180°C), and line a large baking sheet with parchment paper. In a dry frying pan, toast almonds over medium heat until they are a light brown colour. Set aside to cool.

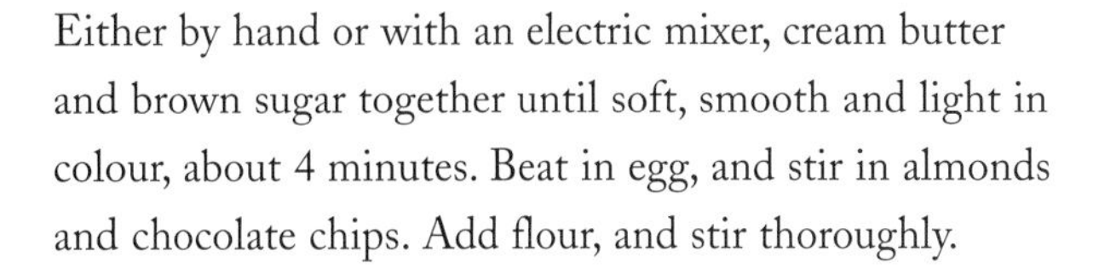

Either by hand or with an electric mixer, cream butter and brown sugar together until soft, smooth and light in colour, about 4 minutes. Beat in egg, and stir in almonds and chocolate chips. Add flour, and stir thoroughly.

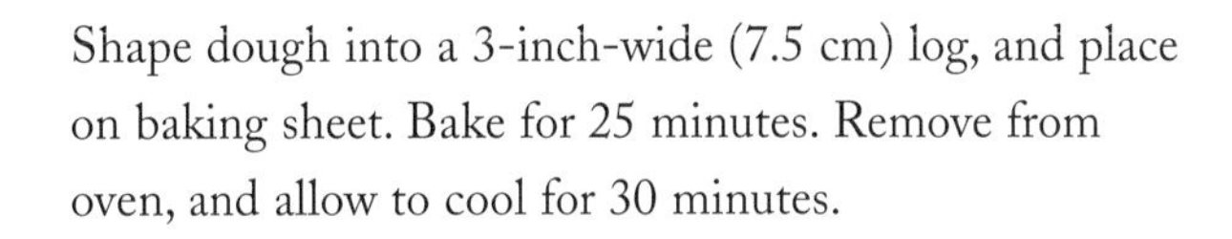

Shape dough into a 3-inch-wide (7.5 cm) log, and place on baking sheet. Bake for 25 minutes. Remove from oven, and allow to cool for 30 minutes.

Reduce oven temperature to 325°F (160°C). With a serrated knife, cut log into slices just under 1/2 inch (1 cm) thick. Lay slices on baking sheet, and bake for 20 minutes. Biscotti can be stored in an airtight container for up to 3 weeks.

Makes 20 biscotti

rocky mountain cookies

Simple ingredients and honest flavours make this mouthwatering cookie one of our favourites. But be careful not to overbake — when these cookies are ready to come out of the oven, their centres should still be light in colour.

1 cup	unsalted butter	250 mL
1 cup	packed brown sugar	250 mL
1 1/2 cups	white sugar	375 mL
2	large eggs	2
2 Tbsp.	2% milk	25 mL
2 tsp.	vanilla extract	10 mL
3 cups	all-purpose flour	750 mL
1 tsp.	baking powder	5 mL
1 tsp.	baking soda	5 mL
1 tsp.	salt	5 mL
1 1/3 cups	rolled oats	325 mL
3/4 cup	chocolate chips	175 mL
1 cup	chopped walnuts	250 mL

Preheat oven to 325°F (160°C), and line two large baking sheets with parchment paper.

In a large bowl, cream butter and sugars together until light and fluffy. In a small bowl, whisk together eggs, milk and vanilla. Slowly blend egg mixture into butter mixture, frequently scraping down sides of bowl. Combine flour, baking powder, baking soda and salt. Add to batter all at once, and mix just until combined. (Mixing can be done by hand, but if using an electric mixer, use paddle attachment.) Add rolled oats, chocolate chips and walnuts, and continue mixing until they are evenly distributed.

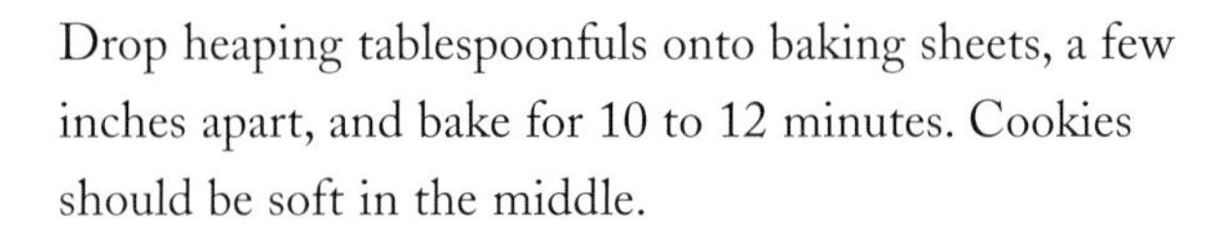

Drop heaping tablespoonfuls onto baking sheets, a few inches apart, and bake for 10 to 12 minutes. Cookies should be soft in the middle.

Makes 6 dozen cookies

clockwise from top: brazil nut cookies, ginger cookies, triple chocolate almond biscotti and rocky mountain cookies

brazil nut cookies

Simple to make and unbelievably delicious, these cookies are perfect with cappuccino.

2/3 cup	icing sugar	150 mL
1	large egg white, lightly whisked	1
1/2	pkg. frozen puff pastry, defrosted	1/2
2/3 cup	chopped brazil nuts	150 mL

Stir together icing sugar and enough egg white to make a very thick, smooth icing. Cover, and set aside.

On a floured board, roll out pastry to a 9-inch (23 cm) square. Prick surface repeatedly with a fork to prevent puffing as pastry bakes. Spread icing evenly over pastry. Sprinkle with nuts, and chill in refrigerator for 1 hour.

Preheat oven to 375°F (190°C). Cut pastry into three 3-inch-wide (7.5 cm) strips, then cut each strip into individual cookies, 1/2 inch (1 cm) wide. (If pastry becomes too soft to handle, return to refrigerator for 30 minutes.) Bake on an ungreased baking sheet for 15 minutes or until light golden brown and puffy.

Makes about 50 cookies

ginger cookies

Sweet, spicy, chewy — we've created more than a few ginger-cookie addicts with this recipe.

2 cups	all-purpose flour	500 mL
1 Tbsp.	ground ginger	15 mL
2 tsp.	baking soda	10 mL
1 tsp.	ground cinnamon	5 mL
1/2 tsp.	salt	2 mL
3/4 cup	unsalted butter	175 mL
1 1/4 cups + 2 Tbsp.	white sugar	325 mL
1	large egg	1
1/4 cup	fancy molasses	50 mL

Preheat oven to 325°F (160°C), and line two large baking sheets with parchment paper. In a medium bowl, stir together flour, ginger, baking soda, cinnamon and salt. Set aside. Cream butter and 1 cup plus 2 Tbsp. (275 mL) sugar until mixture is light and fluffy. Beat in egg, scraping sides of bowl well. Add molasses, and combine. Add dry ingredients, and mix just until incorporated.

Shape dough into 24 balls, and toss in a plastic bag with remaining 1/4 cup (50 mL) sugar. Place a few inches apart on baking sheets, and bake for 17 to 20 minutes. When done, cookies will be crinkly and golden.

Makes 24 large cookies

extras

extras

preserved lemon

To achieve their desired mild taste, these lemons must be cured at least a month before using.

6	whole lemons, washed	6
6 Tbsp.	coarse sea salt	75 mL
1	stick cinnamon	1
1 Tbsp.	coriander seed	15 mL
3	juniper berries, crushed	3
3–4	whole dried chilies	3–4
1 Tbsp.	black peppercorns	15 mL
2 1/2 cups	lemon juice	625 mL

Cut each lemon lengthwise into 6 sections to within 1/4 inch (6 mm) of stem so that lemon will hold together. Pack 1 Tbsp. (15 mL) salt inside of each lemon. Place lemons, cinnamon, coriander, juniper berries, chilies and peppercorns in a large sterilized glass jar. Completely fill jar with lemon juice. Cover, and refrigerate for at least 1 month. Use rind only.

pear + cranberry compote

Created to complement our cheese plates, this fruit compote is excellent company for a wide variety of cheeses.

4	pears, small dice	4
2 cups	frozen cranberries	500 mL
2 cups	dry white wine	500 mL
2 Tbsp.	sherry vinegar	25 mL
1	2-inch (5 cm) stick cinnamon	1
	Pinch ground nutmeg	
2 Tbsp.	finely grated fresh ginger	25 mL
2 Tbsp.	honey	25 mL
	Zest of 1 lemon	

Preheat oven to 350°F (180°C). Combine all ingredients in a roasting pan, and bake for about 1 hour, stirring every 15 minutes, until most of the liquid is absorbed. Remove cinnamon stick, spoon into a bowl, and chill.

Compote can be stored in refrigerator in a covered container for up to 2 weeks.

Makes 3 cups (750 mL)

mango salsa

This salsa enjoys a stellar — and long-standing — reputation at Pan Chancho. It's a perfect condiment with either salmon or chicken, and it's a great fresh dip with spring rolls. Canned mango purée is available at Asian markets.

1	ripe mango, finely diced	1
1 1/2 cups	mango purée	375 mL
1/2	red bell pepper, finely diced	1/2
1/2	green bell pepper, finely diced	1/2
1	small red onion, finely diced	1
1/3 cup	lime juice	75 mL
1/2 cup	chopped cilantro	125 mL
1–2	Thai chilies, minced	1–2
	Pinch sea salt	

Mix all ingredients together in a medium bowl.

Salsa can be stored in refrigerator in a covered container for up to 5 days.

Makes 4 cups (1 L)

roasted grape compote

Served on slices of baguette with Stilton pâté, this compote is delightful.

4 cups	whole red + green seedless grapes	1 L
1 Tbsp.	canola oil	15 mL
2 Tbsp.	brown sugar	25 mL
2 Tbsp.	brandy	25 mL
2 Tbsp.	apple cider vinegar	25 mL
	Pinch sea salt	
	Pinch freshly ground black pepper	

Preheat oven to 350°F (180°C). Combine all ingredients in a baking dish, and bake for about 1 hour, stirring every 15 minutes, until about half of the grapes have popped.

Compote can be stored in refrigerator in a covered container for up to 5 days.

Makes 3 1/2 cups (875 mL)

orange + sun-dried tomato relish

This relish peps up any kind of grilled cheese sandwich, from traditional to exotic. We serve it with Asiago and smoked mozzarella on Olive + Rosemary Sourdough (see page 18).

6	oranges	6
	Small pinch saffron threads	
3/4 cup	dry white wine	175 mL
1/2 cup	red-wine vinegar	125 mL
1/2 cup	white sugar	125 mL
3/4 cup	tomato paste	175 mL
1 cup	sun-dried tomatoes	250 mL
2 Tbsp.	extra-virgin olive oil	25 mL
1/4 cup	diced red onion	50 mL
	Zest of 1 orange	
1	48 oz. (1.5 L) can diced tomatoes, drained	1
	Pinch cayenne	
	Sea salt	
	Freshly ground black pepper	

Peel, section and seed oranges over a small bowl to catch juice. Set orange segments aside, and reserve juice.

Place saffron and wine in a medium saucepan over medium heat. Simmer for 5 minutes, then add vinegar and sugar. Increase heat to medium-high, and boil to reduce to a thin syrup, about 20 minutes. Add tomato paste and reserved orange juice. Continue to boil until mixture is reduced to a thick syrup. Set aside.

Meanwhile, soak sun-dried tomatoes in hot water until soft, about 20 minutes. Drain, and discard soaking liquid. Julienne tomatoes, and set aside.

Heat olive oil in a small frying pan over medium-high heat, add onion, and sauté for about 2 minutes.

In a large bowl, combine reduced syrup, onion, orange segments, orange zest, diced tomatoes, sun-dried tomatoes and cayenne. Add salt and pepper to taste.

Relish can be stored in refrigerator in a covered container for up to 2 weeks.

Makes about 3 cups (750 mL)

chive purée

A lovely coating for chicken, chive purée is also an ideal base for salad dressings and a great spread on garlic bread.

2 cups	loosely packed, roughly chopped fresh chives	500 mL
1 cup	grapeseed oil	250 mL
$^{1}/_{8}$ tsp.	sea salt	0.5 mL

Place chives in a blender, and purée while gradually drizzling in oil. Add salt.

Can be stored in refrigerator in a covered container for up to 2 weeks.

Makes about $1^{1}/_{2}$ cups (375 mL)

basil oil

What wouldn't benefit from a splash of basil oil? Experiment with other herbs as well.

4 cups	loosely packed, washed + dried basil leaves	1 L
$1^{1}/_{2}$ cups	grapeseed oil	375 mL
$^{1}/_{8}$ tsp.	sea salt	0.5 mL

Blanch basil by immersing briefly in boiling water, then drain and plunge into cold water. Drain again, and squeeze out excess water with paper towels.

Place basil in a blender, and purée while gradually drizzling in oil. Add salt.

Can be stored in refrigerator in a covered container for up to 2 weeks.

Makes about 2 cups (500 mL)

pepita cilantro butter

Try this light, nutty butter with our Cornmeal, Cilantro + Jalapeño Rings (see page 28).

1/2 cup	pepitas	125 mL
1 1/2 tsp.	cumin seed	7 mL
1 cup	unsalted butter, softened	250 mL
3 Tbsp.	finely chopped cilantro	40 mL
1/2 tsp.	freshly ground black pepper	2 mL
1/2 tsp.	sea salt	2 mL
3/4 tsp.	chili powder	4 mL
2	cloves garlic, minced	2

In a small, dry frying pan over medium-low heat, toast pepitas, shaking pan, until lightly browned. Allow to cool, then grind in a spice grinder or with a mortar and pestle. Set aside. Repeat process with cumin seed, toasting until fragrant, then coarsely grinding.

In a small bowl, combine all ingredients. Taste, and add more salt if needed. Can be stored in refrigerator in a covered container for up to 2 weeks.

Makes about 1 1/2 cups (375 mL)

pumpkin seed vinaigrette

This is our house dressing. A beautiful colour of green, it gets its distinctive flavour from pumpkin seed and sesame oils, while a hint of sweetness from the maple syrup mellows out the vinegar.

1 Tbsp.	pumpkin seed oil	15 mL
1 Tbsp.	toasted sesame oil	15 mL
2/3 cup	grapeseed oil	150 mL
2 Tbsp.	sherry vinegar	25 mL
1 Tbsp.	maple syrup	15 mL
1/2 tsp.	sea salt	2 mL
1/4 tsp.	freshly ground black pepper	1 mL

Place all ingredients in a jar with a secure lid, and shake well to mix.

Can be stored in refrigerator in a covered container for up to 2 weeks.

Makes 1 cup (250 mL)

sri lankan eggplant pickle

Here's a pickle that can go anywhere and do anything. Making it is a bit of a process, but you'll soon see how completely addictive and fantastically versatile it is. Serve with any Indian dish.

4–5 cups	1-inch-dice (2.5 cm) eggplant	1–1.25 L
1 tsp.	sea salt	5 mL
1 tsp.	turmeric	5 mL
1/4 cup	tamarind pulp	50 mL
1/2 cup	water	125 mL
1 1/2 tsp.	black mustard seed	7 mL
1/4 cup	white vinegar	50 mL
1	small cooking onion, finely chopped	1
2	cloves garlic, sliced	2
2 tsp.	finely chopped fresh ginger	10 mL
	Canola oil for frying	
2–3 tsp.	Sri Lankan Curry Powder (see page 52)	10–15 mL
3	Thai chilies, minced	3
1	1-inch (2.5 cm) stick cinnamon	1
1/2 tsp.	chili powder	2 mL
1 tsp.	white sugar	5 mL

In a large bowl, rub eggplant with salt and turmeric, and allow to sit for at least 1 hour. Meanwhile, combine tamarind pulp and water in a small saucepan. Place over low heat, and simmer for about 10 minutes. Strain through a fine-mesh sieve set over a small bowl, pressing as much pulp through as possible. Discard seeds, and reserve tamarind liquid.

Coarsely grind mustard seed in a spice grinder or with a mortar and pestle, and place in a blender. Add vinegar, onion, garlic and ginger, and blend into a smooth paste. Set aside.

Drain eggplant, and spread pieces on paper towels to dry. Pour 1 1/2 inches (4 cm) oil into a medium cast-iron frying pan, and set over medium-high heat. When oil is hot but not smoking, add a single layer of eggplant, and fry, turning to brown on all sides. Transfer to a large bowl, and repeat process until all the eggplant is browned.

Pour off all but 1/2 cup (125 mL) of the oil, and place frying pan over medium heat. Add mustard seed paste, and fry for 3 to 5 minutes, stirring constantly. Do not let it burn. Stir in curry powder, chilies, cinnamon, chili powder and reserved tamarind liquid. Add eggplant, stir well, then cover and simmer for 10 minutes. Remove from heat, remove cinnamon stick, and stir in sugar. Taste, and add more salt, if needed.

Allow to cool completely, then store in refrigerator in a clean glass jar for up to 2 weeks.

Makes 2 cups (500 mL)

yogurt dipping sauce

Cool and fresh-tasting, this sauce is the perfect accompaniment for lamb kebabs or pita sandwiches. It cools a spicy dish but adds a bit of zing at the same time.

1½ tsp.	cumin seed	7 mL
16 oz.	10% M.F. yogurt	450 g
2	cloves garlic, minced	2
2 Tbsp.	finely chopped fresh mint	25 mL
2 Tbsp.	finely chopped fresh dill	25 mL
½ tsp.	ground sumac	2 mL

In a small, dry frying pan over medium-low heat, toast cumin seed, shaking pan, until fragrant. Allow to cool, then coarsely grind in a spice grinder or with a mortar and pestle.

In a small bowl, mix together all ingredients.

Can be stored in refrigerator in a covered container for 5 to 6 days.

Makes 2 cups (500 mL)

arugula pine-nut pesto

Did we mention that we love arugula? Its unique peppery flavour gives this pesto just a little extra something. Use baby arugula to avoid the bitter taste that more mature leaves can develop.

⅓ cup	pine nuts	75 mL
4 cups	tightly packed, washed + dried arugula	1 L
½ cup	extra-virgin olive oil	125 mL
3–4	cloves garlic, minced	3–4
⅓ cup	freshly grated Parmigiano-Reggiano	75 mL
⅛ tsp.	sea salt	0.5 mL
⅛ tsp.	freshly ground black pepper	0.5 mL

In a small, dry frying pan over medium-low heat, toast pine nuts, shaking pan, until lightly golden. Set aside.

Process arugula and olive oil in a food processor until well blended. Add remaining ingredients, and pulse until well combined. Taste, and add more salt and pepper, if needed.

Can be stored in refrigerator in a covered container for 5 to 6 days.

Makes 2 cups (500 mL)

olive + caper relish

We serve this relish with the all-Italian Calabrese Sandwich (see page 121), but it's also tasty with our Marinated Mediterranean Tuna Salad on Olive + Rosemary Sourdough (see page 108) or simply on a baguette with chèvre.

1/3 cup	thickly sliced roasted red peppers	75 mL
6	pitted colossal green olives, cut lengthwise into sixths	6
1 Tbsp.	drained capers	15 mL
2 Tbsp.	extra-virgin olive oil	25 mL
	Pinch sea salt	
	Pinch freshly ground black pepper	

In a small saucepan over low heat, combine all ingredients. Warm through for 5 minutes to blend flavours. Serve at room temperature.

Can be stored in refrigerator in a covered container for up to 2 weeks.

Makes about 1/2 cup (125 mL)

chili machismo

This amazingly simple hot sauce is just the kick your Mexican and Central American cooking might be missing. You can substitute jalapeños or finger-hot chilies for the serranos. We serve it with our breakfast wraps.

1 cup	whole fresh serrano chilies	250 mL
2 Tbsp.	extra-virgin olive oil	15 mL + 15 mL
	Sea salt	
	Freshly ground black pepper	
1 Tbsp.	minced garlic	15 mL
1 Tbsp.	lime juice	15 mL

Preheat oven to 300°F (150°C). Lightly toss chilies with 1 Tbsp. (15 mL) of the olive oil, and season with salt and pepper. Spread in a roasting pan, and roast for 30 minutes, stirring occasionally, until liquid has evaporated. Allow chilies to cool, then remove stems.

Purée chilies in a food processor or a blender with garlic, lime juice and remaining 1 Tbsp. (15 mL) olive oil. Taste, and add more salt and pepper, if needed.

Can be stored in refrigerator in a covered container for up to 2 weeks.

Makes about 1 cup (250 mL)

diablo hot sauce

We heat up Salade Diablo (see page 153) with this sauce, but you can use it to turn up the temperature on almost anything.

1	6 oz. (170 g) can piquillo peppers, drained	1
7	cloves garlic	7
1 tsp.	crushed dried chilies	5 mL
1/3 cup	red-wine vinegar	75 mL
3/4 cup	grapeseed oil	175 mL
1/2 tsp.	sea salt	2 mL

Purée all ingredients together in a food processor or blender.

Can be stored in refrigerator in a covered container for up to 2 weeks.

Makes 2 cups (500 mL)

sweet barbecue sauce

Hoisin and orange give this sauce its sweetness, but garlic, ginger and chilies lend it a little attitude. Toss with some deep-fried tofu and vegetables or add to stir-fries.

1 cup	hoisin sauce	250 mL
1/2 cup	dry sherry	125 mL
	Zest of 1 orange	
	Juice of 2 oranges	
1/3 cup	Kung Fu soy sauce	75 mL
1/4 cup	minced garlic	50 mL
2 Tbsp.	finely chopped fresh ginger	25 mL
1–2	Thai chilies, finely chopped	1–2

Combine all ingredients in a medium saucepan over medium-high heat, and bring to a boil. Immediately remove from heat, and allow to cool.

Can be stored in refrigerator in a covered container for up to 1 month.

Makes 2 cups (500 mL)

ranchero sauce

With a little jolt from Mexican Chili Paste, this simple sauce partners beautifully with enchiladas and breakfast burritos.

1 Tbsp.	extra-virgin olive oil	15 mL
1/2 cup	finely diced cooking onion	125 mL
2 tsp.	minced garlic	10 mL
1	28 oz. (796 mL) can diced tomatoes, with juice	1
1/4 tsp.	sea salt	1 mL
	Pinch freshly ground black pepper	
2 tsp.	Mexican Chili Paste (see see page 228)	10 mL

Heat olive oil in a medium saucepan over low heat. Add onion and garlic, and cook until soft but not browned, about 10 minutes. Add tomatoes, salt and pepper. Increase heat to medium, and simmer, stirring frequently, for 20 to 30 minutes. Stir in chili paste, and remove from heat. Taste, and add more salt and pepper, if needed.

Can be stored in refrigerator in a covered container for 4 to 6 days.

Makes 2 cups (500 mL)

chez piggy chili sauce

This unbelievably tasty chili sauce adds a rich dimension to eggs and grilled meats that you won't soon forget.

3	medium cooking onions, thinly sliced	3
2 Tbsp.	canola oil	25 mL
9	tomatoes, cored + coarsely chopped	9
1 1/4 cups	white vinegar	300 mL
1 1/4 cups	white sugar	300 mL
1 1/2 tsp.	freshly ground black pepper	7 mL
1 1/2 tsp.	ground ginger	7 mL
1 1/4 tsp.	sea salt	6 mL
1/2 tsp.	cayenne	2 mL
1/2 tsp.	ground allspice	2 mL
1/2 tsp.	ground cloves	2 mL
1/2 tsp.	ground cinnamon	2 mL

In a large heavy-bottomed pot over medium-high heat, cook onions in oil until soft, about 10 minutes. Add remaining ingredients, and bring to a boil. Reduce heat to low, and simmer uncovered, stirring occasionally, for 2 hours or until sauce thickens.

Can be stored in refrigerator in a covered container for up to 1 month.

Makes about 4 cups (1 L)

tomato butter

Okay, it's actually a sweet and spicy textured ketchup. We serve it with anything cheesy or eggy, and you should too.

3	whole cloves	3
3	allspice berries	3
3–5	black peppercorns	3–5
2	28 oz. (796 mL) cans diced tomatoes, with juice	2
$\frac{1}{3}$ cup	white-wine vinegar	75 mL
$\frac{1}{2}$ cup	packed brown sugar	125 mL
$\frac{1}{2}$ tsp.	sea salt	2 mL
	Pinch cayenne	
1	$\frac{1}{2}$-inch (1 cm) stick cinnamon	1

Combine cloves, allspice and peppercorns in a cheesecloth sachet, and place with remaining ingredients in a large heavy-bottomed pot over medium-high heat. Bring to a rolling boil, reduce heat slightly, and boil gently, stirring occasionally, for 30 minutes.

Reduce heat to low, and simmer uncovered, stirring frequently, for about $1\frac{1}{2}$ hours. Remove cinnamon stick, and continue to cook for 3 to $3\frac{1}{2}$ hours more, stirring frequently, until mixture is thick and jamlike. Keep heat low enough so that mixture does not burn. Remove from heat, and allow to cool.

Can be stored in refrigerator in a covered container for up to 1 month.

Makes 2 cups (500 mL)

caramelized onions

These versatile onions show up in the strangest places, all of them delicious. We add them to everything from quiche and stuffed chicken to spreads and breads.

9 cups	thinly sliced cooking onions	2.25 L
$\frac{1}{3}$ cup	butter	75 mL
$\frac{1}{4}$ cup + 2 tsp.	white sugar	60 mL
$\frac{3}{4}$ cup	dry sherry	175 mL
3 Tbsp.	sherry vinegar	40 mL

Cook onions in butter in a heavy-bottomed saucepan over very low heat until onions are soft, 15 to 20 minutes. Add sugar, and continue cooking for 10 minutes. Add sherry and vinegar, and cook, stirring frequently, until liquid is incorporated and onions are a toffee-brown colour. As Zal used to say, you should cook your onions as an old Jewish woman would, with a lot of time and patience.

Makes $2\frac{1}{4}$ cups (550 mL)

pickled red onions

While this hot pickling method is quick, the red onions lose their brilliant colour within a day, so it's best to serve them shortly after they're chilled. Excellent as a side with sandwiches or as a condiment with Mexican dishes. If you're planning to serve these with Chicken Chimichangas (see page 50), slice onions paper-thin.

2 cups	rice-wine vinegar	500 mL
1 Tbsp.	sea salt	15 mL
2 1/2 Tbsp.	white sugar	35 mL
1 Tbsp.	yellow mustard seed	15 mL
1 tsp.	black peppercorns	5 mL
1	bay leaf	1
1	medium red onion, cut into 1/4-inch (6 mm) rounds	1

In a small saucepan over medium-high heat, bring vinegar, salt, sugar, mustard seed, peppercorns and bay leaf to a boil. Remove from heat, and stir to dissolve salt and sugar, about 1 minute. Immediately add onion. Let stand in hot vinegar for 15 to 20 minutes, until onion is bright red but still crunchy. Remove onion from vinegar mixture, and chill before serving.

Makes about 1 1/2 cups (375 mL)

note

The leftover pickling vinegar can be strained and stored indefinitely in a covered container in refrigerator for use in another batch.

east indian onion salad

Simple but fabulous. Try it with pappadam, make it part of a thali, or use it as a fresh side dish with Green Curried Haddock Steamed in Banana Leaves (see page 151).

1 1/2 cups	thinly sliced red onion	375 mL
1/4 cup	grated carrot	50 mL
1 Tbsp.	lemon juice	15 mL
	Large pinch sea salt	
1 1/2 tsp.	coarsely chopped cilantro	7 mL

In a medium bowl, combine all ingredients. Taste, and add more salt, if needed.

Can be stored in refrigerator in a covered container for up to 2 days.

Makes 2 cups (500 mL)

mexican chili paste

Essential to Mexican cooking, chili paste is the key to unlocking a whole range of authentic-tasting dishes. Experiment with the flavour by using a single chili variety or different combinations of chilies.

8	cloves garlic, unpeeled	8
1	dried guajillo chili	1
1	dried pasilla chili	1
2	dried chipotle chilies	2
6	dried ancho chilies	6
2/3 cup	Ham Broth or Chicken Stock (see pages 75 and 60)	150 mL
1 1/2 tsp.	dried oregano	7 mL
1/4 tsp.	ground cumin	1 mL
	Pinch ground cloves	
1 tsp.	sea salt	5 mL
1/2 tsp.	freshly ground black pepper	2 mL

In a cast-iron frying pan over medium heat, char garlic, turning occasionally, until skin begins to blacken and garlic is soft, 10 to 15 minutes. Remove garlic from pan, allow to cool slightly, then peel off skin and discard. Set aside.

Meanwhile, cut dried chilies in half, and remove stems and seeds. In the same frying pan used to char garlic, roast chilies over medium-high heat a few at a time, about 30 seconds on each side. Watch closely to prevent burning.

To rehydrate chilies, soak in a saucepan of hot water over very low heat for up to 30 minutes. Drain, and discard soaking liquid.

Place a little broth or stock, chilies, garlic, oregano, cumin, cloves, salt and pepper in a blender, and blend, drizzling in additional broth or stock as needed, to make a thick purée. Press through a sieve or food mill.

Covered with a thin layer of olive oil, chili paste can be stored in refrigerator for up to 1 month or in freezer for up to 6 months.

Makes about 1 1/4 cups (300 mL)

madras curry paste

One of the cornerstones of Indian cooking, this paste is so easy to make, why buy it already prepared? Add to soups, chickpeas, eggs, scrambled tofu and anything else you want to put a curry spin on.

1/2 cup	ground coriander seed	125 mL
1/4 cup	ground cumin	50 mL
1 1/2 tsp.	freshly ground black pepper	7 mL
1 1/2 tsp.	turmeric	7 mL
1 1/2 tsp.	black mustard seed, ground	7 mL
1 1/2 tsp.	chili powder	7 mL
1 1/2 tsp.	sea salt	7 mL
1 Tbsp.	minced garlic	15 mL
1 Tbsp.	grated fresh ginger	15 mL
1/3–1/2 cup	white vinegar	75–125 mL
3/4 cup	canola oil	175 mL

In a blender, purée all ingredients together, except oil, until smooth.

In a medium heavy-bottomed pan, heat oil over high heat until almost smoking. Add spice mixture, being careful not to splatter the oil. Immediately reduce heat to low, and cook, stirring constantly, until oil reseparates from spices, 25 to 30 minutes. Remove from heat, and allow to cool.

Can be stored in refrigerator in a covered container for up to 1 month or can be frozen in small quantities and kept for up to 6 months. Simply pop the frozen portion into soups and stews.

Makes 1 cup (250 mL)

guacamole

There are guacamole recipes, and then there are guacamole recipes, but take it from us, this is the best. Our thanks to Reyna Belsham for sharing it. Serve alongside Chicken Chimichangas *(see page 50)**, with our Fish Tacos with Salsa Fresca* *(see page 161)**, in sandwiches or as a dip.*

5	ripe avocados, halved, peeled + pitted	5
1	medium tomato, diced	1
3 heaping Tbsp.	sour cream	40 mL
$^1/_2$	large red onion, diced	$^1/_2$
	Juice of 1 lime	
2	Thai chilies, minced	2
2	cloves garlic, minced	2
2 Tbsp.	chopped cilantro	25 mL
	Sea salt	

In a large bowl, mash avocados into a chunky purée. Fold in tomato, sour cream and onion. Stir in lime juice, chilies, garlic and cilantro, and add salt to taste. Chill.

Makes about 5 cups (1.25 L)

crème fraîche

A quick and easy method for making a thickened cream for use in a variety of recipes, from savoury to sweet.

$^1/_2$ cup	sour cream	125 mL
$^1/_2$ cup	35% M.F. cream	125 mL

In a small bowl, stir sour cream and cream together. Spoon mixture into a clean cheesecloth or coffee filter, and place in a colander over a bowl. Allow to drain in a warm place for 12 to 24 hours. Discard liquid.

Can be stored in refrigerator in a covered container for 5 to 6 days.

Makes $^3/_4$ cup (175 mL)

plain mayonnaise

Here's our foolproof mayonnaise method. The whole egg makes emulsification a dream.

1/4 tsp.	Dijon mustard	1 mL
1 tsp.	lemon juice	5 mL
1 tsp.	red-wine vinegar	5 mL
3/4 tsp.	sea salt	4 mL
1/4 tsp.	freshly ground black pepper	1 mL
1	large egg	1
1 cup	canola oil	250 mL

Place mustard, lemon juice, vinegar, salt and pepper in a blender, and purée. Add egg, and purée. While blender is running, slowly drizzle in oil until a thick mayonnaise forms. Taste, and add more salt and pepper, if needed. Refrigerate until ready to use.

Can be stored in refrigerator in a covered container for up to 4 days.

Makes about 1 cup (250 mL)

tartar sauce

Our tartar. Sure, you can try it with fish, but you'll be pretty happy if you whip up some to dress your next potato salad.

1 cup	Plain Mayonnaise (see above)	250 mL
3 Tbsp.	coarsely chopped drained capers	40 mL
3 Tbsp.	finely diced dill pickles	40 mL
2	cloves garlic, minced	2
2 Tbsp.	minced shallots	25 mL
3 Tbsp.	coarsely chopped green olives	40 mL
1 Tbsp.	finely chopped fresh Italian parsley	15 mL

In a small bowl, combine all ingredients.

Can be stored in refrigerator in a covered container for up to 4 days.

Makes about 1 1/2 cups (375 mL)

highland blue cheese dressing

Who doesn't love a good old-fashioned buttermilk-and-sour-cream-based blue cheese dressing? We use it to dress Salade Diablo (see page 153), but you can serve it as a dip for chicken wings or drizzle it over a wedge of iceberg lettuce.

1/3 cup	Highland Blue cheese	75 mL
1/4 cup	Plain Mayonnaise (see page 231)	50 mL
2 1/2 Tbsp.	sour cream	35 mL
2 Tbsp.	buttermilk	25 mL
2 tsp.	lemon juice	10 mL
1 tsp.	minced garlic	5 mL
1/2 tsp.	grated cooking onion	2 mL
1/4 tsp.	white sugar	1 mL
2 tsp.	coarsely cracked black peppercorns	10 mL

In a small bowl, mix all ingredients together, mashing some of the blue cheese but leaving some chunks.

Can be stored in refrigerator in a covered container for up to 4 days.

Makes about 1 cup (250 mL)

caesar dressing

There are many standard Caesar dressing recipes, but we keep coming back to this one.

4	cloves garlic	4
	Pinch sea salt	
3	anchovies, rinsed	3
1 1/2 tsp.	Dijon mustard	7 mL
1/2 tsp.	Worcestershire sauce	2 mL
3	dashes Tabasco sauce	3
1 Tbsp.	lemon juice	15 mL
1 1/2 tsp.	red-wine vinegar	7 mL
	Pinch freshly ground black pepper	
1	large egg	1
2	large egg yolks	2
1/2 cup	extra-virgin olive oil	125 mL
1 1/2 cups	canola oil	375 mL
1/2 cup	freshly grated Parmigiano-Reggiano	125 mL

Mince garlic and salt together, and press into a paste with the flat side of a chef's knife. Finely chop anchovies, and mash into garlic and salt.

Place anchovy mixture, mustard, Worcestershire, Tabasco, lemon juice, vinegar and pepper in a blender, and purée. Add egg and egg yolks, and purée. While blender is running, slowly drizzle in olive oil, then canola oil, until a thick mayonnaise forms. Stir in cheese, taste, and add more salt and pepper, if needed.

Can be stored in refrigerator in a covered container for up to 4 days.

Makes 2 1/2 cups (625 mL)

photo credits

Pan Chancho staff photos:
5 Nick Waterfield, Veronica Desjardins and Zoe Yanovksy
9 Zal Yanovksy and Rose Richardson
16 Left to right: Dean Taylor, Amanda Smith, Chris Gollogly, Veronica Desjardins, Carel Vanderlinden, Mick Richmond, Tim Grass, Paul Muller, Ian Norris
21 Paul Varty
25 Angela Hollywood
29 Paul Muller
34 Carel Vanderlinden
41 Sonny Sadinsky and Victoria Newbury
43 Zoe Yanovsky
67 Julie Burbidge, Bernice Huisman and Manuel Ventura
70 Stephanie Mitchell
77 Alex Amodio and Chris Lawrence
81 Susan Silver
89 Korinne Peachey and Kendra Black
99 Michaela Olesova
112 Emily and Nick Waterfield
119 June Wu
125 Zal Yanovsky
133 Tibrata Gillies
137 Anne Linton, Laura Charrette and Ryan Steffler
145 Mariela Santamaria
155 Veronica Desjardins
161 Christyne Flynn
164 William Wu
175 Anne Linton
177 Danielle Kreps, Jessie Lindley and Adele Swinnard
188 Stefanie Killen
195 Patrick Kelly, Josh Button (middle right) and Stefanie Killen
198 Jen Collins
202 Joy McBride
218 Sonny Sadinsky
230 Anne Linton and Laura Charrette

Photographs by Bernard Clark Photography:
5, 16, 21, 29, 31, 34, 41, 43, 67, 70, 75, 77, 89, 92, 99, 108, 112, 119, 133, 137, 145, 155, 161, 164, 171, 173, 175, 177, 188, 195, 198, 202, 218, 228

Photographs by Janice McLean:
1, 6, 15, 18, 19, 22, 25, 27, 28, 32, 33, 35, 36, 39, 44, 47, 49, 51, 52, 56, 59, 62, 65, 66, 68, 73, 78, 83, 85, 87, 91, 94, 96, 101, 103, 104, 105, 107, 110, 115, 117, 121, 123, 127, 128, 131, 134, 139, 140, 142, 144, 146, 149, 152, 157, 158, 162, 167, 168, 172, 178, 180, 182, 185, 187, 190, 191, 193, 194, 196, 199, 200, 205, 206, 208, 209, 210, 211, 212, 215, 216, 219, 221, 224, 229

Courtesy Nick Waterfield: 81, 230

Courtesy Zoe Yanovsky: 125

Publisher's Note
A very special thanks to Laurel Aziz, for being the go-to friend and editor, and Frank B. Edwards, friend and publishing mentor. Thanks also to architect Rob Crothers for sharing both memories and photos from the 44 Princess Street renovation. Thanks to Connie Morris, Louise Topping, Jean Bruce, Steven Maynard, Pamela Cross and Peter Dundas for their support and care throughout the project, and to Susan Dickinson, Mary Patton, Bernard Clark, David Kennedy and Vicki Newbury, who continue to be a great pleasure to work with. Finally, thanks to Veronica Desjardins for her many kindnesses and to the Pan Chancho chefs for their patience and good humour.

index